Social Science Frontiers

Occasional Publications Reviewing New Fields
for Social Science Development

The Vulnerable Age Phenomenon

By Michael Inbar

Russell Sage Foundation

1976

*H
31
.S67
NO. 8*

Russell Sage Foundation
230 Park Avenue
New York, N.Y. 10017

Contents

Preface

This short monograph discusses a recently documented finding
which suggests that children in about the 6 to 11-year-old
age bracket may be more vulnerable to crises in their
environment than either younger or older youths.

At first sight the finding appears surprising. It runs counter
to the image of a trouble-free latency period. However, as
evidence accumulates, it seems increasingly likely that we shall
have to revise this notion. Moreover, on both empirical and
theoretical grounds we may have to replace it with the broader
concept of *vulnerable ages of transitions*. On the basis of the
presently available evidence, there would seem to be two such
ages. One is in mid-adolescence, around the age of 15; by
common-sense standards this finding is not very surprising. The
other occurs in mid-childhood; it would appear to have been
completely overlooked. For theoretical and practical reasons
the latter might be the most interesting phenomenon of the two.

To date the Vulnerable Age effect has been documented for
one dependent variable—school achievement (operationalized in
terms of college attendance and average years of schooling
completed). The original study in which the finding was first

1

noted was a cross-cultural study of immigrants; there is now evidence that another independent variable—geographical mobility, in particular in the United States—has the same effect. The possibility arises therefore that a variety of crises in the environment of juveniles may have heretofore unsuspected consequences. At the very least, school transfers during grade-school years would appear to be more problematic events than is usually assumed to be the case. In an age of ever-increasing geographical mobility, this fact has obvious implications and may make remedial policies necessary.

A prerequisite for such policies is a sound theoretical understanding of the problem that we are confronting; at this stage such understanding is nonexistent. Nonetheless, as I shall indicate, there are a few hypotheses which appear both reasonable and promising. But before these or other theoretical explanations are investigated, there is a task which should be given priority over all others. This task consists in the urgent need to have additional replications carried out. My overriding aim in writing this monograph is to invite such work. The reasons are twofold.

In the first place it stands to reason that before engaging in serious attempts at theory-building, we must know exactly what it is that has to be explained. This amounts to the requirement that the age curve to be interpreted be specified with as much precision as possible; one way to achieve this aim is to attempt to narrow down the 6 to 11-year age range for which the effect has been documented to date. As we shall see, there are reasons to believe that this might be feasible; indeed, there are already indications that the effect might be concentrated in the middle to upper part of the age range.

Secondly, the replications that I shall report were carried out by me. Because I was also one of the authors of the original study where the effect was first observed, none of the available evidence is as yet independent of one or both of its discoverers.

In short, this is a progress report on the evidence that I have been able to assemble in support of the existence of a Vulnerable Age effect. Should this effect be genuine, it is likely to constitute a finding of theoretical and practical consequence. Presently, however, it has first and foremost to withstand the test of independent replications. In the following pages I shall attempt to show that on both empirical and theoretical grounds it deserves such a test.

The data analyses which will be reported were carried out by means of a double blind procedure. I am indebted in this respect to Peter Abrams for carrying out the analysis of the Canadian sample. Donald H. McLaughlin, director of the Project TALENT Data Bank, was kind enough to supervise all the analyses of the TALENT Data. At times he himself made some of the runs. His help and collaboration for making the computer runs and for coding and adding to the tapes information about large-scale geographic mobility is gratefully acknowledged.

The Israeli and Canadian studies which will be discussed in the "Introduction" and in the chapter, "Additional Evidence," have already been reported elsewhere (Inbar and Adler, 1976a; Inbar, 1976). The analyses of the TALENT Data are reported here for the first time.

The preparation of the manuscript was carried out while I was a Visiting Scholar at Russell Sage Foundation. I owe a special debt of gratitude to its president, Hugh F. Cline, for constant support and encouragement. Without his sustained interest in the project it could not have been carried out. Walter L. Wallace generously spent time discussing with me the finding and its implications. I have taken advantage of some of his ideas; for the sake of his modesty and my ego, I shall use the excuse of our friendship to forego getting into unnecessary details.

Finally, I wish to express my gratitude to Ms. Hilary Silver for her valuable assistance in the library research. Mrs. Hetty de Sterke not only typed the manuscript with unusual competence, but contributed many helpful editorial comments.

Introduction: The Finding

The Vulnerable Age phenomenon was first documented in a
study initiated in Israel by Chaim Adler and myself (Inbar and
Adler, 1976a; 1976b). It revolves around the finding that
children in about the 6 to 11-year-old age bracket may be more
vulnerable to crises in their environment than either younger
or older youths. In the following chapters I shall show the extent
to which the finding is generalizable to Canada and to the
United States and discuss some of the theoretical questions and
research problems that the Vulnerable Age effect raises. As a
background to this discussion, it is useful to say a few words
about the original study in which the effect was first documented.

The precipitating event for the finding was a case study
by Martan (1972), who had investigated a collective village in
Israel. This village—Yad Rambam—had been settled in 1955–56
by Jewish immigrants from Morocco. Martan was interested in
the school achievements of children as a function of the impact
of the Israeli educational system on youths. To ascertain the
modality of this impact, he cross-tabulated the age of the children
upon immigration in 1955–56 against college attendance
(in 1971). On common-sense grounds the expectation was that

a negative relationship would obtain between successful schooling (operationalized by percentage having attended college) and the age of the children upon immigration. This expectation was based on the fact that young children are commonly observed to learn a new language faster than older youths; morever, language problems for adolescents translate as a rule into high-school test and exam failures which are immediately consequential for continued school attendance to a much greater extent than is the case for grade-school children. Furthermore, ever since the publication of the largest available survey on immigrant children at the turn of the century (Dillingham, 1911), the sociological literature explicitly or implicitly assumes an inverse relationship between age upon immigration and school achievement (e.g., Bhatnagar's *Immigrants at School*, 1970). On both intuitive and documented grounds, therefore, the anticipation was that the younger a child was when he immigrated with his family, the better his chances of school achievement would be.

Contrary to this expectation, however, Martan obtained what amounts to a *positive* relationship between age upon immigration and chances to attend college. In particular, in his sample those children who were 14 years of age or older upon immigration were quite likely in 1971 to have completed high school and have entered an institution of higher learning. Conversely, and quite surprisingly, however, their younger brothers and sisters (including those of pre-school age at the time of immigration) exhibited a marked and monotonically decreasing rate of successful schooling. On the strength of his finding, Martan concluded that a process had unfolded in Israel which had hampered the educational achievements of the settlers' *young* children.

Quite clearly, Martan's finding could reflect a process of downward mobility. It could also be idiosyncratic to a small village for any of a number of reasons. In fact, most people— including Adler and myself—felt that this was the most likely explanation for the finding. Nonetheless, because at the time of Martan's report we were planning a cross-cultural study on Moroccan immigrants, we decided to take advantage of the opportunity to scrutinize the finding. Our own impending research was about brothers and first cousins who had settled in France and Israel; it included a control group of Rumanian immigrants (Inbar and Adler, 1976b). Our sample included 238

6

youths who had immigrated with their families to either France or Israel, and who at the time of the research were old enough to have attended college. The analyses pertaining to Martan's finding that we performed were based on this sample.

The relationship between age upon immigration and later college attendance which obtained in these data did not turn out to be the inverse one that we had anticipated; nor did the curve resemble Martan's. Rather, the distribution was curvilinear (see Table 1). Furthermore, this relationship obtained not only

TABLE 1

Percentage of Children

Admitted to College, by Age at Date of Immigration

Age at time of families' immigration	0–5	6–11	12–15	16+
Percentage admitted to college	.26	.13[a]	.25	.29
	(N=47)	(N=77)	(N=65)	(N=49)

SOURCE: After Inbar and Adler (1976a, Table 4).

a. X^2, 1 d.f. (6–11 age group versus others) = 5.23, P < .05.

at the aggregate level, but held also within breakdowns by subsamples (see Inbar and Adler, 1976a, Table 4). Of perhaps even greater interest was the fact that at this point a reexamination of Martan's data showed that he had mistakenly defined one of his age categories, and that in all likelihood his data too were in fact curvilinear (Inbar and Adler, 1976a, pp. 5–6). All of a sudden, therefore, my colleague and myself found ourselves confronted with the fact that we had achieved a replication that we had not expected, to an extent that we had not anticipated. Martan's mistake and his unsubstantiated conclusions were no longer of importance. What was significant is that an unexpected finding had emerged which could be of some consequence.

The analyses which we carried out within the constraints of the limited sample that was available revealed a few additional trends. These can be summarized as follows.

1. The Vulnerable Age phenomenon, while generally predominant in the 6 to 11-year age group of immigrants, was stronger for the 12 to 15-year age group in one of the three subsamples. This suggested the possibility that

chronological age and school (or social) structures may
interact to produce the Vulnerable Age effect; alternatively,
a second problematic period—possibly independent of
the first—might exist in mid-adolescence.

2. The strength of the effects was always sufficient to offset
   the known phenomenon of older children of·immigrants
   (16 years old or more in this case) being sent to work.

3. At the same time, and quite unexpectedly, the effect
   was undetectable at below the college level; that is to say,
   with other cutting points (i.e., earlier measures) of school
   achievement, no trend was distinguishable. We shall see
   later that the Canadian data cast light on this puzzling fact.

As a tentative theoretical explanation for the Vulnerable
Age phenomenon, Adler and I sketched out a rudimentary
model; its essence is that while school transfers are stressful
for all youths, this fact is more likely to go unnoticed for
grade-school children. We reasoned that the desocialization-
resocialization paradigm found in many immigrant studies may
be adequate to explain the Vulnerable Age phenomenon.[1]

This paradigm sees social adaptation to a new environment
as involving a fundamental and usually painful process of
unlearning and relearning, as well as a process which depends
on social power and resources. It is noteworthy, however, that
the unlearning-relearning process is probably not applicable to
infants and/or very young children, at least not as far as a school
environment would be concerned. For children of school age,
however, it clearly is. For these children, then, the difficulties
which accompany a radical change of school environment
may be relatively similar, in any case much more similar than
are the resources that they marshal to ease the crisis. If so, our
finding would be directly interpretable; it would simply be a
consequence of differential resources under conditions of
high but fairly uniform duress.

To buttress the socialization-resocialization paradigm, consider
the following. It is generally true that the older a child, the less
his parents can help him directly with his school work,
irrespective of country of residence. Also, however, the older
the child, the more articulate he is and the more attention and
power he commands inside as well as outside his family. Such
factors combine to make older children better equipped to deal
with school problems they face upon immigration than are

---

1. See, for example, Curle (1947), Eisenstadt (1954), and Bar-Yosef
   (1968).

younger children. These observations specifically suggest that an older child is likely to lose less in terms of direct help from his parents, is likely to articulate his problems to a greater extent, and is able to command more attention and help than younger children.

According to this view, in the very early years of immigration in particular, the problems encountered by young children of school age, especially grade-school children, are likely to be given low priority by many families or go unnoticed altogether. In addition, these children are likely to have little or no independent school-related resources (e.g., peer tutoring). The expected effect of such processes on children who are at a cognitive and school-socialization stage of development would be compatible with the trend exhibited by our Israeli data. (Inbar and Adler, 1976a, pp. 7–8.)

In addition to this environmental explanation, we also recognized that a developmental interference might be responsible for the Vulnerable Age phenomenon. For instance, in the light of some recent sociolinguistic findings (Entwisle and Frasure, 1974), it is quite possible that language development is affected by cross-cultural school transfers during grade-school years. I shall elaborate this interpretation later.

Because, as we shall see, there is now evidence that the Vulnerable Age phenomenon holds also in the case of within-country geographic mobility, and because the finding for youths in mid-adolescence has recurred, it seems likely that these explanations will have to be revised; in addition, it may be, and I shall indeed suggest, that each effect calls for an explanation of its own.

Adler and I made it a point to emphasize that given the lack of prior empirical and theoretical evidence, the first order of priority was to replicate the Vulnerable Age finding. Operationally, this meant recognizing the fact that it is useful to postpone engaging in serious theoretical attempts until the shape of the curve is better specified and, even more importantly, until plausible artifacts are discarded.

With this order of priority in mind, one possible artifact of importance could already be checked with the original data. As the reader will have noticed, the form of the trend observed in Table 1 suggests that the shape of the distribution could be the result of the operation of the first/later-born effect. In particular, older children also being likely to be first-born, it is conceivable that the trend observed could be due to this effect. As the analyses showed, however, this was not the case; the shape of the distribution turned out to be independent of birth order, in particular of primogeniture (see Table 2).

TABLE 2

Percentage of Immigrants' Children Admitted to College by Age at Time of Immigration and Birth-Order

Age at time of families' immigration	Percentages admitted to college	
	First-born	Later-born
0–5	.40(N=5)	.24(N=42)
6–11	.00(N=16)	.16(N=61)
12–15	.22(N=23)	.26(N=42)
16+	.36(N=25)	.21(N=24)
Total	.23(N=69)	.21(N=169)

SOURCE: Inbar and Adler (1976a, Table 5).

This being so a series of additional tasks came to mind which required further research.

The first was, of course, to determine whether the finding could be replicated, in particular with North American data. The second was to further control for possible artifacts, for example, age cohort and SES effects. The third was to document the generality of the phenomenon in terms of causal variables, in terms of populations, and in terms of scope of consequences. That is to say, would the effect hold for migrations? Would it hold for boys as well as for girls? Were variables other than college attendance affected?

In the following pages I shall report the results of two additional studies, and the answers that they presently suggest to some of these and related questions.

Additional Evidence

The first piece of additional evidence bearing on the Vulnerable Age phenomenon stems from a replication carried out with the Canadian Census of 1971.[2]

By implication, the preceding discussion has indicated that attempting to replicate the Vulnerable Age phenomenon requires that a very specific set of data be available. In particular, with "crises" defined as immigration or migration, the following two conditions must be met.

1. *Sample characteristics.* The sample must be of immigrants or migrants, and the respondents must be old enough to have had a chance to attend college; allowing for a margin of security, this means that the sample must be made of respondents who were 19 to 20 years old or more at the time of the interview.
2. *Variables and level of measurement.* a) For each respondent it is necessary to either have information about his/her age upon immigration or migration, or,

2. Public Use Sample Data (Individual File for Metropolitan Areas) derived from the 1971 Canadian Census of Population supplied by Statistics Canada. The responsibility for the use and interpretation of these data is entirely that of the author.

alternatively, data about his/her present age and the date of immigration or migration, so as to be able to generate this information; b) it is also necessary to have explicit information about the respondents' college attendance.

As I shall elaborate later, these minimal conditions are generally not found in most available large-scale data banks. In the 1971 Canadian Census of Population they are—at least to some extent.

The reasons for this qualified statement about the 1971 Census are twofold. In the first place, there is no usable information for migrants. The replication can therefore be for immigrants only. Even for them, however, age upon entering Canada is unknown. What is available is the period of immigration, coded as follows.[3]

    1. Before 1946
    2. 1946–1955
    3. 1956–1960
    4. 1961–1965
    5. 1966
    6. 1967–1968
    7. 1969
    8. 1970
    9. 1971
  10. Canadian born

This variable, in combination with the age of the respondents (in 1971), can nonetheless generate the requested information. The procedure has been reported in detail in Inbar (1976); it allows a cohort analysis of the respondents who were 20, 21, and 22 years old in 1971. In particular, for each of these cohorts, age upon immigration can be determined according to three age brackets which approximate the trichotomy 0–5, 6–11, 12+ years in which we are interested. It should be mentioned, however, that even these categories are not without an element of imprecision. The reason is that the age of the respondents which is reported in the Canadian Census is age at last birthday. That is to say, an unknown number of persons were born in 1970, rather than in 1971. This factor of incertitude generates

3. 1971 Census of Canada, *Public Use Sample Tapes, User Documentation* (Draft), Statistics Canada, March 1975, p. 4.2.15.

TABLE 3
Age Categories upon Immigration to Canada of Three Cohorts of Respondents

Age at time of Census (1971)

A. Individual cohorts

		Age upon immigration		
20	0–(4–5)	(5–6)—(9–10)	(10–11)—(15–16)
21	0–(5–6)	(6–7)—(10–11)	(11–12)—(16–17)
22	0–(6–7)	(7–8)—(11–12)	(12–13)—(17–18)

B. Consolidate cohorts

20 + 21	0–5	6–10	11–16
21 + 22	0–6	7–11	12–17

the (trichotomized) actual age categories upon immigration which are summarized in Table 3A; the parentheses indicate the age-range of incertitude.

Clearly, the 21-year-old cohort yields the best age trichotomization for the purpose at hand. However, depending upon one's assumptions about the distribution of dates of birth, the cohorts of 20 and 22 years old also present advantages when the lower and upper boundaries of the age range with which we are concerned are considered. This being so, the analyses were always carried out twice: once for the consolidated cohort of 20 and 21 years old, and once for the consolidated cohort of 21 and 22 years old. This procedure had the additional advantages of having a built-in test for the robustness of the results, and of increasing the number of cases available for the analyses, a consideration of importance when the number of cases shrank due to the introduction of control variables. The categories of age upon immigration generated when the cohorts were consolidated are presented in Table 3B.[1]

With these clarifications in mind, the results of the replication (which have been reported in detail elsewhere—Inbar, 1976) can be summarized as follows.

In the first place, the U-shaped or J-shaped curve, whose replication was attempted, obtained in each cohort (see Table 4). The results, however, did not reach the .05 level of statistical significance in any individual cohort. At the same time, as a pattern, it should be noted that the probability of the trend recurring in all three cohorts by chance is less than .05 (1/27).

4. Merging two consecutive age cohorts generates a one-year overlap between age categories upon immigration (see Table 3A); I have taken this common value to represent the modal age for the category boundaries of the consolidated cohorts.

TABLE 4
Percentage of College Attendance among Immigrants of Both Sexes
by Age upon Immigration, and by Cohort

Cohort (age at time of Census)	Age upon immigration		
	0–(4–5)	(5–6)—(9–10)	(10–11)—(15–16)
20	.37	.20	.31
(N=126)	(N=43)	(N=51)	(N=32)
	0–(5–6)	(6–7)—(10–11)	(11–12)—(16–17)
21	.33	.18	.21
(N=151)	(N=69)	(N=44)	(N=38)
	0–(6–7)	(7–8)—(11–12)	(12–13)—(17–18)
22	.27	.11	.13
(N=139)	(N=64)	(N=35)	(N=40)

SOURCE: Public Use Sample Data, Individual File for Metropolitan Areas, Canadian Census of 1971.

Second, the weakness of the trend could be traced to an interaction by sexes. Indeed, controlling for this variable, no evidence was found of a Vulnerable Age effect for girls (see Table 5B). On the other hand, the predicted relationship recurred for boys and was in this case both sizeable and robust. In comparison with the children who immigrated during their grade-school years, younger and older male immigrants exhibited a rate of college attendance which was at least 50 percent higher; this relationship was unaffected by the combination of age cohorts which was considered (see Table 5A).

TABLE 5
Percentage of College Attendance among Immigrants, by Sex
and Age upon Immigration

Cohorts (age at time of Census)	Modal age upon immigration		
A. Males	0–5	6–10	11–16
20 + 21	.48	.18	.32
(N=106)	(N=40)	(N=38)	(N=28)
	0–6	7–11	12–17
21 + 22	.40	.23	.35
(N=92)	(N=43)	(N=26)	(N=23)
B. Females	0–5	6–10	11–16
20 + 21	.20	.22	.23
(N=123)	(N=51)	(N=41)	(N=31)
	0–6	7–11	12–17
21 + 22	.15	.12	.08
(N=131)	(N=59)	(N=33)	(N=39)

SOURCE: Inbar (1976, Table 8).

N.B.: The N's for boys and girls do not exactly add up to the total N's reported in Table 4. The reason is that in Table 4 some respondents were already heads of households. These respondents were omitted from later analyses to allow a control by parental SES, which in the Census is only possible for non-heads of households.

Third, the effect now specified for boys, was shown to be independent of the mother tongue of the respondents (mostly English, followed by Italian; only some 5 percent having a French-speaking background); see Table 6.

TABLE 6

Percentage of College Attendance among Male Immigrants, by Mother Tongue and Age upon Immigration

Cohorts (age at time of Census)	Modal age upon immigration		
A. Mother tongue: English	0–5	6–10	11–16
20 + 21	.50	.29	.36
(N=52)	(N=20)	(N=21)	(N=11)
	0–6	7–11	12–17
21 + 22	.27	.17	.22
(N=47)	(N=26)	(N=12)	(N=9)
B. Mother tongue: Other	0–5	6–10	11–16
20 + 21	.47	.09	.24
(N—84)	(N=36)	(N=23)	(N=25)
	0–6	7–11	12–17
21 + 22	.45	.24	.29
(N=87)	(N=42)	(N=21)	(N=24)

SOURCE: Inbar (1976, Table 11).

Finally, the effect was shown to be independent of levels of SES (see Inbar, 1976, Table 10). At the same time, the analyses suggested that the Vulnerable Age phenomenon was quite likely to be obscured by confounding factors wherever the SES background of the respondents was insufficently controlled. This was shown to be a likely occurrence when high-school measures of school achievements are used as a dependent variable, in particular high-school completion (see Inbar, 1976, pp. 13–16, especially Tables 12 and 14).

In short, the finding was replicated. Moreover, it emerged from this study as being both generalized and specified. In terms of generalization, there was now evidence that the effect is not likely to be cohort, SES, or culture (language) specific. In terms of specification, the Canadian data suggest that the effect is probably restricted to boys. We shall see later that these conclusions appear to be valid—with one qualification: the Vulnerable Age phenomenon, although less consistently found among girls, does not appear to be strictly limited to males.

This being so, it may now be useful to confront an epistemological question of importance.

15

Assuming that the finding is a genuine one—as obviously each replication makes this increasingly likely to be the case—how could it have gone unnoticed for so long?

Interestingly, delving into the literature and searching through data banks suggest an intriguing answer to this question. The answer may even constitute—in a manner of speaking—additional evidence *by default* for the finding itself. Specifically, it would seem that the effect could hardly have been documented in the past, given the manner in which the data which are required for observing the effect are usually collected and analyzed. This point is obviously of extreme importance and deserves some elaboration.

As a case in point consider the Canadian Census of 1971. The Metropolitan tape released for public use contains 53,173 respondents. Of them 13,153 (close to 25 percent) are immigrants. This is an extremely high rate, which can only be expected to be found in very few modern societies. Nonetheless, the analyses that I have reported ended up being based on a couple of hundred cases. This stems from the fact that in the Canadian Census periods of immigration have only been recorded in very rough categories, making most cases unusable. In most countries even this type of information is not available; rather, the breakdown is simply by national/foreign-born, occasionally with information about country or continent or origin. Another problem is that large-scale data bases often use collapsed age categories, a frequent one being 0 to 14; the reason for this categorization is that such data are usually collected in connection with studies or surveys which focus on aspects of the labor market. In combination, the lack of information about either or both the precise age or date of immigration of the respondent makes it next to impossible to even attempt to observe the Vulnerable Age phenomenon in most large-scale data banks which are listed.[5] This holds also true if one attempts to shift the focus from the effect of immigration to that of simply migrating. In this case the usual information which is available is merely whether or not the respondent has moved in recent years. Sometimes, but not always, there is also information about the number of moves; in this case whenever the

5. I am extremely indebted in this respect to Mrs. Alice Robbin of the Computer Center of the Department of Sociology, The University of Wisconsin, who searched nationally and worldwide for the existence of usable data banks. It is through her efforts that I became aware of the existence of the Canadian Census of 1971.

information includes dates, it is about the latest moves. The Canadian Census of 1971 is an example in point of some of these shortcomings. (See fields 52, 53, and 54 of the Metropolitan Area File, Statistics Canada, 1971.)

Other potentially relevant data banks have an additional weakness. They focus on youths who are at most of high-school age. In this case the problem for the analyses in which we are interested is compounded by the inadequacy of the dependent variable. As I have indicated, the Vulnerable Age effect is very likely to be obscured at this level by SES factors which are particularly potent at the onset of opportunities to enter the labor market and which require, in order to be neutralized, powerful controls indeed. (See Inbar, 1976, Table 14.) That is to say, in the quasi-totality of the listed data banks the Vulnerable Age phenomenon could not have been observed. Documenting the effect requires not only an appropriate set of data— a very rare occurrence in itself—but also controls and nonparametric analyses which are most unlikely to be performed together if the phenomenon is not hypothesized in advance. To date, however, it has not been. As a result, as we have just seen, neither was it likely to have been found by accident.

In this respect it may be of interest to note that I did come across a couple of studies in which the effect could theoretically have been noticed. What did actually occur in these studies is intriguing. First, it is noteworthy that in both cases there is evidence that the effect may have been present. In each case, however, the author either overlooked the finding or discarded it as a random fluctuation. The first case occurs in Bhatnagar's *Immigrants at School* (1970, p. 97). In this study Bhatnagar presents data about the exact age of immigration to England of a sample of West Indian and Cypriot high-school students; at one point he also relates this variable to a generalized scale of adjustment. Bhatnagar's aim in this specific analysis was to test the usual negative relationship which is assumed to obtain between age upon immigration and school-related variables, in this case adjustment. Interestingly, he did not find evidence of such a relationship. Accordingly, and after recalling his specific source for the hypothesis, he concludes that past evidence "would lead to a prediction that age at the time of immigration is negatively related to adjustment. The data gathered in this study does not support the view" (Bhatnagar, 1970, p. 97). Of course, should his distribution have been curvilinear, this is precisely the result that one would have anticipated, *given that the conclusion is based on correlations.* Unfortunately, Bhatnagar does not present the raw data, and neither does he elaborate on his unexpected failure to replicate a well-established relationship.

In the second study, the author explicitly noted what may be the first published evidence in support of the Vulnerable Age phenomenon. However, in this case the author (Lee, 1956) chose to pursue his unrelated concern and to discard the finding as a likely random fluctuation. The study is a replication of Klineberg's finding (Klineberg, 1935) about the increase in IQ evidenced by Negro children who migrated to the North. It should be noted that the independent variable in this study is migration rather than immigration. Also, the dependent variable is not school attendance but the standardized IQ score obtained at test and retest times by the respondents. Keeping these differences in mind, the author presents in tabular form (Lee, 1956, p. 435) the IQ scores of his subjects as a function of the age (grade) at which the migrant children entered the northern school system. Lee's data span the age range 6 to 14 and are summarized in Table 7.

Interestingly, looking at column 9A one notes two dips in the distribution: one at ages 8 to 9.5, the other at ages 12 to 14. Because the scores are standardized, such comparisons are meaningful; at the same time it should be noted that they might be lacking validity due to the possible confounding effect of retesting. This difficulty, however, can be overcome by considering separately the results of the first test, then the results of the second test, etc.

The IQ scores obtained in the first test by all the subjects are those which appear in the main diagonal of Table 7. Clearly, and although the difference is admittedly small, controlling in this manner for the test-retest effect shows that the group which emerges with the lowest standardized score (86.3) is the group of children who migrated between the ages of 8 and 9.5. Furthermore, pursuing this analysis one step further, it is possible to compare among themselves those children who were retested the same number of times. For the 12 to 14-year-olds no such comparison is possible for lack of data. For the others, however, at least one comparison of this kind is feasible by considering the diagonal which runs from columns 2B to 9A. By the way Table 7 is set up, this diagonal is made of the scores

18

TABLE 7

Mean "IQ's" on Philadelphia Test of Mental and Verbal Ability of Southern-Born Negro Children, by Age (Grade) at which They Entered the Philadelphia School System, and by Grades at which They Were Tested and Retested

Grade in which the children entered the Philadelphia school system	Age range	N	Grade in which test was taken					Test-retest improvement between 1st and 2nd test
			1A	2B	4B	6B	9A	
1A	6	182	86.5	89.3	91.8	93.3	92.8	+2.8
1B–2B	6.5–7.5	109		86.7	88.6	90.9	90.5	+1.9
3A–4B	8–9.5	199			86.3	87.2	89.4	+0.9
5A–6B	10–11.5	221				88.2	90.2	+2.0
7A–9A	12–14	219					87.4	—

SOURCE: After Lee (1956, p. 435, Table 1).

of the children who at the time had been given exactly one retest. Inspecting this diagonal clearly shows that the group of 8 to 9.5-year-olds stands out again as having the lowest IQ scores (87.2). The disutility in this sample of migrating at this age can be summarized in a single measure: the difference between the first and second test. This difference is indicative of a stable handicap; it is presented in the last column of Table 7.

Lee's study is intriguing on several accounts. In the first place, the age group of migrant children which is the most affected falls well within the expected age range; it may even be a first indication that the phenomenon that we are discussing could be narrowed down in the future.[6] Not less interesting is the fact that the shape of the distribution did not escape Lee's attention. He chose, however, to discard the finding as an exception to the trend he was attempting to establish—without further explanation (Lee, 1956, p. 434).

It is unfortunate that the data do not allow a longer and more complete trend analysis of the IQ scores controlled for the test-retest effect. This is particularly true in the case of the 12 to 14-year-olds for which not even one retest score is available. In the light of the evidence found in one of the subsamples of the original study on the Vulnerable Age effect (see the "Introduction"), it would have been intriguing indeed to find that this age group does also exhibit a lower retest score. The structural view that I shall discuss in the next chapter suggests, however, that we should not expect this to have been the case in Lee's data, because this study held constant the school-level subdivision. I shall elaborate this point shortly.

Be this as it may, and unless Lee's distribution is a coincidence, there are grounds to believe that the Vulnerable Age phenomenon might be more general than the two immigration studies that I have discussed may suggest. The effect appears likely to be a function of migrations as well as immigrations, and if so, perhaps more generally of crises in the children's environment (e.g., divorces, parental deaths, school transfers, etc.); in turn, these crises might very well affect more than simply school-related variables. At least these are possibilities

6. We should of course be prepared for possible age shifts as a function of structural and developmental changes. Lee's study was carried out in the early 1950s and on a sample of Negro children. The Vulnerable Age for non-minority children and in the 1970s might conceivably be concentrated at somewhat different points of the age continuum.

20

which should not be discarded without investigation.

Before speculating, however, it is obviously necessary to first establish on firmer grounds than accidental evidence the fact that the Vulnerable Age effect indeed holds in the case of the first conceptual step toward a generalization, i.e., in the case of migrants. Furthermore, the results should be further controlled for possible artifacts. This is the task that I shall now undertake with the TALENT Data.

The TALENT Data

The data bank known as TALENT was started in 1960. It is a nationally respresentative sample of United States high school students in that year. To date there have been three follow-up studies of the original sample. The last was the eleven-year follow-up which at the time of this writing has been carried out for three grades: the 10th, 11th, and 12th.

The master sample includes over 400,000 cases. It is kept and managed in Palo Alto by the American Institutes for Research. The staff in charge of the data bank has developed weighting procedures to overcome the problem of sample mortality in the follow-ups. They have also developed various standard scales, among them an SES and an education variable.

In the following analyses we shall be concerned with the eleven-year follow-up. The samples are those which are standardly made available by the American Institutes for Research to investigators; the N's are about 3,000 cases per grade. Each sample has been calibrated to be nationally representative by the above-mentioned weighting procedure. Details about the sample, the weighting procedures, and a copy of the questionnaires can be found in the *Handbook of the*

Project TALENT Data Bank (American Institutes for Research, 1972).

For the purpose at hand it is useful to note the exact wording and coding of two key variables.

The dependent variable, years of schooling, was made available coded as follows.

Coding		Meaning
0	=	up to grade 8
1	=	up to grade 9
2	=	up to grade 10
3	=	up to grade 11
4	=	up to grade 12, without diploma
5	=	high school diploma only
6	=	high school diploma plus some further education (but no college)
7	=	high school diploma plus some college
8	=	college graduate
9	=	college graduate plus some graduate school education
10	=	college graduate plus Master's degree or equivalent
11	=	Beyond Master's degree but without Ph.D., M.D., or law degree
12	=	Doctorate or law degree

The independent variable—migrations—was operationalized by the answers to a question which was included in the 1960 student questionnaire. The question—SIB167—reads as follows.

> How long have you lived in this community?
> 1—One year or less
> 2—More than 1 year, but no more than 3 years
> 3—More than 3 years, but no more than 5 years
> 4—More than 5 years, but no more than 10 years
> 5—More than 10 years, but not all my life
> 6—All my life.
> (American Institutes for Research, 1972, p. 53.)

Under the assumption that 10th-graders are on the average 16 years of age, this question allows to determine for the three cohorts with which we shall be concerned—the age brackets of migration which are reproduced in Table 8.

TABLE 8
Age Categories upon Migration Generated by the Answers to
Question SIB167 (see Text), for the Respondents who were
10th, 11th, and 12th-Graders in 1960

Cohort	Answers to question SIB167					
	1	2	3	4	5	6(Never)
10th-graders	15–15.5	13–14	11–12	6–10	1–5	—
11th-graders	16–16.5	14–15	12–13	7–11	1–6	—
12th-graders	17–17.5	15–16	13–14	8–12	1–7	—

From Table 8 it is apparent that the age categories in which
we are primarily interested are approximated with various
degrees of accuracy in each of the three cohorts. For instance,
the pre-school age category is best approximated for the 10th-
graders, and less accurately so for the 11th and 12th-graders
(see Table 8, column 5); on the strength of Lee's study, however,
this is likely not to prove too harmful inasmuch as there are
grounds to believe that the Vulnerable Age effect may begin at
about the age of 8. From a different perspective, and for reasons
that I shall elaborate in the theoretical discussion, the choice of
age brackets should additionally allow to capture the effect of
moving from one level of the educational system to another,
e.g., from elementary school to high school. Such structural
transitions are known to have an attrition effect on cohorts and
should be distinguished from the Vulnerable Age phenomenon
proper.

In the United States, transition points in the educational
structure can occur at various ages.[7] In some school systems one
transition occurs at grade 7 and the other at grade 10 (i.e., at
ages 13 and 16 respectively). Another widespread structure
has only one transition point in grade 9, i.e., at age 15. In
addition, at ages 15-16 the end of compulsory education
constitutes a selective transition in and of itself. But the
consideration of importance is that the earliest commonly found
transition point occurs at age 13. For a careful test of the

---

7. Should one prefer to assume that 10th-graders are on the average 15
rather than 16 years old, all the ages of transition which will now be
discussed should be reduced by one year. In this case, however, so
should be the age categories presented in Table 8 and in the tables which
follow. Because of this built-in relationship and of the fact that in the
analyses which will follow the comparisons are always relational (i.e.,
relative to adjacent categories), the validity of these analyses is
independent of the assumption which is chosen. It should be kept in
mind, however, that given the choice that I have made, all the
vulnerable ages of transition which will be discussed represent an upper
age limit estimate of the age of the respondents at the time of interest.

hypothesis at hand it is consequently necessary to avoid depressing the age bracket which is critical for the Vulnerable Age test by inadvertently including in it the potentially confounding effect of the beginning of high-school selection. In other words, we must be careful not to have 13-year-olds or older children in any of the age groups in which on the basis of the previous studies we expect to find evidence of the Vulnerable Age effect.

Operationally, this requirement, together with the constraints of the data, means that in the TALENT samples the confirmation of the 6 to 11-year-old Vulnerable Age hypothesis requires that dips in years of schooling be found in the following categories of Table 8.

A) *In the 10th grade*: in categories 4 and 3 as opposed to 2 and 5.

B) *In the 11th grade*: in category 4 as opposed to categories 3 and 5.

C) *In the 12th grade*: in category 4 as opposed to categories 3 and 5.

On the other hand, because in the United States the most significant transition to a higher level of the school structure occurs upon entering high school proper, i.e., at the ages of 15 (in the 8-4 systems), and 16 (in the 6-3-3 systems), and because of the end of compulsory education, the selection explanation suggests that we should expect to find evidence of an independent and relative structurally induced dip in the following categories of Table 8.

A) *In the 10th grade*: in category 1 as opposed to 2.

B) *In the 11th grade*: in categories 2 and 1 as opposed to category 3.

C) *In the 12th grade*: in category 2 as opposed to categories 1 and 3.

These predictions are summarized in Table 9. The structural predictions are obviously incidental to our main concern. They are useful, however, because they will put the findings pertaining to the Vulnerable Age effect in mid-childhood in perspective and will document another possible reason for its having been overlooked in the past.

With the hypothesis listed in Table 9 in mind, the aims of the analyses are fourfold.

TABLE 9

Hypotheses to be Tested about Average Years of Schooling Completed
by Children who Migrated at Various Ages

Cohort	Vulnerable age predictions		Structural predictions	
10th-graders	$5,2 > 3,4$[a]	(A)	$2 > 1$	(D)
11th-graders	$5,3 > 4$	(B)	$3 > 1,2$	(E)
12-graders	$5,3 > 4$	(C)	$1,3 > 2$	(F)

a. The numbers in this table are those of the columns listed in Table 8.
This inequality, for instance, reads as follows: the average levels of
schooling completed by the respondents who migrated between the
ages of 1 to 5 (column 5) or 13–14 (column 2) are greater than the
averages of those who migrated between the ages of 11–12 (column 3)
or 6–10 (column 4).

1. To examine the extent to which the Vulnerable Age
   finding can be generalized to the United States.
2. To examine the extent to which it holds in the case of
   migrations.
3. To diversify the criterion variable by using a measure
   of school achievement which encompasses the *whole*
   educational cycle.
4. To refine the findings by beginning to differentiate between
   effects which are anticipated on the basis of the selective
   structure of school systems, from those which require
   a different explanation.

We can now turn to the results of the analyses. The overall
distribution of means of levels of schooling achieved by the
various groups of migrants in each of the three cohorts is
presented in Table 10. For the reader's convenience, Tables 11
and 12 present the same data split-up according to the age
range which is relevant to the test of the Vulnerable Age
phenomenon and to that of the selectivity of secondary
education, together with the effect predicted from these
explanations.

Considering first the extent to which the hypotheses listed in
Table 9 are borne out by the findings, Table 11 shows that,
although the differences are at times small, all the predictions
based on the existence of a Vulnerable Age effect are consistently
supported by the data, without exception. As a trend (whose
probability of occurring by chance is less than .05 for these
data alone, and infinitesimal if we consider the results of Table
10 together with those obtained in the Canadian study), it would
seem that the existence of a pre-adolescent vulnerable age is
now, if not established, at least highly probable.

TABLE 10

Average Levels of Education Achieved by Migrants and Non-Migrants by Cohort and Age upon Migration in Childhood

A. Key to age categories upon migration (see Table 8)

Cohort	1	2	3	4	5
10th-graders	15–15.5	13–14	11–12	6–10	1–5
11th-graders	16–16.5	14–15	12–13	7–11	1–6
12th-graders	17–17.5	15–16	13–14	8–12	1–7

B. Data

	1	2	3	4	5	Mean	Standard Deviation	Never Moved 6	Grand Mean	Standard Deviation
10th-graders	6.44	6.68	6.55	6.48	6.69	6.59	.10	6.49	6.54	.09
(N)	(133)	(189)	(239)	(362)	(520)	(1443)		(1330)	(2773)	
11th-graders	6.57	6.72	6.83	6.79	6.89	6.81	.09	6.71	6.76	.08
(N)	(145)	(189)	(228)	(475)	(654)	(1691)		(1537)	(3228)	
12th-graders	6.85	6.77	6.85	6.82	6.95	6.88	.07	6.72	6.80	.09
(N)	(84)	(142)	(210)	(422)	(746)	(1604)		(1668)	(3272)	

TABLE 11

Visual Partition of Table 10: Elementary School Age Range

A. *Key to age categories upon migration, and predicted dips (underlined)*

Cohort	2	3	4	5	Mean (untruncated distribution— see Table 10)	Standard Deviation
10-graders	13–14	11–12	6–10	1–5		
11th-graders		12–13	7–11	1–6		
12th-graders		13–14	8–12	1–7		

B. *Data and matching dips (underlined)*

Cohort	2	3	4	5	Mean	Standard Deviation
10-graders	6.68	6.55	6.48	6.69	6.59	.10
11th-graders		6.83	6.79	6.89	6.81	.09
12th-graders		6.85	6.82	6.95	6.88	.07

TABLE 12
Visual Partition of Table 10: High-School Age Range

A. *Key to age categories upon migration and predicted dips (underlined)*

Cohort	1	2	3	Mean (untruncated distribution— see Table 10)	Standard Deviation
10th-graders	15–15.5	13–14			
11th-graders	16–16.5	14–15	12–13		
12th-graders	17–17.5	15–16	13–14		

B. *Data and matching dips (underlined)*

	1	2	3	Mean	Standard Deviation
10th-graders	6.44	6.68		6.59	.10
11th-graders	6.57	6.72	6.83	6.81	.09
12th-graders	6.85	6.77	6.85	6.88	.07

30

In terms of the magnitude of the effect, it lies between one-fifth of a standard deviation to about one standard deviation below the grand mean (of the untruncated distribution), depending on the cohort which is considered. In comparison to the age categories which are adjacent to those where the Vulnerable Age phenomenon is predicted to occur, the differences are of course larger. It should be noted, incidentally, that to the extent that there is a selectivity effect from one level to another of school systems, the size of the Vulnerable Age phenomenon is underestimated in function of the independent dampening effect that this selection may start having on 13-year-olds (column 2 for 10th-graders, and column 3 for 11th and 12th-graders; see Table 11).

In this connection Table 12 shows that as far as the upper level of high-school selection is concerned (i.e., for 15 and 16-year olds), the anticipated effect is clearly documented; indeed, all the differences are in the predicted direction (see Table 12).

In short, the image which emerges is that the Vulnerable Age and the selectivity of various levels of school structures create for learning an empirical sequence of vulnerable ages of transition. This conclusion is strengthened by a theoretically derived additional test of the hypotheses that we have just examined.

Consider the wording of the question about migrations (see page 24). It is imprecise about the periods of migration, a shortcoming which is found in most data banks; in point of fact, it is fortunate that this question is as detailed as it is and that it was included in the study, otherwise the TALENT Data would have been useless for the purpose at hand. But the question has another weakness: it does not allow to distinguish between uprooting in some real sense and trivial geographical moves; it does not allow to distinguish either between one or repeated moves. In short, the independent variable is noisy, a fact which raises two possibilities. The first is that the results may be artifactual. The second is that the underlying phenomena may be powerful enough to be noticeable despite the inadequacies of the measure.

In an attempt to refine this measure, one could reason that the importance of moving has two major components: frequency and geo-cultural magnitude. The frequency variable does not require any elaboration. The geo-cultural continuum, on the other hand, can be conceptualized as having immigration at one of its ends and a trivial move at the other.

For lack of data, I shall have nothing to say about the frequency variable. The magnitude of the geo-cultural transitions, however, can be estimated in all three studies where the Vulnerable Age phenomenon has been documented to date. In the Israeli and Canadian immigration studies this magnitude lies at one extreme of the continuum; in the TALENT Data it lies somewhere along the continuum, in part because we are dealing with the concept of migration, but also because we have a diluted measure of this variable. Conceptually, therefore, a better definition of migrations—for instance, migrations across large geographical boundaries—should yield a magnitude which falls between these two points. In theory, we would thus expect that in this case the size of the Vulnerable Age effect should also be intermediate.

Because the sets of data are not directly comparable, this test cannot be fully carried out. The TALENT Data, however, allow to determine who are the respondents for whom migration took place from one large geographical area of the United States to another. This in itself is of interest because on the basis of the foregoing reasoning we would expect that in this subsample the Vulnerable Age effect should be present in a somewhat stronger form. This derivation, however, applies only to the segment of the curve where a developmental interference is suspected to have occurred. Indeed, in the case of the effect of school selection no such accentuation of the dips can be predicted. This follows from the consideration that developmental patterns are relatively invariant, much more so in any case than school structures. Hence, the size of an interference effect on a developmental pattern may be expected to be primarily a function of the magnitude of the interference—a magnitude which in the present case is estimated by the size of the geo-cultural move. Large geographical subdivisions, however, do not bear any predictable relationship to the selectivity structure and policies of school systems, inasmuch as these vary no less within than across regions; furthermore, some migrations are likely to be undertaken by parents with precisely the aim of overcoming the difficulties that high-school students experience at certain selective junctions of their secondary school career. Together, the non-specificity by region of high school selectivity and the reactive nature of some migrations to this obstacle, on the one hand, and the probable developmental nature of the problem for the 6 to 11-year-old migrants, on the other, suggest that concentrating on interregional moves should help clarify the existence of a Vulnerable Age in mid-childhood and, at the same time, differentiate further between the developmental and selective explanations which may apply at different points of the age curve.

This logically derived test was carried out, and its results will now be presented. For the purpose of the analyses, the following six geographical regions were used.

1. New England and Middle Atlantic States (Maine, New Hampshire, Vermont, Massachusetts, Rhode Island, Connecticut, New York, New Jersey, Pennsylvania).

2. East and West North Central States (Ohio, Indiana, Illinois, Michigan, Wisconsin, Minnesota, Iowa, Missouri, North Dakota, South Dakota, Nebraska, Kansas).

3. South Atlantic, East South Central, and West South Central States (Delaware, Maryland, District of Columbia, Virginia, West Virginia, North Carolina, South Carolina, Georgia, Florida, Kentucky, Tennessee, Alabama, Mississippi, Arkansas, Louisiana, Oklahoma, Texas).

4. Mountain States (Montana, Idaho, Wyoming, Colorado, New Mexico, Arizona, Utah, Nevada).

5. Pacific States (Washington, Oregon, California, Hawaii, Alaska).

6. United States possession (Puerto Rico, Guam, etc.) and Foreign.[8]

Focusing then on the subsample of respondents who migrated from one of these regions to another, Table 13 presents the overall distributions which obtain in their case. For visual convenience, these data are again split up according to the age range which is relevant to the test of the Vulnerable Age phenomenon proper (Table 14) and to that of the selectivity of secondary education (Table 15). Each of these two tables also presents the magnitude of the migration effect (relative to the adjacent age categories) for the whole sample (from Tables 11 and 12) and in the present case.

8. This turned out to be a residual category with an insignificant number of cases.

TABLE 13

Average Levels of Education Achieved by Inter-Regional Migrants,
by Cohort and Age upon Migration in Childhood

A. *Key to age categories upon migration (see Table 8)*

Cohort	1	2	3	4	5	Mean	Standard Deviation
10th-graders	15–15.5	13–14	11–12	6–10	1–5		
11th-graders	16–16.5	14–15	12–13	7–11	1–6		
12th-graders	17–17.5	15–16	13–14	8–12	1–7		

B. *Data*

	1	2	3	4	5	Mean	Standard Deviation
10th-graders	6.66	6.83	6.52	6.45	6.96	6.71	.21
(N)	(37)	(48)	(59)	(80)	(114)	(338)	
11th-graders	6.49	6.87	6.97	6.90	7.04	6.91	.15
(N)	(33)	(49)	(50)	(94)	(109)	(335)	
12th-graders	7.07	7.12	7.11	6.82	7.33	7.12	.20
(N)	(15)	(42)	(48)	(84)	(124)	(313)	

34

TABLE 14

Visual Partition of Table 13: Elementary School Age Range

A. *Key to age categories upon migration, and predicted dips*
(underlined)

Cohort	2	3	4	5	Mean (untruncated distribution— see Table 13)	Standard Deviation
10th-graders	13–14	11–12	6–10	1–5		
11th-graders		12–13	7–11	1–6		
12th-graders		13–14	8–12	1–7		

B. *Data and matching dips (underlined)*

10th-graders	6.83	6.52	6.45	6.96	6.71	.21
11th-graders		6.97	6.90	7.04	6.91	.15
12th-graders		7.11	6.82	7.33	7.12	.20

C. *Comparative size of the effect relative to adjacent category*

10th-graders (whole sample)[a]	+.13	—	—	+.21
10th-graders (present sample)	+.31	—	—	+.51
11th-graders (whole sample)[a]		+.04	—	+.10
11th-graders (present sample)		+.07	—	+.14
12th-graders (whole sample)[a]		+.03	—	+.13
12th-graders (present sample)		+.29	—	+.51

a. See Table 11.

Considering first the Vulnerable Age in childhood, Table 14B shows that the predicted effect recurs among the interregional migrants. The critical test, however, lies in the magnitude of the effect. Table 14C shows that without exception the effect is magnified for all three cohorts. Thus, in the case of interregional moves the 12th-graders who migrated at ages 1–7 and 13–14 achieved a level of schooling which was respectively .51 and .29 points higher than that of the children who migrated during the Vulnerable Age period (see Table 14C); in the case of the whole sample, these differences are only .13 and .03 points, respectively. The same pattern obtains for 11th and 10th-graders; in particular, in the latter case the children who made an interregional move at age 1–5 achieved a level of schooling which is .51 point above that of the 6 to 10-year-old migrants, and the children who moved at age 13–14 achieved a level which is .31 point above that of the 11 to 12-year-old migrants; the comparable differences in the case of the whole sample are only .21 and .13, respectively.

In short, and to the extent that interregional moves subsume greater disruptions in the children's homes and environments than lesser moves, the finding would seem to lend strong additional support to the existence of a Vulnerable Age in mid-childhood.

Turning now to the selection effect of schools, Table 15 shows that in this case no consistent trend emerges. In the first place the selection pattern itself is inconsistent; in particular in the case of the 12th-graders the empirical dip does not occur in the predicted category (see Table 15A and 15B); as we shall shortly see this is due to an interaction effect. More importantly, where the effect does recur (in the cohorts of 10th and 11th-graders), its relationship to magnitude of migration is erratic. Thus in the whole sample of 10th-graders, those respondents who moved at age 13–14 achieved a level of schooling which is .24 of a point higher than that of the 15 to 15.5-year-old migrants. In the case of interregional migrations no accentuation of the effect is noticeable; on the contrary, it is now only .17 (see Table 15C). In the case of the 11th-graders (for the whole sample) the 12 to 13-year-old migrants achieved a level of school education which is .26 of a point higher than that of the 16 to 16.5 movers, and .11 higher than that of the 14 to 15-year-old migrants (see Table 15C); for interregional movers the comparable differences are .48 and .10, respectively. That is to say, in one case we find an accentuated effect, in the other not.

In short, no demonstrable relation exists between size of geographical mobility and variations in the effect of the selectivity of schools. If anything, the data would suggest a mild inverse relationship. Such a trend would be consistent with a reactive interpretation of the cause of migrations in the case of some parents of high-school students. It would also be consistent with what would be expected if most parents are aware of the selection problem; on psychological grounds the salience of this problem is not unlikely to be a function of the geographical size of the move contemplated, and the magnitude of migrations may well therefore be related to the efforts which are made to overcome the anticipated difficulties.

Be this as it may, the Vulnerable Age effect and the effect of school structures bear a predictable relationship to migrations; these effects are analytically different and appear to be

36

TABLE 15
Visual Partition of Table 13: High-School Age Range

A. *Key to age categories upon migration, and predicted dips (underlined)*

Cohort	1	2	3	Mean (untruncated distribution— see Table 13)	Standard Deviation
10th-graders	15–15.5	13–14			
11th-graders	16–16.5	14–15	12–13		
12th-graders	17–17.5	15–16	13–14		

B. *Data and matching dips (underlined)*

10th-graders	6.66	6.83		6.71	.21
11th-graders	6.49	6.87	6.97	6.91	.15
12th-graders	7.07	7.12	7.11	7.12	.20

C. *Comparative size of the effect relative to adjacent category*

	1	2	3
10th-graders (whole sample)[a]		—	+.24
10th-graders (present sample)		—	+.17
11th-graders (whole sample)[a]		—	— (+.26,+.11)[b]
11th-graders (present sample)		—	— (+.48,+.10)[b]
12th-graders (whole sample)[a]	+.08	—	+.08
12th-graders (present sample)	—.05	—	—.01

a. See Table 12.
b. Category 3 relative to categories 1 and 2, respectively.

empirically distinguishable. This is clearly an important result which should help avoid confusions in the future.

I shall now summarize some additional findings of interest.

One is negative in nature. As in the case of the Canadian study, no systematic pattern of effect by SES emerged in the present data. However, Table 16, which presents the SES distributions for the cohort of 10th-graders (interregional movers) documents a shift which is of interest. This shift occurs in the Vulnerable Age range for high SES respondents—between categories 4 and 3 (see Table 16); the shift seems also to be characteristic of boys, as we shall shortly see.

Because of the constraints of the data, the trend can only be documented in the case of the 10th-graders and is therefore difficult to interpret. It could be indicative of maturation differences among levels of SES (or sexes), or of earlier entrance into junior high school. It could also indicate, however, that the Vulnerable Age phenomenon is concentrated in the upper part of the 6 to 11-year age range, and that the reversal in the rank order of the two categories which span the Vulnerable Age period is a function of fluctuations in dates of birth (and perhaps also of maturation) within, say, the age range 8 to 11. Which of these or other interpretations is the correct one is a question which cannot be answered with the present data.

Another result of interest consists of the partial replication of the finding documented in the Canadian study about sex differences. As it turns out, in the TALENT Data too the results of interregional migrations—upon which much of my argument is based—hold consistently for boys, with only one exception. This occurs among the 11th-graders and concerns the effect of school selection; specifically, the expected dip occurs only among the 16 to 16.5-year-olds, rather than both among them and the 14 to 15-year-olds. The relevant data are presented in Table 17.

For girls, the picture is more complex. The Vulnerable Age effect in mid-childhood is present among 12th-graders. It is also present among 10th-graders; in this case, however, it is limited to the 6 to 10-year age group. Among 11th-graders, finally, it is absent. With regard to school selection, the effect is only present in the case of the 11th-graders. The relevant data are presented in Table 18.

Two conclusions appear to be warranted by the analyses by sex. The first is that, as the Canadian study has suggested, there are important sex differences for the phenomena under consideration. The second is that these differences are less pronounced for the Vulnerable Age phenomenon in mid-childhood than is the case for the effect of school structures. I shall return to the question of sex differences, in particular for the Vulnerable Age phenomenon, in the next chapter.

The last finding of interest is that in all three cohorts the average level of schooling achieved by non-movers is consistently lower than that of the migrants. This trend can be observed in Table 10, by comparing the average of the respondents who never moved (category 6) with the average of the movers, which appears two columns to the left of category 6. In part, of course, this difference reflects an SES effect. Controlling for levels of SES, however, does not completely reduce the differences (data not presented); in any case, never does the average of non-movers rise above that of the migrants. This finding may be due to an

TABLE 16

Average Levels of Education Achieved by the Cohort of 10th-Graders (Interregional Movers) by Parental SES, and by Age upon Migration in Childhood

A. *Key to age categories, with Vulnerable Age predictions (under-lined twice), and school selection predictions (underlined once)*

	1 15–15.5	2 13–14	3 11–12	4 6–10	5 1–5	Mean	Standard Deviation

B. *Data and matching dips (underlined)*

SES Level

	1 15–15.5	2 13–14	3 11–12	4 6–10	5 1–5	Mean	Standard Deviation
low	5.05	5.95	5.31	5.21	5.42	5.40	.29
(N)	(14)	(17)	(12)	(23)	(27)	(93)	
medium	6.59	6.82	6.40	5.89	6.82	6.47	.39
(N)	(5)	(13)	(20)	(27)	(35)	(100)	
high	7.50	7.58	6.97	7.56	7.92	7.57	.34
(N)	(20)	(20)	(30)	(32)	(55)	(157)	

39

TABLE 17

Average Levels of Education Achieved by Male Interregional Migrants, by Cohort and Age upon Migration in Childhood

A. *Key to age categories, with Vulnerable Age predictions (under-lined twice), and school selection predictions (underlined once)*

Cohort	1	2	3	4	5
10th-graders	15-15.5	13-14	11-12	6-10	1-5
11th-graders	16-16.5	14-15	12-13	7-11	1-6
12th-graders	17-17.5	15-16	13-14	8-12	1-7

B. *Data and matching dips (underlined)*

	1	2	3	4	5	Mean	Standard Deviation
10th-graders	6.53	7.25	6.63	7.12	7.77	7.21	.47
(N)	(19)	(27)	(30)	(41)	(60)	(177)	
11th-graders	6.77	7.59	7.35	7.02	7.41	7.25	.24
(N)	(14)	(19)	(25)	(50)	(59)	(167)	
12th-graders	7.31	6.85	7.51	7.42	6.68	7.47	.25
(N)	(6)	(18)	(27)	(41)	(66)	(158)	

TABLE 18

Average Levels of Education Achieved by Female Interregional Migrants, by Cohort and Age upon Migration in Childhood

A. *Key to age categories, with Vulnerable Age predictions (underlined twice), and school selection predictions (underlined once)*

Cohort	1	2	3	4	5
10th-graders	15-15.5	13-14	11-12	6-10	1-5
11th-graders	16-16.5	14-15	12-13	7-11	1-6
12th-graders	17-17.5	15-16	13-14	8-12	1-7

B. *Data and matching data (underlined)*

	1	2	3	4	5	Mean	Standard Deviation
10th-graders	6.79	6.30	6.41	5.75	6.07	6.16	.32
(N)	(18)	(21)	(29)	(39)	(54)	(161)	
11th-graders	6.28	6.41	6.59	6.77	6.60	6.57	.16
(N)	(19)	(30)	(25)	(44)	(50)	(168)	
12th-graders	6.91	7.32	6.59	6.25	6.94	6.76	.37
(N)	(9)	(24)	(21)	(43)	(58)	(155)	

insufficient control of the respondents' socioeconomic background. It could also reflect the frequently documented fact that adult migrants are a better motivated group than non-migrants (see, for example, Spilerman and Habib, 1976, pp. 804-805). Even within SES levels one could therefore expect that their children should also be better motivated, including scholastically, than the children of non-migrants. The finding, however, could also have a very different kind of explanation. It could stem from the fact that moving has an *enrichment* effect at certain points of the age curve. In point of fact, some experts believe that the most important learning experience during puberty—roughly around the ages of 12 to 13—consists in being exposed to cultural and social stimuli (Maeroff, 1975). Migrations obviously mediate such experiences, and the shape of the age curves that we have examined could therefore reflect this process, as well as those that we have discussed. I shall not presently elaborate on this possibility, although it is useful to keep it in mind for the discussion of needed research to which the last chapter is devoted.

Theoretical Interpretations

It is probably fair to say that one conclusion which emerges from the evidence that we have reviewed is that a Vulnerable Age effect in mid-childhood is clearly and recurrently observable for boys; for girls too, the effect is noticeable, although not invariably so. A school selection effect is distinguishable as well; however, its impact on migrants is somewhat less predictable for boys, and even less so for girls, than is the Vulnerable Age phenomenon proper.

These, then, are the trends which require a theoretical explanation. In this chapter I shall attempt to provide a few plausible interpretations of this kind. I wish to stress, however, that I shall engage in this task with the utmost caution. My motive is to avoid repeating some of the mistakes made in the context of another serendipitous finding—the first-born effect. As is well known, the effect—although of great importance in itself—does not hold for only children, and hence much of the early theoretical explanations are groundless. The lesson is, of course, that the first task with a serendipitous finding is to specify its exact nature. In our case this means that the first order of priority is to determine the exact shape of the age curve which has to be explained. Before this is done, theoretical explanations can only be speculations. The point of this remark is that we are at the earliest stage of the documentation of a finding. We are therefore moving on uncharted territory. The cues presently available are not only few in number, but also noisy, due to both the limited number of replications performed and the imperfections of the age categories which were available for the analyses. Accordingly, what is presently needed above all is replications. My overriding aim in writing this monograph is to invite such work; it is emphatically not to provide a theoretical explanation for the finding.

The task of reliably specifying the age curve which will ultimately have to be explained (perhaps a different one for different societies), is likely, however, to take years of concerted efforts. Some theoretical guidelines—no matter how tentative— are therefore necessary along the way. The following ideas are offered to fulfill this function. They are of a general nature by design.

Theoretically, then, the explanations which might account for the Vulnerable Age phenomenon fall into two categories: one is based on developmental factors, the other on environmental ones. I shall illustrate in turn the form that these explanations could take.

One developmental process whose disruption might conceivably account for the Vulnerable Age effect in mid-childhood could be cognitive. Specifically, recent research suggests that language and cognitive development may interact in an as yet unspecified but important way between the ages of 6 and 11. As opposed to the long-held belief that fundamental syntax and grammar are acquired by age 5, the latest studies show that a considerable amount of improvement occurs between ages 5 and at least 9 (Frasure and Entwisle, 1973; Entwisle and Frasure, 1974). It should be noted that the age of 9 does not constitute a ceiling; it simply represents the age limit which has presently been investigated. In future research the true limit may have to be extended to the age of 10, or perhaps even 11. To an extent which remains to be determined, the vulnerability of children in mid-childhood to significant crises and changes in their social or school environments may therefore reflect an interference with language development which might be quite general.

Another developmental explanation could be social in nature.

44

It was advanced more than two decades ago by Henry Stack
Sullivan. Sullivan (1953) suggests that one stage of
development, the juvenile era, is critical; as he puts it, "the
importance of the juvenile era can scarcely be exaggerated, since
it is the actual time for becoming social" (Sullivan, 1953, p.
227). This era lasts from about the entrance in school to around
the age of 10; it is bounded by the chum period with which
it overlaps from around ages 8.5 to 10. The juvenile era is a
prerequisite for establishing fundamental patterns of social
adjustment. Sullivan has spelled out how the disruption of this
era usually comes about.

One of the things which time and time again has shown itself
to have been quite disastrous in the history of patients, was
the social mobility of the parents, which took the juvenile
from one school to another at frequent intervals. . . . Other
things being equal, if one is getting on at all fortunately in
juvenile society, it is a very good thing to stay in that group of
juveniles throughout the period, or certainly until near the end of
the juvenile era. . . . continuous upheavals in schooling—and
this is strikingly true with service personnel—is apt to leave a
very considerable handicap in this and subsequent development.
(Sullivan, 1953, pp. 241–242.)

In other words, as far as the number of environmental
disruptions and school transfers are concerned, there is both
evidence and a theory for the existence of a Vulnerable Age at
almost precisely the points of the age curve with which we
are concerned. It is entirely conceivable, of course, that a single
but very drastic change of social and/or school environment
should have all or part of the effects that milder repetitive
changes or transfers have. In point of fact, it is curious that
this possibility does not seem to have been entertained. It is
even more bewildering that Sullivan's advice as it stands
commands so little attention. To illustrate the extent of this
disregard, the reader is asked forgiveness for a short digression. I
recently came across the advice that the American Movers
Conference gives to parents. It may be enlightening to quote
from a leaflet distributed by this organization.

Each child, because of differences in age and life experience,
will view the move differently . . . the pre-school child can pose a
real problem. . . .
The grade school-age child has a more highly developed sense
of self. . . . His developing sense of discovery may make the

45

idea of moving exciting to him. While he will be leaving friends, they will not be the deep, vital friendships of older children. . . .

The teenager, of course, usually has enough problems even in a stable environment. (From a leaflet of the American Movers Conference, undated, obtained by mail, March 1976.)

I do not know whether this image of a problematic age in adolescence and pre-school years, as opposed to a non-problematic one during grade-school years, is widely shared or not. As I have indicated in the "Introduction," on the surface of it the grade-school years are likely to appear to be tranquil years. But theoretically and empirically, as we have seen, there is evidence suggesting that, stereotypes to the contrary, mid-childhood years may be as much if not more developmentally problematic than other ages.

Returning to our main concern, it is noteworthy that for the age range 8.5 to 10, Sullivan explicitly states that on the basis of his data his generalizations hold *for males only* (Sullivan 1953, p. 248; also p. 249). Because Sullivan does not elaborate, neither can I. Nonetheless, the relevance of Sullivan's remark for the finding under discussion and for future theoretical work is obvious.

Still another developmental explanation could be related to the disruption of the transition to autonomy—the acceptance of cooperation and social control through socially agreed-upon rules —which has been identified by Piaget as occurring between the ages of 7 and 11 (Piaget, 1965). Because in this chapter my aim is notional, I shall not attempt to go into the details of this explanation. It is however of interest to note that for this process there would again appear to be important sex differences inasmuch as for girls the transition is more rapid and seems to be over by age 8, almost at the onset of the stage of cooperation (Piaget, 1965, p. 80). Of course, for the purpose at hand it might very well turn out that Sullivan's and Piaget's interpretations are the two sides of the same coin. Indeed, from the standpoint of the Vulnerable Age phenomenon, Sullivan would appear to have stressed the independent variable, and Piaget the dependent one. In substance, however, and granting small variations, it is intriguing to note how much their observations agree in form and content, down to specific sex differences which in the light of the empirical findings that we have discussed are obviously of great interest.

Turning now to environmental factors, Table 19 illustrates the type of effect that one might anticipate this class of variables to have. This table presents the survival and transition rates in high school, year after year, of two selected cohorts. The data are from Germany and are taken from the sequence of fifteen cohorts presented by Boudon (1974, p. 57, Table 3.11). The cohorts are the first and last for which there is complete information from the 7th grade to graduation.

TABLE **19**

Survival and Transition Rates in Secondary School, for
Two Selected Cohorts, Germany

	1952		1959	
	Survival Rates	*Transition Rates*	*Survival Rates*	*Transition Rates*
Number of students	14,077		10,170	

	1952 Survival	1952 Transition	1959 Survival	1959 Transition
"Quarta" 7th grade	100		100	
		89.1		90.7
8th grade	89.1		90.7	
		87.7		91.2
9th grade	78.1		82.7	
		93.3		94.1
10th grade	72.9		77.8	
		62.7		86.1
11th grade	45.7		67.0	
		93.4		92.5
12th grade	42.7		62.0	
		94.4		93.7
"Oberprima" 13th grade	40.3		58.1	
		95.5		95.9
High-school degree	38.5		55.7	

SOURCE: After Boudon (1974, p. 57, Table 3.11).

A feature of this table is that for the 1952 cohort there is a clear drop in transition rates between the 10th and 11th grades. In the 1959 cohort, on the other hand, the drop is almost unnoticeable. The reason for this difference is that "a traditonal turning point, the *mittlere Reife* (literally: middle maturation), underwent drastic change over the period. . . . [Up to about] 1955, the *mittlere Reife* was perceived by many students as a terminal point, but some years later it had become just an intermediate step" (Boudon, 1974, p. 56).

The sociological explanation of this phenomenon is that from the standpoint of the students and their families each year is a decision point where success in school (marks) and socioeconomic costs and opportunities are taken into account to decide whether or not to remain in school. Transitions from one formally or normatively defined level (or sublevel) of schooling to another are also decision points of this kind, only more so. This fact is well documented for non-movers in all educational systems, as Table 19 illustrates. It stands to reason, therefore, that the effect should also be found among migrants and immigrants, although in this case it is reasonable to anticipate that it should be magnified.

In other words, the theoretical expectation is that all age curves, including of course those of migrant or immigrant adolescents, should exhibit one or more vulnerable ages of transition, the specific age or ages being a function of the formal and normative structure of the school systems under consideration.

It should be noted that, given the structure of the selective process in school systems, we would expect the school structure effect to apply only to teenagers.[9] Additionally, this structural effect may conceivably be accentuated by a developmental interference; however, I have not yet found in the literature a clearcut set of consequences that one could expect from school disruptions occurring within a specific age range during adolescence. This question obviously deserves further theoretical attention.

In any case, we have seen that there is some evidence of a structural effect of schools in the TALENT Data. This segment of the curve, however, was not of primary interest in the studies that I have carried out and was consequently the least analyzed. Nonetheless, the results clearly point to one additional reason which is likely to account for the fact that the Vulnerable Age in mid-childhood has been overlooked for so long. Indeed, depending

9. However, I should like to mention a variant of a structural explanation which might have some bearing on the Vulnerable Age phenomenon in grade school. In certain schools what has been learned in a given grade is reviewed in the next grade at the beginning of the school year; in certain schools it is not, or there is one or more breach of continuity— one often noted occurring in the 3rd grade. It could be that in such school systems being transferred at this juncture constitutes a handicap of some consequence. For another variant of an explanation which is environmental in nature, see the original interpretation advanced by Adler and myself ("Introduction").

on the number and intensity of the selection points and on random fluctuations in the data, the segment of the curve pertaining to high school years clearly can at times overshadow the Vulnerable Age effect and even impart to the whole curve a shape which makes unavoidable the conclusion that schooling and age upon migration or immigration are inversely related. In this sense, the Israeli and Canadian studies may have been fortunate occurrences.

To conclude this brief theoretical sketch, I should like to mention that in the last analysis the main contribution of the studies that I have discussed may well be that they will lead to the rediscovery of theoretical propositions buried for decades in the child development literature. Whether this will turn out to be the case or not is too early to say. It is noteworthy, however, that some of these propositions are phrased in terms which qualify them as predictions. The curves that I have presented may have merely documented their accuracy.

For some reason, however, these predictions were not taken up as a challenge by sociologists. On the basis of the data that I have presented and in an age when geographical mobility keeps growing, I would argue that now they should be.

Needed Research

As I have repeatedly stated, the purpose of this volume is to invite replications of the findings that I have reported. Should I have made my case, I would like to mention a few topics and issues which, to my mind, deserve particular attention in future research.

To put these research problems into perspective, it is useful to distinguish among the tasks of validation, explication, and intervention. (The reader looking for a more detailed discussion of developmental research paradigms than the one which follows, is invited to consult Baltes and Goulet, 1971, and Baltes and Schaie, 1973.)

Validation

The first task is of course to further document and validate the age curves that we have been discussing. In this respect the following aims stand out as deserving preferential consideration.

REFINEMENT OF MEASUREMENT. In the studies that we have reviewed the age categories upon migration or immigration were always age ranges. A satisfactory documentation of the

Vulnerable Age phenomenon and of the effect of school structures calls, however, for more detailed information about the exact age at which a move took place; the estimation of the magnitude of the environmental change or geo-cultural move must also be improved beyond the dichotomous measure which was used in the analyses of the TALENT Data. In short, future research should attempt to improve and refine the operationalization and measurement of the independent variables.

LARGER SAMPLES. As we have seen, the statistical significance of the findings which were reported could only be established as a trend. This was primarily due to the fact that as soon as controls were introduced into the analyses, the size of the subsamples became rather small. One consequence of this fact is that the magnitude of the effect with which we are dealing is not very clear. Future research should attempt to clarify this question.

GENERALIZATION. As part of the documentation-validation effort, the findings should also be generalized to their natural limits. We have seen that they appear to hold in the case of immigrations and migrations; in terms of consequences, an effect on schooling, and perhaps also on IQ, is noticeable. These independent and dependent variables, however, may not be the only ones which are related to the findings under discussion as causes or effects. Furthermore, there is evidence that males and females are differentially affected. Together, these considerations suggest that for guiding serious attempts at theory-building, the scope of the effects—in terms of the variables and the populations affected—must be further clarified.

These three aims could be advanced in a first step by cross-sectional studies. The size and composition of the samples which are needed are largely a matter of choice. There is only one constraint. The respondents must be old enough to permit the proper measurement of the dependent variables which are assumed to have been affected (e.g., schooling). Presently, there is also one desirable feature that the samples should have: they should be large. Indeed, the time has come when possible confounding variables should be *simultaneously* controlled in one set of data. We have seen that although there is some overlap between the studies that we have reviewed, this has not been the case to date; the aims listed also implicitly or explicitly assume the availability of large samples.

With regard to the questions which should be included in such studies, they have a rather simple format. In summary form, they fall under the following five headings.

1. A set of background questions, e.g., date of birth, parental SES, etc.
2. A set of questions to determine the exact age at the time of a move or crisis.
3. A set of questions to evaluate the frequency and intensity of these moves and crises.
4. A set of questions about possible mediating variables, (e.g., loss of friends, specific school difficulties, etc.)
5. A set of questions about the dependent variables of interest.

Such questions can easily be included in any survey. Conceptually, the last set is contemporary in nature and does not present any methodological problems. The other sets are theoretically about historical events. Except for set number 4, however, the questions involve little measurement difficulties, inasmuch as they are about events which are unlikely to be distorted by memory and which can be ascertained by simple or well-tested questions (e.g., fathers' occupation). The intervening variables are another matter. But their investigation comes properly under the heading of explication.

Explication

Once an age curve is well specified, its interpretation is more than a continuation of research. In many ways the explication work which must follow starts a new phase of enquiry.

Cross-sectional studies can be appropriate for documenting an age function. Its genuine interpretation, however, usually requires experimental work and longitudinal studies. In terms of research goals, the emphasis shifts from external to internal validity, in an endless spiral (Campbell and Stanley, 1963).

In the present case, and assuming that a reliably estimated age curve is available, the major problem is to discard the notion of chronological age. Indeed, in the last analysis age is simply a summarizing measure of an ordered succession of substantive events. As Flavell (1963, p. 36) put it, "Age is a vehicle rather than a cause in itself."

The translation of a chronological age range into questions of developmental processes which are affected, and of the substantive events which affect them, rests on theoretical considerations. Presently, it would seem that these could be best tested and that new insights could be sought in a series of micro studies.

Such studies might usefully have three focal points: 1) the children themselves; 2) their parents; and 3) the teachers and school environments of the youths.

Methodologically, it is probably too early to adopt the experimental and simulation paradigm suggested by Baltes and Goulet (1971). On the other hand, studies in depth (e.g., classroom observations, sociometric measures before and after postulated crises, etc.), and longitudinal case studies would appear to be both feasible and promising. Among other things, such studies could conceivably cast light on the question of whether or not the Vulnerable Age in mid-childhood is followed by a period where changes in environment constitute enriching rather than disruptive experiences (see the chapter, "The TALENT Data").

Intervention

This last task marks the end of what can be said in this small volume, because it is presently a heading with no substance. Indeed, the necessity and feasibility of interventions, in the sense of preventive and remedial steps, depend on both the validity of the findings that I have discussed and on their theoretical interpretation. Presently, therefore, we could only speculate about the nature, feasibility, and effectiveness of such steps. Obviously, however, should the answers to the previous research question warrant it, these issues and the evaluation research that they imply will rapidly become salient.

Before this stage is reached, however, we are confronted by a research agenda which is already enormous. Its size is a measure of the extent to which the sociological study of the phenomena that I have documented is overdue—provided, of course, that the findings reported withstand the acid test of independent replications.

I should like to conclude with the question that this last remark raises.

By definition, it is a question that I cannot answer. It is therefore also the first which must now be answered.

References

American Institutes for Research, *The Project TALENT Data Bank: A Handbook*. Palo Alto, Calif., April 1972.

American Movers Conference, *Moving and Children*. Undated leaflet, A.M.C., Suite 806. 1117 North 19th St., Arlington, Va.

Baltes, P.B., and R.L. Goulet, "Exploration of Developmental Variables by Manipulation and Simulation of Age Differences in Behavior," *Human Development*, 14 (1971), 149–170.

Baltes, P.B., and K.W. Schaie, "On Life-Span Developmental Research Paradigms: Retrospect and Prospects," in P.B. Baltes and K.W. Schaie (eds.), *Life-Span Developmental Psychology: Personality and Socialization*. New York: Academic Press, 1973.

Bar-Yosef, R., "Desocialization and Resocialization: The Adjustment Process of Immigrants," *International Migration Review*, 12 (Summer, 1968), 27–45.

Bhatnagar, J., *Immigrants at School*. London: Cornmarket Press, 1970.

Boudon, R., *Education, Opportunity and Social Inequality: Changing Prospects in Western Society*. New York: John Wiley & Sons, 1974.

Campbell, D.T., and J.C. Stanley, *Experimental and Quasi-Experimental Designs for Research*. Chicago: Rand McNally, 1963.

Census of Canada, *Public Use Sample Tapes. User Documentation (Draft)*. Statistics Canada (March, 1975).

Curle, A., "Transitional Communities and Social Reconnection," *Human Relations,* 1, No. 1 (1947), 42-68.

Dillingham, W. P., *The Children of Immigrants in Schools,* Vol. 1. Reports of the Immigration Commission, Sixty-first Congress (3rd Session), December 5, 1910–March 4, 1911. Senate Documents, Vol. 13. Washington, D.C.: Government Printing Office, 1911.

Eisenstadt, S.N., *The Absorption of Immigrants.* London: Routledge & Kegan Paul, Ltd., 1954, p. 6.

Entwisle, D.R., and N.E. Frasure, "A Contradiction Resolved: Children's Processing of Syntactic Cues," *Developmental Psychology,* 10, No. 6 (1974), 854–857.

Flavell, J.H., *The Developmental Psychology of Jean Piaget.* Princeton, N.J.: Van Nostrand, 1963.

Frasure, N.E., and D.R. Entwisle, "Semantic and Syntactic Development in Children," *Developmental Psychology,* 9, No. 2 (1973), 236–245.

Inbar, M., and C. Adler, "The Vulnerable Age Phenomenon: A Serendipitous Finding," *Sociology of Education* 49, No. 3 (July 1976a), 193–200. [Quotations in this text were taken from a mimeographed draft of this article.]

Inbar, M., and C. Adler, *Ethnic Integration in Israel: A Case Study of Moroccan Brothers Who Settled in France and Israel.* New Brunswick, N.J.: Transaction Books, 1976b, forthcoming.

Inbar, M., "Immigration and Learning: The Vulnerable Age," *The Canadian Review of Sociology and Anthropology* (1976, forthcoming). [Quotations in this text were taken from a mimeographed draft of this article.]

Klineberg, O., *Negro Intelligence and Selective Migration.* New York: Columbia University Press, 1935.

Lee, E.S., "Negro Intelligence and Selective Migration: A Philadelphia Test of the Klineberg Hypothesis," in J.J. Spengler and O.D. Duncan (eds.), *Demographic Analysis: Selected Readings.* Glencoe, Ill.: The Free Press, 1956, 432–437.

Maeroff, G.I., "Junior High Is Not Easy to Handle." *The New York Times Week in Review,* December 14, 1975.

Martan, M., *Comparative Study of the Communities of Yad Rambam in Israel, and Sarcelles in France.* Paper presented at the World Congress of North African Jews, Jerusalem, 1972.

Piaget, J., *The Moral Judgment of the Child.* New York: The Free Press, 1965.

Spilerman, S., and J. Habib, "Development Towns in Israel: The Role of Communities in Creating Ethnic Disparities in Labor Force Characteristics," *American Journal of Sociology,* 81 (January, 1976), 781–812.

Sullivan, H.S., *The Interpersonal Theory of Psychiatry.* New York: W. W. Norton & Co., 1953.

New Library of Pastoral Care
GENERAL EDITOR: DEREK BLOWS

———

FAMILY MATTERS

The Pastoral Care
of Personal Relationships

———

Sue Walrond-Skinner

First published in Great Britain 1988
SPCK
Holy Trinity Church
Marylebone Road
London NW1 4DU

British Library Cataloguing in Publication Data

Walrond-Skinner, Sue
    Family matters.
    1. Christian church. Pastoral work with
    families
    I. Title
    259

    ISBN 0-281-04350-7

        Filmset by Pioneer, Perthshire
        Printed in Great Britain by
        the Anchor Press, Tiptree

*In gratitude for our
newly formed family*

Contents

Foreword

The *New Library of Pastoral Care* has been planned to meet the needs of those people concerned with pastoral care, whether clergy or lay, who seek to improve their knowledge and skills in this field. Equally, it is hoped that it may prove useful to those secular helpers who may wish to understand the role of the pastor.

Pastoral care in every age has drawn from contemporary secular knowledge to inform its understanding of man and his various needs and of the ways in which these needs might be met. Today it is perhaps the secular helping professions of social work, counselling and psychotherapy, and community development which have particular contributions to make to the pastor in his work. Such knowledge does not stand still, and a pastor would have a struggle to keep up with the endless tide of new developments which pour out from these and other disciplines, and to sort out which ideas and practices might be relevant to his particular pastoral needs. Among present-day ideas, for instance, of particular value might be an understanding of the social context of the pastoral task, the dynamics of the helping relationship, the attitudes and skills as well as factual knowledge which might make for effective pastoral intervention and, perhaps most significant of all, the study of particular cases, whether through verbatim reports of interviews or general case presentation. The discovery of ways of learning from what one is doing is becoming increasingly important.

There is always a danger that a pastor who drinks deeply at the well of a secular discipline may lose his grasp of his own pastoral identity and become 'just another' social worker or counsellor. It in no way detracts from the value of these professions to assert that the role and task of the pastor are quite unique among the helping professions and deserve to be clarified and strengthened rather than weakened. The theological commitment of the pastor and the appropriate use of his role will be a recurrent theme of the series. At the same time the pastor cannot afford to work in a vacuum. He needs to be able to communicate and co-operate with those helpers in other disciplines whose work may overlap, without loss of his own unique role. This in turn will mean being able to communicate with them through some understanding of their concepts and language.

Finally, there is a rich variety of styles and approaches in pastoral work within the various religious traditions. No attempt will be made to secure a uniform approach. The Library will contain the variety, and even perhaps occasional eccentricity, which such a title suggests. Some books will be more specifically theological and others more concerned with particular areas of need or practice. It is hoped that all of them will have a usefulness that will reach right across the boundaries of religious denomination.

DEREK BLOWS
Series Editor

Acknowledgements

My thanks are due first to Judith Longman of SPCK who invited me to write this book. It has provided me with a series of challenges in trying to see how far family therapy is a relevant and appropriate tool for the Church's ministers to use. I have learned a lot in the process. Canon Derek Blows made invaluable suggestions at the outset and provided much encouragement. I am grateful to Elizabeth Carter and Monica McGoldrick and their publishers for permission to reproduce and adapt tables 2 and 3, I would like to thank the Revd Michael Taylor and the Revd Clare Herbert for reading and commenting most helpfully upon the manuscript, also the Revd Michael Monaghan whose discussion of his own thesis with me helped me to think afresh about a theology of the family in chapter 10. I would also like to thank Mrs Sandra Webb for preparing the typescript with great care, and Mrs Joan Sutcliffe for constructing the tables and overseeing the final stages of the typescript's preparation.

Most of the clinical material described in this book is derived from my own case work with families and couples. I would like to thank them for helping me to learn and grow and change, and to thank also my co-therapist, with whom I habitually work, Phil Kingston. He is a continuous source of inspiration, and skill and Christian hope. The marriage preparation work described in chapter 8 was conducted with my husband, the Revd Graeme Parfitt, whose wisdom and tolerance and that of his parishioners has helped me to learn a lot about applying a systemic approach within the parish situation. My special thanks to him for all I have learned from him while writing the book—and for putting up with it all!

Introduction

This book is about one way of helping families and other kinds of personal relationships. It sets out to describe the theory and practice of family therapy and to illustrate some techniques of working effectively with family problems. Family therapy is not the *only* way of working with families, nor is it always the most *appropriate* way of working with many of the contrasting pastoral situations which present themselves. It does however offer a useful set of tools which pastors might adopt in their entirety in some situations or from which they might pick and choose as seems to them to be useful. The purpose of the book is not to transform pastors into family therapists but to offer some theoretical frameworks and perhaps some new skills for making the most of the wonderfully rich opportunities that the pastor's role affords.

The book provides an introduction to the method of helping families known as family therapy—but it is *only* an introduction, and anyone wishing to understand more about this method of work would be well advised to go on a course, read some of the extensive literature on the subject and link up with other people from the helping professions from whom pastors can gain help and support for the work they are trying to do. On the other hand the book can be used in a more wide-ranging way by people who have no intention of ever conducting a family therapy session as such. These people may still find it useful to understand more about how families 'work' and to glean new ideas about the ways in which one can intervene more effectively to bring about change, even during a once-off meeting with a family group.

To introduce a book on family therapy in a series devoted to pastoral care and counselling might be seen by some as a contradiction in terms. Care and counselling, with or without

1

the prefix 'pastoral', can sometimes denote a curative, or ameliorative, non-directive approach to dealing with an individual's pain or distress. The effect of the intervention may be successful in terms of the effort to *remove or change* the problem or it may be unsuccessful, necessitating the continuing *supportive interventions* of a skilled and compassionate counsellor. Or, more negatively, it may simply act as a repressive agent, silencing the cry for radical structural change.

Kenneth Leech has offered a swingeing attack on the way in which pastoral counsellors have followed the individual paradigm, mirroring their secular counterparts, and he points to the dangers which ensue: 'Casework and counselling are always in danger of degenerating into tools of reaction . . . To establish a 'Casework theology' is an extremely dangerous exercise which threatens to imprison theology within the confines of a passing outlook, as well as to privatize its concerns.'[1] And, in his most recent book, Leech asserts: 'Pastoral care must be located within the framework of struggle for the Kingdom of God and his justice'.[2]

Anderson and Guernsey also draw attention to the individualistic bias of those who have attempted to examine the family from a Christian point of view and the way in which Christian approaches to the study of the family are 'naively influenced by psychology'.[3]

Family therapy on the other hand is associated with a restructuring of *the system* in which problems are embedded, rather than the removal of symptoms of individual pain. Moreover, it shifts the balance of responsibility from the activity of the counsellor to the activity of the family system itself. Some writers suggest that a more appropriate term than family therapy/counselling would be 'systems intervention', as it clearly redefines the *target* of change as being the system and the *substance* of change as being to do with participation by the family rather than instrumentation on the part of the counsellor.[4] Moreover, it alters the basic model from a medico/psychological one to a social and communicational one, implying a philosophy and theology of intervention more in line with liberating the oppressed than with shepherding the afflicted.

But pastoral care has recently been more broadly defined

to include the political and social dimensions of change, and the inclusion in this series of the volume entitled *Liberating God* indicates that the editors of the 'New Library of Pastoral Care' understand pastoral care in this broad, inclusive sense. I will argue later in this introduction that family therapy should indeed commend itself to Christian pastoral counsellors as an important and effective tool in equipping them for pastoral ministry and that therefore a volume on the theory and practice of family therapy in a library of pastoral care is entirely appropriate.

But it makes many demands upon the pastoral counsellor as well. Since the family brings together the individual and the corporate dimensions of human existence, the counsellor, in working with the family group, is challenged to unite in some sort of creative tension the polarising tendencies with which we are surrounded, both in secular society and in the Church. By engaging in family therapy, the pastoral counsellor, whether a Christian lay person or an ordained minister, is further challenged to reflect theologically both upon the meaning and purpose of the family and upon his or her approach to intervening in its difficulties. The polarising tendencies, by which we are all affected, include the split between the needs and demands of the individual versus the needs and demands of the body or group. In theology this is reflected in the different accounts of salvation history, concerned on the one hand with the individual in more or less spiritual isolation and on the other with the community in both its social and material aspects.

Then there is the division, which follows from this, between those who argue for an individually orientated gospel of private obligations and those who preach a political gospel of community and social imperatives. And thirdly, there is the division between those who perceive their social and religious obligations as being privatised and concerned with the care and support of individuals in trouble and the cure or amelioration of their problems, and those who believe that structural and political solutions to problems may sometimes demand the abandonment of the individual in her private pain, in order that that pain may become usable in a heightened demand for social change.

Pastoral counsellors who direct their attention to the family group, rather than to the individual members of it, are engaging in an area which brings together both sides of these polarities. For the family unites the concerns of the individual with those of the group; it unites the inner world of the psyche with the outer world of a wider community; and it unites the personal with the political, combining the intimate psychotherapeutic concerns of the consulting room with the radical engagement of the community activist.

But my concern in this introduction is to consider, not what the pastoral counsellor might do for the family, but what a focus on the family might do for the pastoral counsellor and for the discipline of pastoral counselling as a whole. In parallel with its sister disciplines in the secular field, pastoral counselling developed out of a concern and focus on the individual person in distress. As they have become progressively more aware, during the last two or three decades, of the explosion in knowledge and skills in the secular fields of counselling and psychotherapy, pastoral counsellors have become even more concerned to refine their skills in relation to helping their individual clients. The American literature on pastoral counselling[5] has more recently been matched by excellent British publications[6] and there has been a proliferation of training courses and private institutes offering training and supervisory resources.

Out of these developments there has undoubtedly emerged a more sophisticated and more mature approach to the emotional, psychological and material problems of individuals. But there have also been some adverse consequences, seen in an over-concentration on skills relevant to the individual client at the expense of those required for the community or group; a growth in élitism whereby the concept of counselling has become 'owned' by the few who have received recognised training from one of the many training courses and a movement towards the professionalisation and clericalisation of its practitioners. Many of these negative effects only shadow what has been happening in the secular world and as in so many other ways, it is only too clear how closely the Church and its members can uncritically absorb the received wisdoms of their secular counterparts.

An exception to this individualistic focus has been of course the interest that pastoral counsellors have shown in marriage.

Dominated by one name, that of Jack Dominian, pastoral counsellors have, largely through his influence and writings, taken a keen interest in counselling marriages in trouble and in preventative premarital counselling. Dominian has been instrumental in encouraging pastoral counsellors to take the small but significant step away from an almost exclusive concern with individuals to the individual-in-relationship.[7] The initial approach to marital problems had again been an individual one, with the partners being seen either collaboratively (individually by two different counsellors) or concurrently by the same therapist at different times. In practice these methods are still frequently adopted by pastoral counsellors, but Dominian and others now clearly favour the conjoint approach whereby the couple are seen together and counselled as a unit.

This shift to the couple has been a significant one in pastoral counselling, and it remains hard to explain why the further logical shift to an engagement with the family group is only just emerging and is almost exclusively confined to the American scene. Browning calls attention to the need to develop a practical theology of family life and to raise crucial questions around the situation, definition and norms of the modern family.[8] He is concerned too that pastoral counsellors develop suitable strategies for influencing the family. The challenge has at last been taken up and there are several recent examples of books introducing the ideas of family therapy into the pastoral ministry.[9]

The purpose of this book is to continue the process of introducing pastoral counsellors to some of the riches which reside within the family therapy paradigm. There are several reasons why I believe this to be a useful thing to do.

(1) The conjoint approach has been shown to be an effective and economical way of helping those people who present with relationship problems as well as many of those who appear at first glance to locate their difficulties largely within themselves.

(2) It has been shown reasonably conclusively via empirical research that counselling an individual who presents with problems in his or her relationships frequently has a detrimental effect upon those relationships, and is thus much

best avoided, even at the cost of offering no help at all. The natural tendency to want to 'rescue' an individual who presents us with their pain may make such a statement quite hard and shocking to hear, especially for a Christian. This position will be developed and explained later in the book.

(3) Even problems which appear to be unconnected with the individual's significant relationship are often relieved through an individual counselling approach to the detriment of the person's relationship network (see chapter 2 for the theory behind this statement).

(4) Family therapy is often much more economical in time and effort than individual counselling and has the added advantage of acting preventatively upon people who, because they have not been 'identified' as having a problem would not normally enter a counselling situation.

(5) Family therapy combines insights from the fields of sociology, psychology, communications theory and social systems theory and bridges that gap between the individual and the individual-in-his/her-psycho-social-context instead of widening the polarisation between the two. For, paradoxically, whilst a great deal of the family therapy that is practised takes place within the four walls of the counsellor's office or in the families' home, it is nevertheless a highly political activity, shifting the emphasis from healing the victim to challenging and changing the dysfunctional or sinful structure.

(6) By its nature, family therapy opens the doors of the private world of the study or consulting room and lets in the eyes and ears of others onto the hitherto private relationship between counsellor and client. Not only is the client's family admitted, but family therapists often invite the help of a fellow counsellor—or even a team of colleagues—to work alongside the family with them. This greater openness to scrutiny and the sharing of one's counselling work with others, combined with the critical expertise that the family itself holds in terms of its own life struggles, is a useful safeguard against élitism.

But there are of course some caveats. The pastoral counsellor who is used to the one-to-one counselling situation may be aghast at the apparently unmanageable chaos of a family therapy session. He or she may fear that verbal or even physical violence may overwhelm the therapeutic effort, or that overt issues of sexuality may be hard to handle in front of young children or older relatives. The complexity of the verbal and non-verbal data offered to the counsellor by a family group is daunting and it is hard at first to know how to manage it productively. On a personal level, the pastoral counsellor is often thrust into a family situation which reminds him all too clearly of his own current or original family. He or she may well find that the emotional material being struggled with by the family mirrors too closely his or her own current personal dilemma. Whilst this of course may also be true in individual counselling,[10] the chances of it happening in family therapy are far greater because the number of individuals who comprise the family group multiply the potential for mirroring experiences. Lastly, it is often hard to be clear about the extent to which the counsellor is seen as having made a constructive contribution to the family's greater well-being, even if its functioning has markedly improved during the course of the counselling. The rightful satisfaction that the individual counsellor may experience and the overt expressions of thanks he or she may receive are often notably absent in family therapy! This is of course particularly and inevitably true of the strategic approaches discussed in chapter 6.

Notwithstanding these provisos, an acquaintance with the premises, theories and skills of family therapy would, I believe, be enormously helpful to the minister or lay Christian who practises pastoral care. But is there anything that is specific to the Christian's approach to the family, that he or she in turn might contribute to the field of family therapy? Although there may be nothing *exclusively* Christian, one would expect there to be some *specifically* Christian emphasis apparent in the pastoral counsellor's approach. For example, the family therapist's tendency to 'lose' the needs and concerns of the individual in his focus on the group may well be redressed by the Christian's underlying basic assumption concerning the unique value and worth of each individual's soul.[11] Secondly, the Christian brings to his or her work, an ultimate optimism about the human condition. Because of the promises of Christ, he or she should be able to act as a

container of meaning and hope for those who, for the time
being, can find no meaning or hope in the distress of their
current situation. This ultimate optimism is sustained by a
particular tool available to the Christian counsellor—that of
prayer. Prayer sets in its proper perspective the whole of the
counsellor's pastoral activity. His task is to acquire and use
the skills available to him to the best of his ability, but the
outcome of his interventions must always be left, through his
prayer of intercession, in the hands of God.

It should also be the case that some of the more
manipulative treatment techniques would receive the censure
of the Christian counsellor. One would expect that, although
Christians do not hold a monopoly of the truth or of a concern
for ethical imperatives, they would nevertheless be in the
fore-front of current debates regarding the ethical justification
of using covert and deceptive means to achieve particular,
desirable ends in terms of treatment outcome.[12] More
crucially, one would hope that the Christian's longer time-
perspective, which frames life in this world within the context
of eternity, would encourage him to make an important
contribution to the debate which surrounds the pragmatics
versus the aesthetics of family therapy and the efforts to
rescue the modality from an over-emphasis on short-term
problem solving. Whilst the pastoral counsellor may have
much to learn from some of the refined and extremely effective
techniques developed by family therapists, her own insight
into family members' necessary search for meaning and
purpose, beyond their immediate problems, is important to
re-state to the field as a whole. It may be too that the
Christian's sense of tradition and the value of accumulated
past wisdom can stand as a healthy corrective to what is
essentially a present and future-oriented therapeutic modality.
Ultimately though, the question as to whether the Christian
pastoral counsellor has any significant or distinctive
contribution to make to the field of family therapy must
stand or fall on whether he or she is able to elucidate a
credible theology of the family and whether, in addition, he or
she can integrate the theory and skills of family therapy
within an over-arching understanding of the existence of God
and of his purposes in the lives of human beings. I will

discuss some of the implications of these issues in the final chapter.

Notes

1. K. Leech, *Soul Friend,* Sheldon Press 1977.
2. K. Leech, *Spirituality and Pastoral Care,* Sheldon Press 1986.
3. R. S. Anderson and D. B. Guernsey, *On Being Family,* Grand Rapids, MI, Eerdmans, 1985.
4. P. Kingston, 'Family Therapy, Power, and Responsibility for Change', in S. Walrond-Skinner and D. Watson, eds., *Ethical Issues in Family Therapy,* Routledge & Kegan Paul 1987.
5. W. E. Oates (ed.), *An Introduction to Pastoral Counselling,* Broadman Press 1959; H. Clinebell, *Basic Types of Pastoral Counselling,* Nashville, TN, Abingdon Press, 1966; D. Browning, *The Moral Context of Pastoral Care,* Philadelphia, PA, Westminster Press, 1976; T. Oden, *Pastoral Theology,* New York, Harper & Row, 1983.
6. Contributions to the 'New Library of Pastoral Care' (SPCK) represent useful British contributions. In addition, the following are helpful: A. Campbell, *Rediscovering Pastoral Care,* Darton, Longman & Todd 1981; F. Wright, *The Pastoral Nature of the Ministry,* SCM Press 1980; F. Wright, *Pastoral Care for Lay People,* SCM Press 1982.
7. J. Dominian, *Make or Break,* SPCK 1984; J. Dominian, *An Introduction to Marital Problems,* Collins 1986.
8. D. Browning, 'Mapping the Terrain of Pastoral Theology', a lecture delivered at the International Conference of Pastoral Care, Manchester, 1986.
9. D. Anderson, *New Approaches to Family Pastoral Care,* Philadelphia, PA, Fortress Press 1980; H. Anderson, *The Family and Pastoral Care,* Philadelphia, PA, Fortress Press, 1984.
10. D. Brandon, *Zen in the Art of Helping,* Routledge & Kegan Paul, 1976.
11. J. Carpenter, 'For the Good of the Family', in Walrond-Skinner and Watson, eds., op.cit.
12. Walrond-Skinner and Watson, eds., op.cit.

ONE

Preparing the Ground

What is Family Counselling?

Helping family groups as distinct from individual family
members has a rather recent history within professional
counselling practice. As with many things, its appearance
was a result of a convergence between old ideas looked at in
new ways, the pressure of practical necessity and, so far as
the British development was concerned, a misunderstanding.

But first we need to define 'family therapy' or 'family
counselling'—two terms which will be used interchangeably
throughout this book.

*Family therapy can be defined as a method of counselling,
offered to a family group as a whole, using as its primary
means of intervention, conjoint interpersonal interviews.*

Whether or not we use the term *counselling* or *therapy* has
been discussed in relation to work with individuals in many
other places. For our present purpose either is equally
appropriate, and the choice is likely to relate more to the
professional background of the worker than to the means of
help that he or she is offering. Within the traditions of
pastoral care adopted by clergy and others in the Church, the
term 'counselling' will probably feel more comfortable. The
term 'family counselling' when used in this book does not
therefore imply (as it has in some clinical circles) any
distinction or difference from the term 'family therapy'. Both
are used to describe the treatment or pastoral care of the
family group as a whole, using the whole range of methods
and techniques which have been developed and refined over
the last forty years.

Family counselling is offered to *the family group as a
whole.* In other words, it is the family, not any one member of
it that is the counsellor's primary focus of concern. Much

10

follows from this different emphasis in terms of the methods of help which will be adopted and, for most pastoral counsellors trained and experienced in helping individuals, working with the family group as a whole entails a significant conceptual leap and a whole new orientation to pastoral care.

At this point it may be useful to make a few points about the definition of the term 'family'. Nothing that is written in this book should be understood as supporting any one, narrow definition of family form or structure, such as the nuclear family unit made up of a husband, wife and one or more immature children. On the contrary, as I have written more fully elsewhere,[1] the pastoral counsellor can only engage effectively in assisting families in difficulties, if he recognises and accepts the multiplicity of family forms which characterise social life in most parts of the world in the latter half of the twentieth century. Thus we must avoid sacralising one kind of family structure — the nuclear unit — and defining it as the norm. Not only does this marginalise the majority of people who do not belong to such a structure; it also marginalises the potential usefulness of the family counsellor. The *variety* in form which characterises family life is in fact a necessary means by which the structure of the family becomes adapted to and therefore remains viable within the changing conditions of its social environment. For the purposes of this book therefore the term family should be deemed to include this variety, and we might define the family simply as:

> a dynamic, interdependent psychological unit, made up of individuals and the interactions between them, a nucleus of whom form a household over time and may be related by either blood or law in addition to their emotional bonds. Whilst a family will evolve and change through the course of its life-cycle, its members will retain crucial emotional significance for one another, of both a positive and negative kind.

It is with this definition of 'family' in mind that this book is sub-titled 'The Pastoral Care of Personal Relationships'.

Because family counselling is offered to *the family group as a whole,* it has much in common with group work or group counselling. The worker abandons the intimacy of the one-to-one counselling situation and involves himself with the complex network of relationships within the group and the many layers and levels of communication between the group's members. But the family group is a very particular *kind* of group, for it existed before the counsellor made contact with it and it will continue to exist in some form or other long after he has ceased to be involved. This is quite different from working with a 'stranger' group, where members of the group—perhaps depressed young mothers or unemployed men or even a Bible study group—depend for their existence as a group on being called together by the leader. In all these groups the relationship between group members is to some extent defined by the task for which the group has been convened, and because the counsellor or leader has often decided upon the task, chosen the members and set out the framework for the group's agenda, he or she is in a pivotal position in relation to the group's functioning and existence. These general features of an 'artificially' formed group are in strong contrast with that of the 'naturally' formed family group. Notwithstanding the plurality of shapes and sizes which the family group may take, families have in common the fact that they form and function independently of any outside agent and they possess the means of both creating long-term relationships with many and various adjoining groups and independently perpetuating themselves over very long periods of time. It is in fact the family's ongoing commitment to both a 'vertical' network (its history over time throughout many generations) and a 'lateral' network (its relationships with other families, with schools, work groups, churches, peer groups and other aspects of its social, emotional and political environment) which distinguishes the family from other types of group structure. The family counsellor must therefore concern himself with the family group in its vertical and lateral context and consider both the internal world of the family's relationships and its external relationships with its past and with its current social environment.

The last part of our definition concerns the means by which the counsellor will try to help the family, '*the conjoint interpersonal interview*'. As with other kinds of pastoral counselling, family counselling relies primarily on direct, face to face interventions during a therapeutic interview. Because the interview is offered to the family and not, as a rule, to its individual members, the term 'conjoint' is invoked in order to underline the fact that the counsellor will normally be engaged in face-to-face work with two or more family members. In other words, the counsellor's interventions will be directed towards the relationships between family members as much as to family members themselves, and the primary goal of the counselling process will be to effect changes in the family's pattern of relationships rather than in the behaviour or feelings of its individual members.

Definitions may either be made so inclusive as to lose all meaning or be so circumscribed as to cut off any connection with what lies outside their bounds. The purpose of trying to define family counselling is to indicate its distinctive potential as a method of pastoral care. This should not however imply that there is no connection between family counselling and working with individuals or other kinds of groups. Reference has already been made to some ways in which work with family groups resembles other forms of group work. Similarly, there will be many occasions in which the family counsellor draws upon his knowledge and skills in working with individuals, and there will sometimes be a place for individual counselling within a programme of family counselling. This is why the important word 'primary' is included in the definition. Conjoint interpersonal interviews with the whole family will be the primary means of intervention for the family counsellor, but there will be many occasions when the counsellor will choose to see a variety of sub-groups on their own. These may include the marital couple, the children as a group or perhaps the couple's parents. It may also sometimes be necessary to see individual family members alone and, although this is a more unusual procedure for the family counsellor to adopt, it is very important to retain an understanding of the unique part played by each individual family member in the complex pattern created by the whole.

The family counsellor must operate within the three over-lapping worlds of the family group, its context and its individual members' psyches and he or she will frequently be working at the interface of these three worlds simultaneously. Having said that, it remains the unique aim and contribution of the family counsellor to direct his efforts and attention to the transactional processes of the family group and, in John Bell's words, to bring about 'the transformation of the family into a more perfectly functioning group'.[2] Technically and theoretically the help that comes to individuals through this process, and perhaps to the wider community within which the family functions, is a by-product of this primary focus and goal. Again, this may seem a surprising and perhaps rather shocking statement to those who normally operate as counsellors to individuals.

Historical Development

Although it is often argued that family therapy represents a break in continuity from previous approaches to counselling and psychotherapy, it is, I believe, important to acknowledge the links as well as the differences with the past. When we come to discuss the four main 'schools' of family therapy in chapters 6 and 7 it will become obvious that each approach draws upon a body of theory developed earlier for the treatment of individuals or groups. Although family therapy has contributed a wealth of new ideas and opened out many new possibilities to the whole counselling field, it has also drawn heavily upon the discoveries of the great pioneers of the past. In addition, the British branch of the family-therapy tree has been formed by its own unique ancestry as well as by the rich influences of earlier American developments and, to a lesser extent, by cross-fertilisation with developments which have taken place in Europe.

The beginnings of family therapy are usually dated to the 1940s and 1950s in the United States, when three separate developments began to coalesce. The first was within child psychiatry and is linked with the names of Nathan Ackerman (New York), Murray Bowen (Washington) and with Salvador Minuchin (Philadelphia). These workers began to see how the child's disturbance was inextricably connected with what was going on in the rest of the family. Early papers commented on the way in which the child was apparently being 'scapegoated' on behalf of the 'well' siblings or had become the 'elected member' to somehow bear the troubles of the group as a whole. It became clear to these workers that the disturbed child often seemed to act as a sort of cement, 'gluing' together a family group which would probably otherwise fall apart. The concern and attention of every family member was focused upon Johnny's delinquency or Sara's problems at school and, while the child continued to display these problems, family members were relieved from having to attend to perhaps more fundamental difficulties that existed between them.

Because of the obvious way in which the person displaying the problem was seen to be doing so reactively to his family group, this individual became known as the 'identified patient', rather than simply the 'patient' or 'client'. This has remained the usual terminology for the symptom-bearer in family therapy, as it indicates clearly that, although one person may and often does call attention to the family's difficulties or distress, it is the family as a whole that is, in reality, 'the patient' or the focus for the counsellor's concern. The individual symptom-bearer has indeed identified himself to the outside world and has been so identified by the family as the patient but this is only the beginning of the story.

The second important strand in the development of family therapy was the work of the anthropologist Gregory Bateson and his colleagues at the Mental Research Institute in California. Studying the communication patterns of adult schizophrenic patients, they produced a seminal paper of the most crucial significance in 1951 entitled 'Towards a Theory of Schizophrenia'. Through their researches Bateson, Jackson, Haley and Weakland generated new concepts about family interaction including the famous double-bind hypothesis. They suggested that schizophrenia resulted from a person being placed in an untenable position in relation to someone who was of primary emotional significance to him. Two contradictory messages are received at once, so that there is no way in which the loved person can be pleased or obeyed. For example, a parent holds out his arms to his small child in welcome but his facial expression indicates anger or hostility. The child perceives both love and hostility in the parent's non-verbal messages and is left confused.[3] From the early work of Bateson and his colleagues, a rich field of studies in communication theory has developed, giving rise to many new and productive approaches to both the understanding and treatment of family problems.

The third strand in the American development of family therapy was the growing concern with marriage and its break-up. Early pioneering centres were opened by Abraham and Hannah Stone and by Emily Mudd. Although from early on in its history the field of marital therapy viewed the marriage relationship as the patient rather than the individual partners, the treatment focus was often on one or other of the couple separately. Early methods of work tended to be either *concurrent* or *collaborative,* rather than conjoint, whereby each partner was seen either *concurrently by the same* counsellor at different times or *collaboratively by two different* workers at different times. Nevertheless these interpersonal approaches to marriage problems gave impetus to the shift away from an individualistic understanding of relationship problems. Because the marriage relationship is central to many family groups, it was but a short step to relate the new knowledge coming from the field of marital studies to a better understanding of how families themselves function.

At the beginning of this chapter I mentioned that the British development of family therapy owed its start to a misunderstanding. The story is told of the American psychiatrist, John Bell, coming to Scotland to visit John Sunderland. In conversation, Bell understood Sunderland to say that John Bowlby had begun treating family groups at the Tavistock Clinic, London. Although this was not in fact the case, the idea filled John Bell with enthusiasm to try something similar and his enthusiasm in turn inspired John Bowlby to experiment with a practice which he was already believed to have begun.[4] It was not until the mid-1960s that British practitioners began to take a serious interest in the developments in the United States. Gradually an awareness of family therapy began to creep into the curricula of training courses for social workers and psychiatrists, and in 1972 The Family Institute, the first agency in Britain specialising entirely in family therapy, was established in Cardiff. In 1976 the first two British texts on family therapy were published.[5] British family therapy has in no sense been simply a matter of importing the American version lock, stock and barrel, important though its American antecedents have been.

British family therapy owes much of its character and sturdiness to the influence of other theoretical strands as well, and to three in particular — group analysis, attachment theory developed by John Bowlby, and the 'radical' school of psychiatry led by Laing and Cooper.[6]

The 1970s and 1980s have seen an enormous development of interest in family therapy amongst counsellors and other practitioners in Britain. As in the United States, the field of marital studies has also been influential. The work of the Institute of Marital Studies, highlighted the marriage relationship as a focus of treatment and, as in America, there has been a gradual development from concurrent and collaborative treatment to conjoint counselling.[7] This development has also been reflected in the work of the Marriage Guidance Council, now significantly retitled 'Relate', and there has been a growing convergence between the fields of family and marital work. In 1976 The Association for Family Therapy was established, producing its own *Journal for Family Therapy* with an international circulation. Family therapy has 'come of age', gaining respectability amongst all the major mental health disciplines and showing itself to be an effective means of assisting families in difficulties and bringing about positive change. It is not a panacea and it is not an appropriate method to adopt in all situations in the parish, but it is worthy of consideration by clergy and others who are involved in pastoral care.

Equipping Ourselves for the Task

Before considering the theory and practice of family counselling in more detail, it might be useful to review the many resources that the clergy person brings to aid him or her working with distressed families. We can conveniently divide these sources of knowledge into three: (1) the knowledge we derive from being ourselves members of a family; (2) the general knowledge of family life which we acquire through hearing about the families of others — sometimes in real life and sometimes through fiction; (3) the knowledge of other kinds of pastoral counselling and the general skills of relating to and helping people, which we have acquired both through training and experience. Far from being daunted by the considerable body of specialised theory and technique which has been built up around the practice of family therapy, we should first review with confidence the many areas of relevant knowledge and skills which we already possess.

It is often said that we are all experts when it comes to understanding the family. And there is a deep truth here which should always be borne in mind when the so-called 'experts' appear to be given too much authority. The expertise to which almost every human being is a party is his or her own experience of family life. It is of course true that a very small number of people have almost no experience of what it means to live in a family. For most of us however the experience of family is immediate and tangible, and stretches from childhood to our current living situation in a complex kaleidoscope of ever changing patterns and colours. We, like those we seek to help, are embedded in a lateral and vertical network of relationships in which we naturally see ourselves as the centre point. Throughout our lifetime we will struggle to maintain some comfortable balance in our intimate relationships between attachment and intimacy on the one hand and separation and independence on the other. Human beings need both to belong and to be alone, and we will have different needs in relation to both, depending upon the stage we are at in our life cycle and on a variety of other factors which are affecting us at different moments in our lives.

Each of us has at our disposal a range of social and familial experiences which we can make available for our use as helping persons. To be female, to be white, to be an only child, to be married, to be in my mid-forties are all factors defining a range of my own intimate experience which helps me understand some things about families better and differently than others.

For example, I cannot know from the inside, what it is like to be a man, to be black, to have brothers and sisters or to be any age that is older than I am at present. I know what it is like to be *unmarried* but I will not know what it is like *never to have been married*. I may however study books on male sexuality, black culture, the effects of one's sibling position on personality development, the ageing process and the experience of life-long singleness and thus gain a good deal of knowledge and understanding about situations I have never, and can never experience. The first kind of knowledge (inside, subjective knowledge) is not necessarily better than the second kind (outside, objective knowledge) but the two are different and we need to be able to distinguish these different sources of knowledge one from the other and to understand their effects upon us. We may, for example, inappropriately believe that we 'know' how someone who is an unmarried mother, or divorced or childless feels because we have had those experiences ourselves. On the other hand we may believe that we 'don't know' how someone in those situations feels because we have not encountered them ourselves. We will never live through the whole range of experiences known to human beings in their intimate relations, and yet we can increase our understanding of both our subjective and objective knowledge and make it more useful to us in our counselling work with families.

A very good way of increasing our subjective knowledge is to use a tool known as a genogram or family tree to examine our own family experiences. Figure 1 shows the genogram of a woman who was professionally engaged in family counselling for some years. In Chapter 7, we will examine the full potential of the genogram for helping families in distress. For the present we will view it as an aid in helping the family counsellor understand his or her own experiences more fully. When we look at Sara's genogram, we can see at a glance how some experiences, such as death and bereavement are very prominent in Sara's experience of family, but she has only had one experience of divorce or marital separation in her immediate family. Also, she has had very little experience of or contact with children, having been brought up without any living siblings and by parents who were aged thirty-eight and forty-four when she was born. Only one of her six potential aunts and uncles married or has children, and of these two first cousins one remains single and the other marries late and emigrates to America. Sara herself marries late and has no children. We might guess from these rather limited experiences of family life, that one of the factors motivating Sara to work with families might be curiosity! We might further guess, from the data so far, that in her work

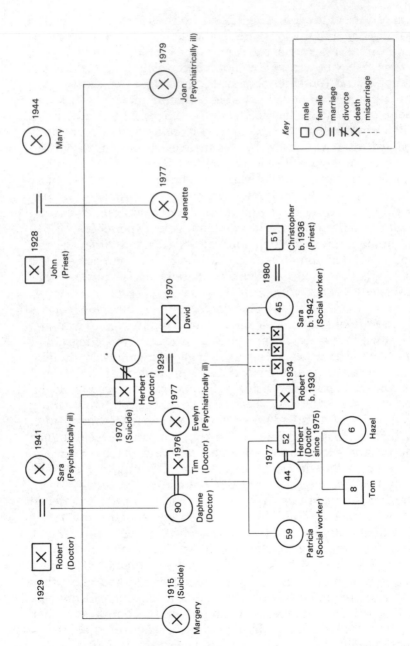

Figure 1   Sara's Genogram

with families Sara will find it easier to understand both the difficulties and the potential of older family members but may be alarmed and disturbed by the threat of loss or separation. She may need to review how far she has worked through the multiple losses that she sustained during the 1970s and, depending upon her relationships with these five pivotal family members, examine the extent to which her feelings of guilt, fear, rejection and attachment have been integrated and accepted. Her late marriage occurs soon after these multiple losses took place and, since it is very common for lost family members to be replaced by new ones and for the loss not to be fully integrated, some examination of this juxtaposition of events might serve to strengthen the foundations of Sara's marriage which in turn would strengthen her ability as a counsellor. Her primary childhood experience is that of being a replacement child, following the death of a male sibling and three miscarriages. This suggests that she may have experienced both the positive and negative attentions of her elderly parents in a particularly sharp and intense way and that she might have had to try to fulfil their expectations, unrelieved by the existence of brothers and sisters with whom she could have shared this burden. Her experience of triangular relationships will have been powerful and this will give her important insights into the many triangles that form in families around children, in-laws or extra-marital partners. Although she is actually the second-born child, she in fact carries the role of the eldest and with it responsibility for her parents and unmarried paternal aunts, all in their seventies, when she herself is in her thirties. (Toman has drawn attention to the significance of people's sibling position in their family of origin in determining some of the roles they may play and some of the functions they may continue to carry in their family of procreation and throughout life.[8]) Sara and Christopher get married at the same age as her parents were when they produced her. She might therefore need to review how far her own parents' urgent need to conceive and bear a live child has been transmitted to her and the extent to which she and her husband can make free choices in this matter, rather than reacting to deep emotional pressures from her past. Sara's mother in fact came from a family where there had been a strong need to produce a boy and where Sara's mother had been the third 'disappointment' before the much needed boy appeared. We can assume therefore that the death of Robert, her parents' first-born, was of added significance over and above the obvious trauma of childhood death. The fact that Sara was female, when she 'should have been' male in order to be a full replacement for Robert, may have affected her experience of her own sexuality in ways which she would need to clarify in order to be free to engage fully in work with families. Finally, almost every member of Sara's family is either a 'helper' or a 'patient'. They are either in clearly defined helping roles such as doctor, social worker or priest or they have been the subjects of psychiatric care themselves. Sara would need therefore to be clear as to the part played by this dialectic between sickness and healing in her own formation as a helping person. (Choices of first names are interesting to note in this respect.)

Each family counsellor needs continuously to review the meaning of his or her own family experiences. The past does not remain static or unchanged, for it is affected by our movement through the present toward the future, making us re-evaluate it continuously in the light of new experience. It needs to be understood in such a way that the counsellor can be freed of its constraints as well as guided by the inner wisdom it provides. Each of us reworks certain crucial themes throughout both our personal and our ministerial lives. The more we can gain understanding of what these themes are, the better equipped we will be as helping people. (In chapter 9 we will consider further ways in which the pastor can aid and extend his personal understanding of himself and his own family context.)

The second main source of knowledge about family life which we all have at our disposal is hearing about the families of others. Listening to our friends and colleagues, overhearing the experiences of others when one is out shopping, and becoming part of other people's family experiences through our friendship with them. Quite apart from the massive literature on the family drawn from sociology, psychology and anthropology, one of the best and most accessible sources of objective knowledge is fiction. Every soap opera centres around family life, and television plays frequently take family relationships as a central theme. We may sometimes find the type of family experiences they describe as bizarre, distasteful or quite outside our range of experience, but they can often, for these very reasons, extend our repertoire of knowledge and understanding and, hopefully, our empathy and insight.

Stories from a wide variety of sources can teach us both by their contrast and by their similarity to our own experience of family. The story of the Holy Family in Luke 2.41—50 describes the archetypal need of teenagers to 'do their own thing', find their own vocation and be separate from their parents, as well as telling us of the anguish and misunderstanding of parents, faced with loss and change. Even though the culture and the context are very different from our own, we can recognise here some themes of family life which do not change over time. 'All happy families resemble one another; each unhappy family is unhappy in its own way,' Tolstoy reminds us in *Anna Karenina,* and it is certainly the case that the novelist and playwright can often pin-point the unique and particular unhappiness of a family in distress. But out of the particularity of individual pain, we can extend our understanding of the universal truths about family life. Shakespeare's plays, for example, provide a rich hunting-ground for learning about many complex relationship problems, and so do the novels of Dickens, Jane Austen and George Eliot, and of contemporary writers such as Iris Murdoch, Fay Weldon and Graham Greene. Plays by Arthur Miller, Eugene O'Neill and T. S. Eliot give us enormous insight into the complex pattern of family dynamics.[9] The marital relationship, too, has been examined from every possible point of view by novelists and playwrights.[10]

The third body of knowledge which will assist us in trying to help families in difficulties is the whole range of learning and skills which we have already acquired in becoming ministers or lay pastors. Our training and experience in helping individuals can be built upon, and although we often need to approach a family group differently from the way we would approach its individual members, much of what we know already can be used.

For example, the *qualities* which go to make up an effective family counsellor will not be markedly different from those of an individual counsellor. He or she will equally need to possess self-awareness, energy, courage, compassion, an inner authority and a sense of humour for, as Friedman so rightly comments, 'self-definition is a more important agent of change than expertise'. He goes on: 'there is an intrinsic relationship between our capacity to put families together and our ability to put ourselves together,'[11] and anyone who works for long with troubled families will know that there is often an uncanny relationship (which can be exploited for the good of the family one is trying to help) between the family's problems and those which the counsellor is trying to solve himself. Developing these general therapeutic qualities and increasing one's own sense of integrity, self-definition and spiritual power is as essential in family counselling as it is in working with individuals.

The generic *skills* of counselling are also important. These have been thoroughly described in a variety of excellent books on pastoral counselling.[12] For example, the family counsellor must also be a good listener, an even better one in fact than the individual counsellor, since there is so much more to listen to as well as to watch in a family counselling session. He or she must learn to convey what Carl Rogers described as the core conditions of the helping process, the empathy, genuineness and non-possessive warmth which enables human beings to risk trying to change.

He or she must also acquire the detailed range of *micro-skills* which have been identified as part of effective counselling behaviour, learning to ask open-ended questions, interpret the words and actions of family members correctly and reflect back to them the counsellor's observations in an appropriate way and at an appropriate moment. Many of these skills will be learned through prolonged experience of the many pastoral situations in which the clergy person will be engaged and they will now often be made easier to acquire through formal training courses in counselling either at theological college or elsewhere.

We have reviewed briefly the definition and history of family counselling, as well as examining the knowledge and experience already owned by the potential family counsellor. We are now in a position to discuss the theoretical base that underpins the family counselling approach.

Notes

1. S. Walrond-Skinner, 'Creative Forms of Family Life: Can the Church let it happen?' in Furlong, M., ed., *Mirror to the Church*, SPCK 1988.
2. J. E. Bell, 'Family Group Therapy', *Public Health Monograph 64*, US Department of Health, Education and Welfare, 1961.
3. For a more detailed discussion of the double-bind theory see P. Watzlawick et al., *The Pragmatics of Human Communication*, Faber 1968. The material is summarised in S. Walrond-Skinner, *Dictionary of Psychotherapy*, Routledge & Kegan Paul 1986, under the entry 'Double bind'.
4. J. Bowlby, 'The Study and Reduction of Group Tension in the Family', reprinted in S. Walrond-Skinner, *Developments in Family Therapy*, Routledge & Kegan Paul 1981.
5. These were A. C. R. Skynner, *One Flesh, Separate Persons*, Constable 1976 and S. Walrond-Skinner, *Family Therapy — The Treatment of Natural Systems*, Routledge & Kegan Paul 1976.
6. The following provide introductions to these theoretical strands: M. Pines (ed.), *The Evolution of Group Analysis*, Routledge & Kegan Paul 1983; J. Bowlby, *Attachment and Loss*, 3 volumes, Penguin 1969, 1973, 1980; D. Cooper, *Psychiatry and Anti-Psychiatry*, Penguin 1967; and R. D. Laing, *The Politics of Experience*, Penguin 1967.
7. See for example K. Bannister and L. Pincus, *Shared Phantasy in Marital Problems*, Codicott Press 1965, and H. V. Dicks, *Marital Tensions*, Routledge & Kegan Paul 1967.
8. W. Toman, *Family Constellation*, Springer 1961.
9. For example: Arthur Miller's *Death of a Salesman*, Eugene O'Neill's *Long Day's Journey into Night* and T. S. Eliot's *Family Reunion* and *The Cocktail Party*.
10. For example: Ingmar Bergman's *Scenes from a Marriage*, Henrik Ibsen's *The Doll's House*, Edward Albee's *Who's Afraid of Virginia Woolf*, Harold Pinter's *Betrayal*.
11. E. H. Friedman, *Generation to Generation*, New York, Guilford Press, 1985.
12. For example, M. Jacobs, *Still Small Voice*, SPCK 1982, and *Swift to Hear*, SPCK 1985.

TWO

Theoretical Frameworks

Over the last forty years, a well delineated body of specialist theory has been developed. In this chapter, we will examine three major theoretical constructs which underpin the practice of family therapy.

General Systems Theory

The most promising theoretical framework to become available for use by the family therapist has been general systems theory, developed specifically in order to describe the theory of interacting *wholes* and not the behaviour of individuals. General systems theory was first formulated in the 1940s by Ludwig von Bertalanffy, and this 'appeared' at exactly the right moment for those counsellors and practitioners who were concerned to shift their focus from the individual to the family group.[1]

Yet this idea of the interconnectedness of human beings has in fact a much longer history. We find it permeating the writings of the Eastern mystics; for example, Lao Tzu's *Tao Te Ching* is redolent with 'systems concepts'. Yet the individualistic bias of Western philosophy and culture has been, until quite recently, a stumbling block to understanding the deep wisdom of these truths. The method and means of understanding phenomena both in science and philosophy has been essentially reductionist, in that wholes are reduced to parts for analysis and study. It is not difficult to see how, given this scientific and cultural context, the work of the founding fathers in psychology—Freud, Adler, Skinner—was consciously directed towards the individual, deliberately divorced from his psycho-social context. As counsellors, we inherit that model and are deeply affected by its implications. The family counsellor must redirect his interest away from

26

the individual and towards 'the pattern that connects', the space that lies between, and the systems model acts as a crucial aid in enabling us to make that conceptual leap from the individual to the individual-within-his/her-psycho-social-context.

Fritjof Capra, in an important book in which he examines the development of the 'new physics' and its implications for the political, social and economic order of Western society, describes the importance of systems theory in helping us to change direction:

> The systems view looks at the world in terms of relationships and integration. Systems are integrated wholes whose properties cannot be reduced to those of smaller units. Instead of concentrating on basic building blocks or basic substances, the systems approach emphasises basic principles of organisation . . . The same aspects of wholeness are exhibited by social systems — such as an ant hill, a bee hive or a human family . . . all these natural systems are wholes whose specific structure arises from the interactions and interdependence of their parts. The activity of systems involves a process known as transaction — the simultaneous and mutually inter-dependent interaction between multiple components.
>
> Systemic properties are destroyed when a system is dissected, either physically or theoretically, into isolated elements. Although we can discern individual parts in any system, the nature of the whole is always different from the mere sum of its parts.[2]

I have included this lengthy quotation from Capra's book, because in it is contained the first element of systems theory that is vital for the family counsellor to grasp — the concept of wholeness or non-summativity. The whole is *more than* the sum of its parts and it is therefore impossible to understand the whole (i.e. the family group) simply by understanding its individual parts (i.e. the family members) and 'adding up' one's impressions of them. The character of the family system transcends the sum of the characteristics of its individual family members and therefore the family counsellor's contact with the family group yields radically different data and different opportunities for intervention from a counselling contact with individual family members.

The second element of systems theory follows from this principle, that every system has a boundary, which circumscribes its identity in time and space. Boundaries provide the interface between the system and its environment (i.e. between one family and other families or community groups) and, within the system, between its parts (i.e. between subgroups such as the marital couple and the children). Bronfenbrenner has described the individual's environment as 'a set of nested structures', each of which relies upon its boundary to protect it and to enable it to have contact with the next level in the structure.[3]

An important part of the family counsellor's initial task is therefore to try to determine the boundary of the family system correctly. Which people constitute this family and what important adjoining systems lie in its immediate or more remote environment?—these are important early questions for the counsellor to ask. Unless the family counsellor determines the system's boundary correctly, she will end up working, not with a system, but merely with a random collection of its parts. Having plotted the family system's boundary correctly, the counsellor may *then* decide to work at the interface of one or more of its sub-systems, as we will note in later chapters. But she will then be doing so from within an understanding of the family system as a whole and its relationships with its environment.

Every family system is engaged in transactions between itself and its environment. The family's boundary with the outside world may be so rigid and *impermeable* that the family is all but isolated from friends and neighbours. These families are described as 'enmeshed'. Because their energy is so inwardly directed, a considerable strain is placed on relationships and for the same reason they may have little outside support to draw upon when they are experiencing stress. On the other hand, the boundary of some families is so *diffuse* that it provides little security in terms of a stable membership or clear guidelines as to what matters can rightly be considered 'private' to the family and what can rightly be shared with others. These families are described as 'disengaged'. Members enter and leave the family system in a chaotic way, providing no enduring hope for the family's continuing identity. Ideally, the family system's boundary will be sufficiently permeable to allow a free and dynamic exchange with the outside world, but sufficiently clear that the family's stability and identity over time is safeguarded.

Thirdly, every system, including the family system, is engaged in a continuous process of internal transaction between its sub-systems. The inputs of the system's components (in the family's case, the behaviour of its individual members) are *simultaneous* and *mutually inter-dependent* not *sequential and linearly connected.* This brings us to the crucial notion of *causality.* Because a system operates as a whole and the activity between its parts is *transactional,* we cannot talk about event A causing event B in a straight linear sequence. Because we are all so steeped in a linear causal model, we tend to view events this way almost automatically. When a couple have a disagreement, each is usually concerned to establish 'who started it'. If one of them can prove that it was the other, then it follows that the other was 'to blame'. This preoccupation with a 'blame game' version of events stands in the way of any resolution of the couple's or family's difficulties or in their ability to construct new patterns of interaction which will be more mutually satisfying. Figure 2 illustrates the difficulty (and irrelevance) of deciding 'who started it' or 'who is to blame'.

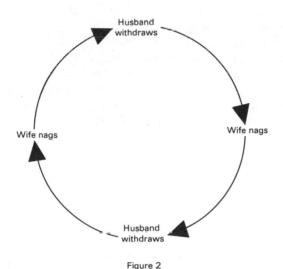

Figure 2

Even within a simple dyadic relationship such as this, the transactional situation is highly complex. Both husband and wife would argue that they are engaged in a sequential process of interaction. Whereas the husband would 'punctuate' the sequence in one way, his wife would 'punctuate' it in quite another. The wife would argue, for example, that when her husband comes home from work, all he wants to do is to put his feet up and bury himself in the newspaper or the television. All she does is to try and alert him to the fact that some friends are coming round later and unless they get on with what needs to be done now, they will not be ready for their guests. He gets angry and slams out of the room. He on the other hand would say that the minute he comes home from work, his wife regales him with all the disasters of the day saying that before he sits down he must attend to the broken catch on the bathroom door because some friends are coming round later and will need to use the bathroom. All he does is to ask for a few moments peace to recover from the day before getting started on home maintenance. Both versions of events are 'true' but partial. Neither party is able to look at the 'pattern that connects' or the circular process of transaction that occurs between them.

The fourth systems concept that is useful for the family counsellor to understand is that of homeostasis or morphostasis, meaning 'steady state'. Within every system, there are always two contrary pulls operating—the pull towards maintaining stability (morphostasis) and the pull towards change (morphogenesis). There is a constant tension between these two tendencies which is held in balance by a regulator and governed by a process known as feedback, which may be either positive or negative. Feedback is the means whereby new information from the environment is introduced into a system, leading either to change and variation (positive feedback) or to stability and homeostasis (negative feedback). In a mechanical system, the regulator may, for example, be a thermostat which enables the temperature of a house to change or stay the same according to the positive or negative feedback received.

In a family system, one member may act as the system's regulator. He or she, by becoming the identified patient, enables the family to engage in one or other of these two contrary activities, depending upon how the system responds to the identified patient's regulating messages. For example, the identified patient may be used by the family as the signal of distress, indicating that the family as a whole is in need of outside intervention, in order to help it to change. Such a signal is nearly always expressed ambivalently. Other family members will want to disassociate themselves from the identified patient's 'ownership' of the problem, yet they will often dimly perceive that they are connected in some way with it and that they may stand to gain, as well as perhaps to lose, by becoming part of the counselling process. On the other hand, the identified patient's problem may be used to prevent change and growth in the system for months or years.

For example, a mentally handicapped teenage boy is kept at home even though there is adequate provision in the community for him to go to a day centre or even live independently in a hostel. His mother goes nowhere without him and the whole family continues to give him the care and support which they appropriately gave when he was a small child but which he now no longer needs. As a result, the family as a whole has got 'stuck' at an early developmental stage and, instead of being able to move on and face the new challenge of adolescent children and a mature marital relationship between the parents, individual family members are left to create their own solutions independently of one another. The father spends less and less time at home and starts an affair; the mother becomes more and more desperate to cling on to her son and keep him a child; the daughter feels obliged to mother her mother and, in the process, she is able to avoid the challenge of making new relationships and starting her own career and/or family. The family system often needs outside help at these moments of imbalance in the relationship between stability and change. These often occur during the periods of natural transition in the life cycle and will be discussed further in chapter 3. It is in order to help correct this imbalance that an outside agent, such as a family counsellor, can effectively be introduced.

Finally, the concept of triangulation, derived from systems theory by family theorists such as Bowen and Minuchin.[4] Because of the family system's need to maintain stability, it develops various 'standard' means of dealing with conflict. These include triangling in a third person, detouring the conflict though a third person and the creation of coalitions. Triangulation may occur when there is stress between spouses and one of them draws one of the children into a close relationship in order to exclude the other parent. The parent sides with the child against the other parent and whilst this may defuse the original cause of conflict between the spouses, it produces stress in both the triangled child and the excluded parent. Triangulation may occur with an extra-marital partner, friend, grandparent or other member of the family system and always acts as a systemic defence against conflict resolution.

Similarly, some families cope with conflict by detouring it through a third party. Minuchin describes two types of detouring strategy: detouring—attacking when a child or other family member is defined as the source of the family's problems and, through the scapegoating that results, the parents are able to retain the myth of marital harmony; and detouring—supportive, when the child is defined as sick or weak and the parents are drawn together to support him. The first type produces 'acting out' or delinquent behaviour in the child; the second produces 'acting in', psychosomatic or withdrawal behaviour.

The forming of coalitions is a third method of diverting conflict and avoiding the search for an appropriate resolution. Coalitions of two or more family members may be formed, creating an alliance against those who do not belong. The discomfort of the excluded/excluding experience creates what Bateson calls 'the infinite dance of shifting coalitions'.[5] A pathological coalition is usually formed across the generational boundary and involves, for example, a grandparent or aunt and the children against one or both parents. This coalition manoeuvre can produce family feuds over several generations, with new members being recruited into one or other side of the coalition without having had the slightest contact with the original source of conflict.

Communications Theory

The second major theoretical base for family therapy is

communications theory. Relying closely upon systems concepts, communications theory was developed by Bateson and his colleagues at the Mental Research Institute, California.[6] The original team's work was further developed by Watzlawick, Fisch and others[7] and has been further extended and applied to many intransigent clinical situations which have seemed impervious to all other forms of help. We will consider the application of communications theory when discussing both structural and strategic family therapy in chapter 6. Because family counselling is concerned with the transactions *between* family members, tools for understanding the way family members communicate are potentially of great use to the counsellor. Communication, as defined in communications theory, is a broad term, encompassing all the external behaviour of a person, both verbal and non-verbal. This behaviour is viewed as being simultaneously both *expressive* of inner feeling for the individual and *communicative* to other people within the family system. Watzlawick and his colleagues present several interrelated axioms of communications theory.

(1) Communication and behaviour are synonymous and it is therefore impossible not to communicate. If, therefore, the family counsellor invites a family to come for an interview, then, even if everyone appears to be sitting in silence, a continuous stream of communication is being emitted through the family members' silence, gestures, exchanges of looks, signs of rising discomfort, etc. Unlike the one-to-one situation, the family interview provides the counsellor with the opportunity of observing and participating in the rich interplay of communicational processes that go on between family members. The seating arrangement chosen by the family, for example, is always a powerful piece of communication about the family's relationships. It is always wise for the counsellor to encourage the family to choose their own seats, because of the rich data that their choices often yield. Sometimes, the data is very explicit. For example, when I said to a family coming into the room for an interview early on in my contact with them, 'Sit wherever you like,' the husband replied quickly and bitterly, 'It doesn't worry me where I sit so long as it's not next to my wife.' After some minutes trying to understand this piece of communication, it

turned out that although it *was* an angry and desperate rejection, it was also an effort at trying to understand his wife better, for he had learned over the previous two or three family interviews, that he would have more chance of listening to and being listened to by her if he was seated so he could see as well as hear her — in other words by not sitting next to her. At other times, small children may insist on clambering over one or other parent, protecting them, stifling them, comforting them, controlling them. The *interpretation* of behaviour has of course to be struggled with, by both counsellor and family members and may take some time to decode.

(2) The second axiom is that human communication involves two types: digital (verbal, symbolic) communication and analogic (non-verbal) communication. So far as we know, no other species (with the possible exception of the dolphin family) has the ability to communicate symbolically through words. Because of the primary importance of verbal language in enabling human beings to communicate complex and abstract messages, solve problems and arrive at a highly sophisticated degree of intellectual development, we tend to overlook our more primitive needs and ability to communicate in non-verbal ways in order to define our relationships. Bateson points out how animals engage in complex non-verbal communication in order to define and express relationships. He comments for example, that when the cat comes and rubs against one's legs when one is opening the fridge door, he is not saying 'I want milk' but 'Be a mother to me' — because such behaviour is only observed in kittens in relation to their mothers, never in relation to another adult animal.[8] It is therefore particularly important for the family counsellor to become aware of non-verbal communication because this kind of communication 'gives away' both the interrelationship experience of the family group as well as the less conscious inner feelings that each person may be experiencing. For example, a person may be denying that he has any difficulty in making new relationships or feeling at ease in strange company. His words and facial expression may look and sound convincing but his bodily posture may indicate (by clasped arms and legs) that he is 'holding in' a great deal of anxiety. Because issues of relationship are the

main focus of family counselling, inner feelings and their response to the stress and demands made by relationships are always revealed non-verbally. Watzlawick goes so far as to say that 'whenever relationship is the central issue of communication, we find that digital language is almost meaningless. This is not only the case between animals and between man and animal, but in many other contingencies in human life, e.g. courtship, love, succour, combat, and of course, in all dealings with very young children or severely disturbed mental patients.'[9]

(3) The third axiom of communications theory is that every communication has two levels — it conveys both *content* and a message about the *meaning* of the content and the *relationship* between the communicators, such that the latter always classifies and interprets the former. 'Have a sweet,' is on one level an invitation to help oneself to a sweet. However, the tone of voice, facial expression and bodily posture of the person offering the sweet significantly affects both how the invitation is perceived and the way in which the relationship between the two parties might be construed.

Thus, the second or relationship level of the communication offers a *metacommunication* both about the content and the relationship. This metacommunication may be congruent with the content and with the relationship, in which case, in the above example, one would expect the metacommunication to be a smiling face, an outstretched hand and be set within the context of a friendship or other congenial relationship. The two communication levels may however be discrepant, in which case the metacommunicative level will disqualify the content. In our example, the verbal invitation would be accompanied by an angry look, a sarcastic voice tone or be given in a highly inappropriate context, such as the middle of a row between husband and wife. If such 'double messages' are conveyed over serious issues for a prolonged period of time, they may lead the recipient to be put into a double bind, an important concept within the aetiology of serious mental disorders and, as we noted in chapter 1, first described by Bateson and his colleagues in their work on communication theory. The family counsellor can learn a great deal about the family by learning to note the congruence or discrepancy between different communication levels. She can use these observations not only to aid her understanding of how a particular family functions and the nature of its problems, but also to turn discrepant communication to good effect, to help the family to change. Methods of doing this will be described in chapter 6 when strategic family therapy is discussed.

(4) The nature of the relationship between the two or more people communicating is dependent upon the way the communication sequences are punctuated. Earlier in this chapter, we noted the way in which a husband and wife might punctuate a circular sequence of behaviour in such a way that a simultaneous phenomenon appears to be sequential, with each person viewing the sequence from a diametrically opposite view point. If, in that example, the husband's punctuation of the sequence prevails, the relationship will be defined as one in which he is a hard-working, brow-beaten man, unreasonably pushed around by his wife at home. If the wife's punctuation of the sequence prevails, the relationship will be defined as one in which she is a conscientious home-maker, struggling single handed to look after everything on the domestic front, whilst her husband treats the place like a hotel. The family counsellor's task is to understand the different punctuation given to the same events by different family members and to enable the family to become aware of the *process* that occurs between them instead of concentrating on trying to unravel the *content* of how each sequence gets started. They need to be helped to examine what goes on between them in terms of the patterns and rules of the process which they *all* help to create. R. D. Laing, in his book *Knots*, gives a wealth of examples which can be used sometimes with family members themselves, to help them understand that it is the way transactions are *punctuated* which actually determines their interpersonal meaning.[10]

(5) All communication is either symmetrical or complementary, depending upon whether it is based on similarity or difference. Every intimate relationship will display more characteristics of one type of communication than the other, so that we can describe some relationships as essentially symmetrical and some as essentially complementary. Neither is either 'good' or 'bad' but they tend to function differently, and they are likely to exhibit somewhat different problems

when the relationship comes under stress. Moreover, if either type of communication becomes exclusive of the other, the relationship system becomes locked and unable to change or adapt to changing external circumstances. In relationships which are basically symmetrical, the couple or family are highly cohesive, similar in their likes and dislikes, in their interests and life goals. Family members tend to mirror each other's behaviour and their interaction is characterised by equality and the effort to minimise difference. This pattern may lead to a cohesive, comfortable pattern of family interaction but it can also easily lead to competition and to the escalation of violence, because when difference must always be minimised, it is difficult to get disagreements resolved.

Complementary patterns of interaction on the other hand are based on difference. Family members bring different interests and preoccupations to the life of the group and, when the family is working well, they are enriched by the differences that exist between them. There can often be a very satisfactory dovetailing of needs and skills between family members, and in their communication patterns each member will tend to offer different aspects of an issue for consideration and complementary views of a particular situation. Typically, some members in a complementary set of relationships will occupy primary and others secondary positions in terms of power and influence—for example, parents and children or an authoritative husband and a compliant wife. Such relationships may continue to work well over a long period of time but may come up against problems when one or other in the complementary 'fit' wishes to change or when a new stage in the family's life cycle is being encountered. For example, a relationship between husband and wife may work extremely well, with the husband acting as breadwinner and making most of the major decisions, and the wife looking after the children and the running of the home, until the children go to school and the wife wants to move into some paid employment. She may then wish to define her relationship with her husband as more symmetrical and less complementary. Intellectually, he may also find this a congenial change but he also may find it highly threatening to the role he has comfortably occupied for

many years. Each person's definition of self in a complementary pattern is highly dependent upon the other playing the
complementary and opposite role. Therefore any shift made
by one will tend to upset the other's sense of identity.

Psychodynamic Theory

Psychodynamic theory provides the third theoretical base for
the family counsellor. He or she is likely to be more familiar
with its tenets and can bring knowledge from previous
training and experience to help in understanding the family
group. While systems theory helps the family counsellor
make the conceptual leap from individual to group and
communication theory helps him to concentrate on the 'here
and now' of observable behaviour, psychodynamic theory
enables him to include in his focus an understanding of the
'there and then' of the family's past and how the past
significantly affects the family's inner world of feelings and
current emotional experience. Because the basic tenets of
psychodynamic theory have been fully described in other
texts on pastoral counselling they will be treated here only in
so far as they can be usefully applied to working with the
family group.

(1) The family can be conceived of as 'a single psychic entity'.
It is not only conscious behavioural acts that are systemically related to one another but also the unconscious parts of
family members' psyches. Freud drew attention to this
possibility long before the practice of family therapy
developed: 'It is very remarkable that the unconscious of one
human being can react upon that of another, without the
conscious being implicated at all.'[11] Family members react to
one another's feelings unconsciously and play parts in each
other's emotional and internal worlds. Thus we can speak of
family members taking on certain emotional tasks and
shouldering certain burdens on behalf of another member or
on behalf of the whole group.

The most obvious example is the way in which the
identified patient will often carry the burden of his or her
symptomatology at great personal cost so that other family

members may be symptom-free or so that the family group may stay together. Although the identified patient and others in the family may sometimes have a fleeting perception of the part they may be playing in relation to others, these phenomena are primarily *unconscious* and act as a group defence against the anxiety of facing threats to the family's survival. There is often a relation between the choice of the identified patient's symptom and the psychic material which the family is avoiding. For example, the parents of a child who was soiling were struggling to find a way to develop a more satisfactory sexual relationship in the face of the wife's extreme distaste of sex, which she considered to be essentially dirty and disruptive to her tidy well ordered life. The child however was 'saying' rather crudely, 'Dirt's OK! Let's have a bit more of it around!' In another highly respectable middle-class family, where the couple had endured an unsatisfactory marital relationship for many years because of the husband's refusal to seek help for his impotence, the teenage daughter became pregnant. She was, if you like, undertaking the sexual and generative function of family life on behalf of her parents. Children and adolescents often act out the forbidden wishes and impulses of their parents, and the question for the family counsellor to have in mind is, 'what *meaning* has this particular symptom for the family as a whole? Is it, for example, calling attention to psychic material which has been repressed and which needs to be released, worked through and integrated?'

In a similar way to the benefits which an individual often gains from his problem or symptom, we can use the term *mutual secondary gain* to describe the 'payoff' both for the individual and the family as a whole which results from maintaining the symptom. These mutual secondary gains may be obvious to an outsider—for example, the company and support which a lonely woman gains from the fact that her youngest child refuses to go to school, as well as the relief for the little boy in not having to face up to new relationships and other new challenges. But family members themselves are usually oblivious of these mutual advantages. Because of the way in which the family operates as a single psychic entity on an unconscious level, the family counsellor must approach his or her work with the same delicacy as he would

when considering how best to approach the defence mechanisms of the individual. In general, the family counsellor needs
to acknowledge the protective and defensive nature of the
identified patient's symptom and seek not to remove the
symptom prematurely but, by aiding the family to explore
and resolve its more fundamental problems, to render the
symptom unnecessary.

(2) The concept of the family myth has provided the family
counsellor with an important theoretical tool. The family
myth helps everyone to gain protection from the skeletons in
the family's cupboard, real or imaginary, as well as avoid
what has proved to them to be unmanageable pain, such as
the pain of separation and death. Byng-Hall has done a
considerable amount of work on the family myth. He suggests
that 'family mythology consists of all those shared family
images and stories which help give the family its continuing
identity, but which, under closer inspection, are judged to be
highly coloured.'[12] The purpose of the family myth is both to
conceal and reveal important but anxiety-provoking truths
about the family's past or present. Sometimes the myth will
relate to the family's present functioning. 'We never have
arguments or anything like that in *our* family,' may conceal
the hidden violence in one or more family members or hide
from present family members a violent and destructive drama
in the family's history. Sometimes a myth can be prescriptive
of expected behaviour: 'I'm thankful to say that none of the
older relatives in *our* family have ever had to go into a home.'
The family's anxiety over separation, rejection and death is
concealed by this comforting story.

Myths may be told about past family figures in which
everyone colludes in the embellishment of the person's good
or bad points and he becomes a hero to be emulated or an
example to be avoided. Sometimes a new arrival is said to
look 'just like Uncle Freddie, who came to no good' and, if
such an attribution sticks, the child may have some difficulty
in disentangling himself from Uncle Freddie's identity when
he gets older. The myth may combine a mixture of concealed
guilt for the past and prescription about the future: 'To be a
real man, a boy needs to leave home early and go abroad to
seek his fortune.' 'A nice feminine woman gets married young.'

Myths about what it means to be masculine or feminine can be particularly powerful and create considerable stress for family members encountering a clash between the expectations of their family's transmitted history and the challenge of current society. In chapter 7, we will be able to see how the family's myths can often be helpfully revealed by using a genogram or a family sculpt.

(3) The third concept from psychodynamic theory which can be helpful to the family counsellor is that of family transference. The psychoanalytic concept of transference relates to the relationship between the counsellor and his client, in which the client 'transfers' onto the counsellor the attributes of authority figures from his past, usually his parents and his feelings towards them. In family counselling family members will inevitably recruit the counsellor into a position of authority in relation to them and he or she will need to understand the projections that are put onto him and work with them.

But the more important concept for the family counsellor to understand is the way in which family members *transfer onto each other* transferences from the past which significantly distort the way in which the family is then able to live in the present. For example, a couple who married late in life found it extremely difficult to perceive each other unclouded by their experiences of the past. The husband transferred onto his wife the punitive, demanding father who had all but annihilated him as a child. At the same time he resented the way in which she failed to resemble his soft and protective mother who had shielded him from his father's attacks. The wife transferred onto her husband the compliant and gentle father who had suffered severely from her dominating mother's tongue. It is often however *relationships*, not simply individual family members, which are transferred from past to present. Thus the wife in this example had inherited an idealised blueprint of marriage from the many 'successful' marriages in her family of origin of which she had often heard tell. The husband's transference was thus confirmed by the wife's projections of her parents' relationship on to their marriage, and their marriage was disturbed by the high and unrealistic expectations which the wife in particular brought to the relationship. In this example, a family counsellor would have to help each of the partners to disentangle themselves from their 'ghosts from the past' so that they could begin to relate to one another as real people.

All three of these theoretical constructs can helpfully be used by the family counsellor. In the following chapter, we will examine a model for understanding the family's life cycle and note the occasions which can be particularly stressful for a family group and when therefore they may be in need of outside intervention.

Notes

1. Ludwig von Bertalanffy, *General System Theory*, Penguin 1968.
2. F. Capra, *The Turning Point*, Wildwood House 1982.
3. U. Bronfenbrenner, *The Ecology of Human Development*, Harvard University Press 1979.
4. M. Bowen, *Family Therapy in Clinical Practice*, New York, Jason Aronson, 1978; S. Minuchin, *Families and Family Therapy*, Tavistock 1974.
5. G. Bateson, *Steps to an Ecology of Mind*, Granada 1972.
6. G. Bateson et al., 'Towards a Theory of Schizophrenia', *Behavioral Science*, vol. 1, 1956, pp. 251–64.
7. P. Watzlawick et al., *Pragmatics of Human Communication*, New York, W. W. Norton, 1968; *Change—Principles of Problem Formation and Problem Resolution*, New York, W. W. Norton, 1974.
8. Bateson, *Steps to an Ecology of Mind*.
9. Watzlawick et al., op. cit.
10. R. D. Laing, *Knots*, Penguin 1970.
11. S. Freud, 'The Unconscious', *Complete Works*, Standard edition vol. 14, Hogarth Press 1915.
12. J. Byng-Hall, 'Re-editing Family Mythology during Family Therapy', *Journal of Family Therapy*, vol. 1, 1979, pp. 2–14.

THREE

Moving through the
Family Life Cycle

Awareness of the great cycle of events that constitute human life for most people is nothing new. Bowen in his Foreword to a most important book on the life cycle comments: 'Life cycle thinking is second nature in all people. The human has always been aware of the sequential stages of life from birth to death. This has been recorded in history, religion, cultural rituals, novels, drama and art since earliest times.'[1]

Certainly, the field of individual counselling has been greatly enriched by the psychoanalytic contributions of Freud's developmental stages and Erikson's eight stages of the human being, as well as Jung's elucidation of the great archetypal images of primordial events, the reflections of which lie deeply rooted in the unconscious. Capps, Carr and others have considered the relevance of a life cycle approach to the pastoral care of individuals.[2]

Strangely, however, the family therapy field has adapted this work to the family unit only rather recently. Haley and Solomon made early attempts, and Minuchin used the family's life cycle to provide a framework for normal family functioning, against which developmental problems could be more clearly highlighted.[3] But it was not until the publication of Carter and McGoldrick's book *The Family Life Cycle* in 1980, that the effort was made to translate the events of the individual's life cycle fully to the life cycle of the family group.[4] Anderson, Anderson and other writers on pastoral counselling have now adopted the concept in their consider-ations of the pastoral care of the family, and it undoubtedly provides the family counsellor with an invaluable framework for a developmental understanding of the life of the family group.[5]

General Features of the Family Life Cycle

The work that was originally undertaken on the life cycle of
the individual by Erikson helped to create the atmosphere
necessary for the development of family therapy. In stating
the importance, potential and hope that existed in each of the
eight stages, he contradicted earlier views on the determining
force of the first few years of life.[6] If there is hope for those
individuals who have been severely damaged in their early
years, then the newly formed family group of adult life may
be the vehicle through which that hope is realised. Because of
the importance of his work, Erikson's eight-stage plan of the
individual life cycle is reproduced in Table 1.

However, just as it is difficult to make the conceptual leap
from the individual to the family group, so it can be difficult,
when approaching the life cycle, to avoid using the theoretical
tools of individual counselling and develop instead new,
specially designed theoretical tools for the job. Using
questions suggested by Carter and McGoldrick, we can try to
do this by discovering *the major points* at which family
members enter and leave the family system; *the emotional
process* involved in transitions from one stage to the next,
and the various *relationship shifts* created by entering and
proceeding developmentally through each new stage of the
family life cycle.

Table 2 makes use of this three-fold analysis, but it divides
the stages differently. In addition, the adaptive work of
pastoral theologians has been included in a fourth column, so
that the unique sacramental and ritualising contributions of
the Church's ministry can be related to these family events.
There can be something trite about relating the Church's
sacraments to stages of the life cycle. And yet, as Carr points
out, 'sacraments are not the Church's possession, but a facet
of common human experience within God's creation'.[7]
Whatever the Church tries to make of them, the majority of
those who come seeking the Church's sacraments from
outside the gathered congregation do so at nodal points in
their life cycle. In some dim way they appear to be seeking
acknowledgement and affirmation of an important life stage
through which their family is passing. Like Carr and Green,[8]
I would want to draw attention to the pastoral potential of the

Table 1 — Erikson's eight stages of the individual's life cycle

	Oral (1)	Anal (2)	Phallic (3)	Latency (4)	Adolescence (5)	Young Adulthood (6)	Adulthood (7)	Maturity (8)
VIII								INTEGRITY vs. DESPAIR
VII							GENERATIVITY vs. STAGNATION	
VI						INTIMACY vs. ISOLATION		
V	Temporal perspective vs. Time confusion	Self-certainty vs. Self-consciousness	Role-experimentation vs. Role fixation	Apprenticeship vs. Work paralysis	IDENTITY vs. IDENTITY CONFUSION	Sexual polarization vs. Bisexual confusion	Leader- and followship vs. Authority confusion	Ideological commitment vs. Confusion of values
IV				INDUSTRY vs. INFERIORITY	Task identification vs. Sense of futility			
III			INITIATIVE vs. GUILT		Anticipation of roles vs. Role inhibition			
II		AUTONOMY vs. SHAME, DOUBT			Will to be oneself vs. Self-doubt			
I	TRUST vs. MISTRUST				Mutual recognition vs. Autistic isolation			

Table 2 — Stages of the family life cycle (based on Table 1.1. in *The Family Life Cycle* by E. Carter and M. McGoldrick, Gardner Press 1980).

Family life cycle stage	Emotional process of transition	Required relationship shift	Sacraments and occasional offices
1 *Conception:* Preparing for family.	Accepting parent/offspring separation.	Differentiation of self from family of origin. Development of intimate peer relationships. Establishment of self in work.	Confirmation.
2 *Birth:* Forming the family.	Commitment to new system.	Marital choices. Forming the marital relationship. Realignment of relationships with extended families and friends to include spouse.	Marriage.
3 *Childhood:* Young family.	Accepting new members into system.	Moving from two-some to three-some and beyond. Taking on parenting roles. Realignment of relations with extended family to include parenting and grandparental roles.	Baptism.
4 *Adolescence:* Adolescent families.	Increasing flexibility of family boundaries, to include children's independence.	Shifting parent/child relationships to permit adolescents to move in and out. Refocusing mid-life marital and career issues. Concern for older generation.	Confirmation/Orders

5 *Young Adulthood:*	Extending the family.	Accepting multitude of exits from and entries into family system.	Renegotiation back to marital dyad. Development of adult to adult relationships between parents and children. Realignment of relationships to include in-laws and grandchildren. Dealing with losses and partings through loss of children, death or divorce.	Conciliation/ reconciliation and healing
6 *Maturity:*	Re-forming the family.	Accepting the shift of generational and/or inter-familial roles.	Renegotiation of roles to enable middle generation to become central and/or to include the joining of 2 new family systems after re-marriage. Exploration of new social and familial options.	Eucharist.
7 *Completion:*	Transcending the family.	Accepting disintegration of family and ultimate detachment.	Dealing with loss of spouse, siblings and other peers. Making room for wisdom *and* dependency of older generation. New realism stemming from life review of unfulfilled hopes and ultimate goals. Preparing for death and new life.	Healing. Last rites and funeral office.

Church's sacraments and occasional offices as they relate to
the transitional experiences of the family group.

As we examine the life cycle of the family group outlined in
Table 2 we see immediately that the shifts and changes relate
to the family system as a whole. As we noted when
considering the way systems work in chapter 2, a change in
one part of the system brings about change in the system as a
whole, because every other part of the system is affected.
Although at first sight it can look a little odd to label the
family stage where children are leaving home and parents are
facing their mid-life crisis as that of 'young adulthood', yet it
is to the *family system* that this description refers not to the
individual members of it. Thus we can adopt some of
Erikson's descriptive terminology shown in Table 1 and adapt
it from the life cycle of the individual to the life cycle of the
family group. The descriptions in Table 2 stretch further in
both directions however, because account is taken here of the
position of the young unattached adult who is between his
family of origin and his family of procreation and is therefore
in a state of 'preparing for family'. During this period, the
new family group is being conceived. At the other end of the
cycle, we can describe the family as reaching completion; the
nuclear or immediate family disintegrates and although it
remains internalised within its individual members, those
members must necessarily pass through the aloneness of
bereavement and death. By using the term 'completion', we
do not imply that the family's purpose and goal-directed
activity has necessarily been achieved, but that the opportunities for doing so in this life are ended and that what is left
unfinished will be completed through the family's continuity
in its new generation and through the mercy of God in the life
to come. There is a certain illogicality in talking about stages
as though they were discrete entities. Such an idea is neither
true to life nor to the systemic framework in which family
counselling is embedded. However, so long as we remind
ourselves that the division is arbitrary and is used as an aid
in conceptualisation, it is a useful theoretical tool.

Structurally, the family life cycle is made up of a series of
historical eras, each of which is marked by a 'plateau',
followed by a period of 'transition'. The plateau periods
represent times of relative stability or homeostasis, in which

the family follows a fairly predictable course. The transitional periods mark times of rapid and discontinuous change, during which the family is often thrown into crisis. As each new stage in the life cycle is reached, the family enters a new period of rapid change and it is often at these crisis points that the family seeks help. Terkelsen suggests that the most pronounced effects occur with first events of a particular type — for example, the birth of the first child usually creates much more stress within the family than subsequent births, because it catapults the family into a new developmental stage and creates a whole series of new and unfamiliar role relationships for each family member.[9] Through learning and experience, the family becomes able to adjust to the entry of new family members and the exit of older ones, although each entry and exit will act as a source of stress on the system. However, these normal developmental crises may be combined with one or more of the many accidental crises assailing the family group from outside its boundaries, and this may alter the intensity and effect of the life-cycle transition. If for example, the *second* child is born handicapped, this second birth may produce a far greater crisis for the family than the birth of the first child and throw the whole system into disarray.

In a similar way, the intensity of the family's life-cycle transition will be heightened if several developmental crises in the family group are juxtaposed. In other words, the way in which family events interconnect laterally, along a horizontal dimension, affects the intensity with which they are experienced. For example, during the adolescent phase of family life, the actual adolescence of one or more of the children may coincide with the mid-life crisis of one or both parents. Just as the adolescent is reaching the height of his or her sexual potency and stands on the verge of his ability to procreate, his father may be experiencing a decline in his sexual powers and his mother is going through the menopause. Because the family counsellor is always cognisant of the interdependence of family events, we need to try to understand these juxtapositions as part of a circular and interlinked process, each part affecting and being affected by every other part. As Terkelson points out,

It is often impossible to determine from clinical observation which change came first . . . growth in one member activates a developmental move in another, which in turn influences the first member, augmenting the initial change and so on.[10]

Not only will events in the family's life cycle interconnect horizontally but they will also interconnect vertically between the family's past and its present. This interconnection may be between the current family's *own* past and present experience or between *the experience of the family of origin* of one of the partners and their current family situation. For example, a couple who came for help because they were experiencing the pain and confusion of the husband's ongoing extra-marital affair, gradually shared with the counsellor the fact that their own twenty-five-year-old relationship had begun when the husband had started an affair with his present wife, while he was still married. Both husband and wife were haunted by the memory of how their relationship had begun, with its attendant shadows of unresolved guilt and pain. The current situation twenty-five years later mirrored only too closely that past experience, when on that occasion the wife had 'won' her husband away from his wife. Was it now her turn to be the abandoned wife she wondered; was he doomed to repeat his past need to desert a long-standing committed relationship for a younger partner?

Likewise, events in the original families of the marital pair will have a compelling effect upon the current family life cycle. For example, a family came for help because of marital difficulties arising from their inability to draw appropriate boundaries between the marital pair and the children. The husband felt torn between his wife and teenage daughter, and when there was a conflict between them he invariably supported his daughter. The wife on the other hand was inseparably 'glued' to their three-year-old son, so that the husband felt he could never relate to his wife without also relating to her little 'appendage'. After doing some work on the wife's genogram, it became clear that her father had deserted her mother when she was three years old. She was therefore compelled, by this shadow from her original family, both to over protect her three-year-old son *and* to cling to him in case her husband left.

We will now examine briefly the specific tasks, challenges and opportunities confronting the family at each of these seven stages.

Stage 1

Stage 1 is neither a beginning nor an end because there are actually no beginnings or endings in the continuous process of family life. Yet, as we have noted earlier, it can be helpful to us to make some arbitrary divisions as it clarifies what is otherwise an impossibly complex process. Stage 1 marks the process of conception during which the new generation is prepared for. During this period the young adult must establish him or herself as separate from and yet continuously linked to his or her family of origin. He must undertake what Bowen calls the task of differentiation—he must become his own person.[11] This will involve establishing strong peer group relationships with both sexes and paying attention to his own inner needs and drives. Discerning his vocation in life may take the form of discovering what work and training he wants to undertake, or simply gaining confidence in his ability to be a productive and creative person even when high levels of unemployment mean that his creativity will not be exercised in return for a wage. When asked what a healthy adult should be able to do, Freud simply replied, 'lieben und arbeiten'—'to love and to work'. It is the task of this first stage to enable the young adult to gain the tools needed for creative love and creative work and to become acquainted with the deep inner resources with which each human being is equipped. Becoming separate and yet remaining intimate with one's family of origin is a major task. Sometimes a person feels that only after the death of their parent(s) will they be able truly to be themselves, and it is often instructive to note the times when a marriage or pregnancy follows soon after the death of a parent or other significant person in the family.

To some extent, full differentiation remains a life-long task and yet, unless a sufficient start is made at this preparatory stage of young adulthood, neither the individual nor his or her family of origin will be equipped to move into the second stage of the family's life cycle. Unless the family has travelled some way along the path of differentiation and allowed its members to stand alone, they will be doomed to create in the next generation relationships that are either fused and over-dependent or disconnected and lacking in ability to create real mutual intimacy. The sacrament of confirmation may offer the young adult the necessary grace and strength for embarking on this phase—but it will be used in this way only for a small number of people since, unlike baptism, marriage and the funeral office, it has not become owned by the wider community and tends to be confined to practising church members. This leaves the Church with little symbolism to offer the young adult.

Stage 2

Stage 2 marks the birth of the new family and the moment when two individuals from two different family cultures join to commit themselves to forming a new family system. Marriage (and other kinds of commitment in partnerships) has rightly been called an event which takes place between two families not simply between two individuals. The work of Dicks[12] and his colleagues has shown that unconscious processes play a major part in our choice of a partner, and, in homosexual coupling, Moberley[13] has described some of the unconscious determinants of the couple's choice. In fact the whole script for our future partnerships—their timing, quality and progress is in some sense already written by the family, over numbers of its previous generations. When we choose a partner, each of us is to some extent unconsciously in search of someone who either *resembles* or *complements* parts of our own personality make-up. We noted in the previous chapter how relationships are either broadly symmetrical or broadly complementary, and it is out of the process of partnership choice that these patterns are developed and maintained.

The process of differentiation may often have been extremely limited during Stage 1 due to a lack of intimacy during childhood, and it is an axiom of family relationships that no true differentiation can occur unless real intimacy has first been established. On the other hand, the extent to which the individual and family have been able to separate will determine the extent to which a free and conscious choice of a partner can be made and the extent to which the new relationship can develop its own direction instead of merely being a means of working out unresolved issues from the individual's and family's past.

Because the task of differentiation takes time, the ability of very young couples to achieve sufficient differentiation to enable their new relationship to succeed is more limited. For the major readjustment which marriage entails for the couple is also required of both their family groups and their separate friendship networks. Each established relationship in both families has to be realigned in order to make way for the inclusion of the marriage partner as an individual *and* the new phenomenon of husband-plus-wife in relationship. Parents have to learn to share their child with another set of parents who have become his or her in-laws, and later the two sets of grandparents have to learn to share their grandchildren with each other. Each partner too has to readjust every aspect of his conscious waking experience to include the fact that he or she is now 'in relationship' with another, and the couple has to negotiate a relationship between the intellectual, social, physical, spiritual and emotional sides of their personalities. What is to be shared, what is to remain separate? How can the intimacy of the new relationship be cherished without sacrificing the hard-won autonomy of each individual person? One of the major avenues for achieving both these apparently contrary needs simultaneously is through the sexual relationship, and throughout his various fine writings on marriage Dominian illustrates the special role of the couple's physical relationship in creating intimacy and separateness simultaneously.[14]

As is the case in the life cycle of the individual, the new family system is at its most vulnerable at the stage of its birth. 49.5 per cent of all divorces have been completed by the ninth year of marriage. Out of a sample of 520 divorced couples, 73 per cent believed their marital problems had become severe by their fifth wedding anniversary.[15] The task for the new family is to begin to create its own identity; its dilemma is to find enough energy and space to work on this task whilst still attending to the many other tasks of the individual partner's young adulthood. The Church's marker for this stage in the family's life cycle is of course the sacrament of marriage. Marriage, uniquely amongst the sacraments, is administered by the couple themselves, and the Church's minister is their guide and their witness. The Church therefore validates the couple's autonomy in taking this step and making this commitment to a new family system. Marriage is a human not a Christian institution, and the Christian minister carries both a symbolic and a practical role on behalf of the couple. In chapter 8 we will note some of the unique opportunities for doing preventive work available to the Christian minister when preparing couples for their marriage.

Stage 3

This is the stage of childhood. The family group is young in years and experience, and this fact is symbolised by the actual presence of very young children. Moving from a two-some to a threesome increases enormously both the number and complexity of possible relationships and propels the couple into living within a new set of triangles. Each partner undergoes an important role accretion, adding a parenting function to their original dyadic relationship. In addition, everyone else's role in the two families of origin changes, and the older generation become grandparents, great aunts, great uncles, etc. The complexity and number of relationships with groups in the wider community also increases, as playgroups, health clinics and schools all impinge upon the family in new and unfamiliar ways.

As with Stage 2, the whole system must be realigned to take account of the new family member. Just as the pressures on very young couples entering marriage are greater, so also are the pressures on the couple who have their first baby very soon after marriage, for the newly formed partnership needs time to establish its relationship before having to integrate new members into the system. Moreover, because of the juxtaposition of developmental crises between parents and children when parents are still young themselves, the pressures upon them to act out their own need for autonomy with toddlers is very great. Conversely, the couple may find it difficult to set boundaries between themselves as a unit and the young children. Each child in turn may sleep in the parents' bed, and all of them together may combine to orchestrate a group resistance to the couple's exercise of their marital roles.

The Church offers the sacrament of baptism to affirm the addition of new family members through birth or adoption. Carr describes eloquently the mixture of motives that bring parents to church for the baptism of their infants. The gap between what the Church is wanting to offer and what the parents want to receive may be wide, for so often the parents may simply be looking for a way to 'do the best for their child' and for a way to 'create the new continuity of the new family'.[16] In Erikson's terminology, the stage of young childhood for the individual involves overcoming the tendency towards shame, guilt, doubt and, later, inferiority and although these emotions will be present to some extent in all young families, they will be particularly present in those who harbour specific negative experiences from the past, such as rejection by a parent, a spouse or a lover. Unmarried parents for example may be particularly keen to have their babies baptised as a sign that they are accepted and belong.

Stage 4

Stage 4 marks the shift into the crisis of adolescence. Both the couple's relationship and some of their children are passing through adolescence with all its attendant opportunities and dangers. The family's task is to increase the flexibility of its boundaries so that some of its members can experiment with being both children and adults simultaneously, moving between these two roles in rather unpredictable ways. Parents need to enable their children's independence, and children need to teach parents and grandparents how to relate to them differently. There is often a juxtaposition between the children's adolescence and the parent's mid-life crisis, when parents must grieve for losses of opportunity and potency in both their work situations and their personal relationships. Adolescents often act out their parents' forbidden wishes and impulses in relation to the need for excitement, potency and lack of restraint. As the children broaden their interests and relationships outside the family, parents may need to refocus their interests and energy on their jobs (if they are in work) and their own social life, in preparation for the time when the children leave home.

Because the parents' own relationship has reached its adolescence, each partner may need to act out needs which are hard to articulate in other ways. A husband or wife may need to begin a sexual relationship with a younger person in order to deny their own increasing age or, sometimes, for more complex reasons. For example, a middle-aged couple came for help, when the husband began an affair with a girl in her mid-twenties. Part of the family's problem surrounded the increasing rift between the two teenage children and their father. They still lived at home and quarrels between them and their father were frequent. Father had also completely lost touch with his twenty-six-year-old daughter by a previous marriage because he did not want to hurt his wife by retaining a relationship with the past. During the course of counselling he began to talk of his sense of loss in not knowing who or how his daughter was. It happened that the girl with whom he had started an affair was also twenty-six and, as the counselling progressed, the couple began to see that this extra-marital relationship was a means whereby the husband might regain a connection with his grown-up children. (Further aspects of this case are discussed in chapter 6.)

The Church offers the sacrament of Confirmation and Orders at this turning point in the family's development. Each complements the other in providing the young adult family members with a means of launching out upon their own lives and moving towards Stage 1 of a reproduced family life cycle. For the older members too, these sacraments can offer occasions when, through their young adult children, they can review their own commitment and redirect their own destinies, sometimes making new vocational commitments themselves or launching into a new interest or occupation.

Stage 5

Stage 5 marks the movement of the family system into its young adult phase. The system must be flexible enough to accept multiple exits and entries from and into the group.

This stage marks what is sometimes called the 'empty-nest syndrome', when the children have left home and have embarked upon their own adult lives. The children will be needing progressively to differentiate themselves from what is now their family of origin, viewed from the perspective of adulthood, and parents and grandparents will need to help them to do so. Many roles need to be renegotiated—the parents are challenged to regain their marital roles in a much less interrupted way, and both parents and children need to develop adult-to-adult relationships with one another. The family system's boundaries will now need to include many new members, with the addition of in-laws and grandchildren. Second only to the early years of marriage, this stage puts great pressure upon the marital pair, and the incidence of marriage breakdown is high. Some of the exits from the family system will therefore include a spouse, where a divorce has occurred, as well as the loss of grandparents and others through death.

Dealing with parting and loss will be an important task for the family, but there will be also the recognition of new hopes and new opportunities which come from the many changes that take place at this stage. O'Collins in his book *The Second Journey* has written eloquently about the opportunities provided by a second start at this stage—a new relationship or marriage partner, new hope through the birth of grandchildren or the start of a new career.[17] In Erikson's terms the family is striving towards fuller intimacy, but its sub-groups may be trying to come to terms with the threat or reality of isolation.

The new field of mediation and conciliation counselling has shown the importance of helping the couple and the family facing divorce to arrive at a 'co-operative win' rather than go through a protracted adversarial process. The relationship system may need help to expand to include new members, to heal deep wounds and to relate to its members in new and constructive ways. It is not impossible for ex-spouses to become friends with new ones, given appropriate help, and for children and grandchildren to learn that separations and partings do not have to mean total catastrophe or the absence of loved ones, although they certainly mean change and the renegotiation of roles and rules within the family.

The Church's sacrament of reconciliation especially in its modern forms, may have much to offer as the family tries to negotiate the many shifts and breaks in their relationship system. Relationships between parents and adult children may need help and healing before they can move on to new growth, and spouses who divorce at this later stage in their relationships may need the help of a ritual for parting and for dissolving their marriage vows before they can move on to make a fresh start.[18] The importance of this work of dis-engagement cannot be overestimated, if unresolved issues from the first marriage are to be prevented from adversely affecting a second marriage and the successful formation of a newly constituted family group. In chapter 8 I discuss ways in which the Church's ministers can make use of the marvellous opportunities afforded by preparing people for a second marriage. Ministers who refuse to conduct new marriages for divorced people undoubtedly sacrifice a unique opportunity for helping them work through many complex and unresolved issues from the past. No other organisation or professional group is provided with this opportunity so freely. It seems folly to forgo it.

Stage 6

At Stage 6 the family reaches maturity. Its members have functioned together as a group for some considerable time and have passed through a good deal of pain and joy on the way. The family has grown in experience and wisdom and it may well include a relationship system of four generations. The challenge of this life-cycle stage, in Erikson's terms is that of generativity; the threat is stagnation. The main concern for the family is its re-formation, to allow a proper place and function for its three or four generations and, where there has been a divorce and remarriage, the re-forming of a new family out of two other family systems. At this stage, the middle generation needs to move into an executive position within the family, taking the main responsibility for both the younger and older generations. This means that both the younger and older generations need to have their own clearly defined tasks and feel appreciated for the contributions they have to offer. Relationships across the generations, between grandparents and grandchildren can be particularly rich and rewarding, unhampered by the closer conflicts between parental and young adulthood roles. The family as a whole will, if it is functioning well, have a wide variety of contacts with the outside world and with many other social systems. It may well have much to offer to the wider community.

Where two families have joined through a new marriage, each new relationship has to be carefully negotiated. If there are children from both previous marriages, the newly formed family may involve losses of sibling positions for oldests and youngests and for only children. Parents will have to learn to be step-parents as well as perhaps embarking upon a new generation of child-rearing from their new relationships, whilst simultaneously becoming grandparents to their children's children from their first marriage. As Sager *et al.* and Furstenberg *et al.* point out, the tasks and potential difficulties facing the remarried family exist over and above the other challenges that operate in the ordinary course of the family life cycle.[19] Therefore, although I have included the remarried family in Stage 6 of the family's life cycle, some of the special features that are unique to remarried families need to be considered separately. These are summarised in Carter and McGoldrick's chart, which is reprinted here as Table 3. Particular problems facing the remarried family are: how to function within roles for which there are inadequate or negative role models (e.g. step-parent, step-grandparent, step-sibling, etc); how to deal with the past in such a way that good experiences are salvaged and bad ones are forgiven; how to enable non-custodial parents to maintain their parenting role, and siblings who do not live in the household, to become in some sense part of the new family group; and how to negotiate the group relationships between what may be three inter-locking remarried family systems.

At this sixth stage, the older generation in the family may, after an absence of many years, resume their church membership. Sometimes this is prompted by their children or grandchildren getting baptised or confirmed. Sometimes this new interest stems from an awareness of their own aging process and the nearer presence of death. The Church's eucharistic sacrament may be sought out for the first time for many years, in response to some perceived need for spiritual

Table 3 — Remarried family formation: A developmental outline[*]

Steps	Prerequisite attitude	Developmental issues
1. Entering the new relationship.	Recovery from loss of first marriage (adequate 'emotional divorce').	Recommitment to marriage and to forming a family with readiness to deal with the complexity and ambiguity.
2. Conceptualizing and planning new marriage and family.	Accepting one's own fears and those of new spouse and children. Accepting need for time and patience for adjustment to complexity and ambiguity of: 1. Multiple new roles. 2. Boundaries: space, time, membership and authority. 3. Affective issues: guilt, loyalty, conflicts, desire for mutuality, unresolvable past hurts.	a) Work on openness in the new relationships to avoid pseudo-mutuality. b) Plan for maintenance of co-operative, co-parental relationships with ex-spouses. c) Plan to help children deal with fears, loyalty conflicts and membership in two systems. d) Realignment of relationships with extended family to include new spouse and children. e) Plan maintenance of connections for children with extended family of ex-spouse(s).
3. Remarriage and reconstitution of family.	Final resolution of attachment to previous spouse and ideal of 'intact' family. Acceptance of a different model of family with permeable boundaries.	a) Restructuring family boundaries to allow for inclusion of new spouse/step-parent. b) Realignment of relationships throughout sub-systems to permit interweaving of several systems. c) Making room for relationships of all children with biological (non-custodial) parents, grandparents and other extended family. d) Sharing memories and histories to enhance step-family integration.

* Reprinted by kind permission from *The Family Life Cycle* by E. Carter and M. McGoldrick (chapter 12), Gardner Press 1980.

food and refreshment or as an instinctive thanksgiving for achievements and gifts that have been given. Church membership may then become part of the new social options which some sub-groups within the family begin to explore. Seeking new spiritual food for the later stages of the journey makes earthy good sense, and it would be unfortunate if the Church simply lamented the fact that many older, more battle-scarred members only join the fellowship at this later stage.

Stage 7

The seventh stage of the family cycle corresponds to Erikson's final stage. The family is challenged by ultimate hopes and fears, and achieves either a sense of its own integrity or despairs at its disintegration. The family must come to terms with both its continuity and its end. On the one hand, because it exists within a circular movement of death and rebirth, the family, unlike the individual, continues in a semi-permanent state of renewal and growth. On the other hand, seen from the point of view of the family members whom we have traced as the focal participants through the seven stages, the family in its current form is coming to an end. The older generations must accept, and through them the younger ones prepare for, the disintegration of the family system and the ultimate aloneness of its individual members. Losses through death and disability are the hallmarks of this stage and the family must find ways of coping with the dependency and perhaps extreme dependency of its older members. A new realism may come from a review of unfulfilled hopes and ultimate goals as well as peace and satisfaction from aspects of family life that have been obviously creative and productive. Shared memories will enable the family's culture to be transmitted on to future generations and, for those who hold a belief in some form of after-life (most people), there is a sense in which their membership of the current family can be transcended through hopes for their own future and for a future reunion with others.

The Church has much to offer at this stage through its healing ministries, last rites and funeral offices. Very few people express a wish to be buried or cremated without any kind of religious ceremony, and Carr helpfully discusses the difficulties and opportunities of the Christian minister's role at this point. The funeral is a ritual which involves not only the family system but often the inter-face between several interrelated systems with which the deceased family member was connected—such as friends, colleagues and work-mates. Carr comments that, 'through the ritual the minister is asked to articulate on behalf of people what they cannot at this moment manage for themselves'.[20] Quoting from Reed, Carr suggests that the funeral is a particularly powerful instance of 'managed regression' in which the family is enabled to regress to dependency within their intra-familial relationships and between the family and the minister and others in the outside world. The funeral and its attendant rituals are therefore tools for the minister to use in enabling this necessary regression to take place, and they can be also used to assist the recovery of responsibility and autonomy. Obviously the way in which the family manages this process will depend upon the nature of the relationship which the deceased had with every other family member and on the position, role and emotional significance he or she held within the family system.

There is an artificiality in writing about death as the significant feature of the final stage of the family life cycle as though it does not have to be encountered at other earlier stages. On the contrary, it often clearly holds even more significance and threat for a family when it occurs at a much earlier stage in the cycle. When deaths occur at this later stage however, they can bring a sense of peace and completion and can help the family to reconsider its boundaries, its identity and its overall purpose. As family members come together to mourn, they often reforge links which have become tenuous and weak, and opportunities sometimes arise for the healing of old rifts and the re-vitalising of lapsed relationships.

Notes

1. M. Bowen, 'Foreword' to E. Carter and M. McGoldrick, *The Family Life Cycle*, New York, Gardner Press, 1980, p. xiii.

2. D. Capps, *Life Cycle Theory and Pastoral Care*, N. Philadelphia, PA, Fortress Press, 1983, and W. Carr, *Brief Encounters*, SPCK 1985.
3. J. Haley, *Problem-Solving Therapy*, San Francisco, Jossey-Bass, 1973; M. Soloman, 'A Developmental Conceptual Premise for Family Therapy' in *Family Process*, vol. 12, no. 12; S. Minuchin, *Families and Family Therapy*, Tavistock 1974.
4. E. Carter and M. McGoldrick, op. cit.
5. D. A. Anderson, *New Approaches to Family Pastoral Care*, Philadelphia, PA, Fortress Press, 1980, and H. Anderson, *The Family and Pastoral Care*, Philadelphia, PA, Fortress Press, 1984.
6. E. Erikson, *Identity, Youth and Crisis*, Faber 1968.
7. Carr, op. cit., p. 54.
8. R. Green, *Only Connect*, Darton, Longman & Todd 1987.
9. K. G. Terkelsen, 'Toward a Theory of the Family Life Cycle' in Carter and McGoldrick, op. cit.
10. ibid., p. 42.
11. M. Bowen, *Family Therapy in Clinical Practice*, New York, Jason Aronson, 1978.
12. H. V. Dicks, *Marital Tensions*, Routledge & Kegan Paul 1967.
13. E. Moberley, *Psychogenesis*, Routledge & Kegan Paul 1983.
14. J. Dominian, *Christian Marriage*, 1967; *Proposals for a New Sexual Ethic*, 1977; *Marriage, Faith and Love*, 1981 (all Darton, Longman & Todd).
15. B. Thornes and J. Collard, *Who Divorces?*, Routledge & Kegan Paul 1979.
16. Carr, op. cit., p. 67.
17. G. O'Collins, *The Second Journey*, Paulist Press 1978.
18. See, for example: 'Form for the Dissolution of Vows', compiled by the Revd Owen Barraclough; R. L. Morgan, 'A Ritual of Remarriage', *Journal of Pastoral Care*, vol. 37, 1983; E. H. Friedman, 'Systems and Ceremonies' in Carter and McGoldrick, op. cit.; and R. Grainger, *Staging Posts — Rites of Passage for Contemporary Christians*, Merlin Books 1987.
19. C. J. Sager et al., *Treating the Remarried Family*, Brunner/Mazel 1983, and F. F. Furstenberg and G. B. Spanier, *Recycling the Family*, Sage 1984.
20. Carr, op. cit., p. 116.

FOUR

Meeting the Family

Some of what I shall describe in this chapter will perhaps seem a counsel of perfection when measured against the untidiness of many of the pastoral situations which the minister encounters. Like other kinds of counselling, family therapy is a creative art form, in which the counsellor is engaged in a continuous dialectic between the urgent practical necessities of the real world of each family situation and the theoretical constructs from which he is trying to work. But he is not alone in this. Practically everyone who tries to use family therapy works within these constraints. It takes effort and ingenuity on the part of social workers, doctors and others in the counselling business to apply the theoretical frameworks of family therapy effectively and begin to engage with the family rather than with the individual as the unit of treatment.

However, family therapy has itself moved on over the last few decades and has become more sophisticated in its understanding of the way its theories should be applied. Few family counsellors would now make it an unvarying rule to refuse to see the family at all unless every important member came together to the counselling session. On the other hand, most family counsellors know that they can easily do more harm than good by seeing the family group in an extremely attenuated form *unless* this is being done as part of a carefully thought-out plan of action.

Initial Contact

Families present their problems to us in one of two ways: *either symptomatically* in terms of one member, who we then describe as the 'identified patient'; or *transactionally* in terms of a relationship that is unhappy or in some difficulty. With families who adopt the second course, it is usually less difficult to work out who should be involved in the counselling process and to persuade them to come. They have already defined their difficulties in terms of more than one person and will therefore be more amenable to talking about problems in terms of relationships. However, by far the greatest number of families adopt the first course and come to the counsellor *as though* the problem belonged entirely to one family member. In these situations the counsellor is being asked to 'do something' for or about the one family member, and others in the family may be genuinely baffled as to how they could be helpful in trying to alter Johnnie's school truancy or father's drinking problem.

A useful theoretical construct in helping to determine who should be involved in the counselling process, is Skynner's concept of the 'minimum sufficient network'.[1] He suggests that whilst it is essential to involve every member of the 'operative system' (i.e. all those individuals who, between them, compose the system of relationships in which the 'problem' is embedded), it is also important, in accordance with the principle of parsimony, to include only the minimum number of individuals in the family or wider social system that are required to make therapeutic change possible. Sometimes the decision as to who to include is made for us — the important family members are dead or geographically absent. In other situations, part of the process of deciding who to include may have to be done by trial and error — the counselling becomes stuck and the counsellor becomes aware for the first time of the existence of an important member of the system. The best initial plan is usually to invite everyone who is living together in the household, but it may often be important to revise this invitation and later incorporate other significant people who do not happen to be living under the same roof.

Having learned how *to determine* who is part of the family system, the counsellor must then learn how *to engage* it in the counselling process. For example, it is unlikely that he will successfully engage a husband and children if he enters into prolonged discussions with their wife and mother first. They will merely conclude that they are either redundant to the process *or* that they have now been discussed to such an extent from one family member's view point that there can be no hope of describing things from *their* point of view or believing that the counsellor will really *hear them.*

Having made his assessment as to who is part of the system, either from a referrer or from the family member who first made contact with him, the counsellor should try to make contact as quickly as possible with everyone he believes should be included. He might do this by sending a letter of invitation addressed to the whole family or to some of the members he feels may find it particularly difficult to see him. Gorell Barnes suggests some useful patterns that can be adopted in writing to a family. As she points out, the emphasis in this letter must be on seeing the family as a resource group not as an aspect of 'the problem'.[2] If the individual family member seems to have sufficient influence within the family, the counsellor may simply 'send a message' via him or her inviting them all to meet with him.

Often however the individual who makes this first contact, may find ways of sabotaging a family meeting if he or she is left with the whole responsibility for convening it. This may be a conscious decision on this person's part because what he or she is really wanting is a 'shoulder to cry on' rather than any intervention which might radically change the family system. More usually it is an unconscious response to the fear of the pain and disruption which may be involved in the counselling process itself. Change is painful and the person who knows or senses this is wise. Part of the work of the initial contact is to help the individual to weigh up the losses and gains of engaging in counselling. In most situations, the counsellor will be wise to refuse to continue to see an individual family member unless, by so doing, he can manoeuvre the family strategically towards change (see chapter 6). If all his attempts to engage the system have failed and a high level of resistance continues, the counsellor is better advised to decline to become involved any further. This may seem a brutal and rejecting course to adopt but it is only too easy, for the best of conscious motives, to be drawn into colluding with the malfunctioning that already exists, whereas to take a firm stand against collusion at this early stage may present the family with an important and useful challenge.

The Brown Family

Initial contact is all important. Many of the minister's first contacts with the family in distress will either be through a chance conversation with a member of the congregation or during some other type of pastoral contact in the wider community such as a request for baptism. The family may be church members and well known to the minister, in which case he will often have suspected that the family is experiencing difficulties before anything has been put into words. One member may gradually become a little braver and find some pretext for drawing the minister aside for a few moments' private conversation. As in any other approach for help, the individual may begin by talking about a matter of small importance that appears to have nothing to do with any kind of serious difficulty.

For example, a woman may begin by telling the vicar that she is finding it too time-consuming to continue as the Enrolling Member of the Mother's Union. She has done the job for several years and it is time to make way for a younger person. In any case, now two of the children are well into their teens, she is finding that there is more rather than less work to do in and around the house. This one might describe as the 'presenting problem' — the first move in the encounter between help seeker and helping person.

Now it is the vicar's turn. He has two main alternatives: first he can accept that the issues so presented are no more nor less than the woman has stated them. All he has to do is to thank her for what she has done and find a new Enrolling Member. Or he can ponder within himself as to whether there might be more to this situation than meets the eye. He may reflect upon his recent contacts with Mrs Brown and her family to see if he can remember anything that seems to be giving them cause for concern. Perhaps nothing in particular strikes him. Or perhaps he recalls that Julia, the teenage daughter, has stopped coming to choir practice for several weeks and has not been to church. This memory may then prompt him to pursue the second approach. He may enquire whether all is well or indicate by some other comment that, whilst accepting Mrs Brown's remarks at their face value, he would nevertheless be open and willing to hear about anything further she would like to discuss. Let us suppose that at this point Mrs Brown breaks down in tears and says she cannot cope any more. The atmosphere at home is unbearable and she's afraid that something terrible is going to happen. The only thing she's sure about is that it would be nothing short of hypocritical for her to continue as Enrolling Member. Encouraged by the vicar's obvious interest and concern, Mrs Brown continues. The problem is that Julia is pregnant and her father is so upset that he is threatening to leave home, unless Julia does first. Mrs Brown desperately needs help and cannot think of anyone else to turn to except the vicar.

At this point the vicar has a crucial decision to make. Either he can encourage Mrs Brown to go on talking or he can begin to suggest that he could probably be more helpful to Mrs Brown and her family if he could meet with them all. It *may* be that Mrs Brown's response to this is one of welcome and relief but she may on the other hand become even more anxious and say that her husband and/or Julia would be furious if they thought she had told anyone outside the family and that on no account would they be willing for the vicar to come and see them. At this point, Mrs Brown and the vicar are entering upon a phase of initial negotiation by which the framework for the family counselling will be established.

If in this hypothetical case, the vicar wants to proceed to do some family counselling, he first of all has to *believe* that this would indeed be the most effective means of helping Mrs Brown and her family. He then has to *convey* that belief to Mrs Brown. A complex interaction will be taking place between these two people — part of which has to do with the vicar building a trusting and caring relationship with Mrs Brown and part of which involves challenging her assumptions as to how best to obtain help with her problems. As in any other potential helping situation, the vicar has to convey a lot of things at once in this first encounter. He has first to register his compassionate concern for Mrs Brown. As Carr points out, 'Whatever the intention of presenting the Grace of God, his welcome to the prodigal, his longing to save all and his universal love — all this will crumble if it is not implicit in and discoverable through the first contact.'[3] In addition to this important fact, the vicar has to redefine the implicit helping contract as being to do with *counselling the*

family group and not simply *supporting Mrs Brown.* It will
already be obvious that Mrs Brown's problems are entrenched
within the current relationship system composed of her
husband, her daughter, her son and herself (and probably,
her parents and parents-in-law as well). The vicar must
therefore convey two apparently contradictory messages at
the same time and, whilst assuring Mrs Brown of his loving
acceptance of both her and her problem *as she has stated it,*
he must also indicate that he can only be helpful if he can
meet with the whole family.

Timing is an important element in these early negotiations,
as it is throughout the counselling process. He may need to
sit down with Mrs Brown at some length and work out with
her how they might involve the rest of the family. Mrs Brown
is the gateway to the family group and the family counsellor
can only proceed at her pace. Yet, the counsellor must at
some stage win what Whitaker calls 'the battle for initiative
and control' of the process of counselling at this early stage
and gently but firmly pursue the task of convening the family
group.[4]

Choice of Venue

If this preliminary negotiation is successfully accomplished,
the family counsellor will be able to set up a first meeting
with the family. He may be in a position to choose whether
to see the family in their own home or in his study or office.
If so, the choice should be made on the basis of how best to
help the counselling to be effective.

It may be that the family will feel more relaxed in their own
home. There may also be special considerations to take into
account such as the inclusion of an elderly or handicapped
person which might be more easily accomplished if the
counselling takes place in the family's home. There is also a
lot of useful information to be gained if at least one of the
sessions is held in the home. The level of chaos or calm; the
way in which individual family members share their space or
guard their territory; the extent to which the family's
boundaries appear to be diffuse and easily crossed by
neighbours popping in and out—all this and much more is
revealed during a home visit and helps the counsellor build
up a picture of the family in its context.

However, it will often be the case that the minister already has a very clear picture of these kinds of facts. He may visit the home regularly in the course of his ordinary pastoral ministry and the family may be well known to him through his other kinds of contact with them. If this is the case, there may be a lot to be said for suggesting that the family meetings are held in the minister's office. This will enable both the family and the minister to set the scene for a focused, problem-solving activity, defining difference as well as continuity in their new contact with one another. The minister needs to establish himself as a family counsellor for the period of time he is working in this way with a particular family and to keep the boundaries as clear as possible between his temporary contact as a family counsellor and his on-going contact with them as priest or minister. With some families this will not be an issue because the family does not come from the minister's regular congregation. But even here, it is important that 'something different' should be perceived about this kind of contact, so that if family members at some future date joined the Church as regular members, they will be able to relate to the minister in a more normal everyday manner.

The family counsellor must also consider his own needs. If he is anxious (which he is likely to be when he starts doing some family counselling) he will probably feel more at home and more in control (in an appropriate way) if he uses his own territory. Again, much will depend upon the facilities he has at his disposal. If his study was only designed for interviewing one person at a time, he may not have the option of using it for family counselling. Most ministers will be able to create the necessary space on their own territory, and it is certainly preferable if this can be an option rather than always having to use the family's own home, with its distractions and the sense of 'invasion' which the family may experience.

The room that is used needs if possible to be informally furnished with chairs of equal size and height. If it is normally used as an office, desks and filing cabinets should be made as unobtrusive as possible. The chairs should be arranged in a half circle so that everyone can see each other and so that the counsellor can see everyone simultaneously without having to move his head from side to side as though he is umpiring a tennis match. There should be sufficient space for children to use play material and for a small blackboard or flip chart to be on hand in case the counsellor wants to compose lists with the family or draw a genogram.

Tasks of a First Family Interview

The family counsellor needs to accomplish various tasks during the first family meeting. Perhaps the most basic task is to enable the family to come to a *second* meeting! In a sense all else can be subsumed within this important aim, and in order to achieve this the family counsellor has to steer a delicate middle course between two potential pitfalls. On the one hand he must make a relationship with each family member so that each person experiences him as concerned, caring and potentially worthy of trust. In essence, he must *join* with them, accommodating himself to their mood, their language, culture and style of interaction. This includes beginning to make age-appropriate relationships with young children, adolescents and older family members. On the other hand he must continually convey the message that it is the *family group as a whole* that is his concern and not simply the individual family member(s) who appear to 'have a problem'. Other family members may ask why they have been invited to come 'when it is clearly Michael or John who needs help'. This means that the family counsellor will probably need to introduce several important ideas about his own counselling beliefs at an early stage in the first interview.

For example, he may need to say that 'in my experience, when one person is upset or in trouble in a family, everyone is affected in some way.' Or, 'I usually find that one person's problems can be helped a lot quicker if we all put our heads together to see what can be done. That's why I asked you all to come along today.' Or, 'Although it seems that Michael is the person who you are all most concerned about, other family members may have things that worry them and which they would like to talk about. We could hear about some of those at the same time.' On the one hand, the family counsellor must convey the message that everyone here (and perhaps others too) are essential if the counsellor is to be helpful. On the other hand, he has to avoid challenging too directly their view of how they see the family problem. Not many families will happily digest a full-blown account of the way families operate as systems, however simply the counsellor explains it! If they need to present their difficulties through an identified patient, they are not likely to agree very easily that 'Michael's behaviour isn't the *real* problem; the *real* problem in your family has something to do with the way you relate to each other.' However theoretically correct, this statement will almost certainly be totally unacceptable to the family. An important rule of thumb to bear in mind is that if the family *needs* an identified patient, this should be treated as a *group defence* and handled as cautiously as any of the defence mechanisms exhibited in an individual counselling relationship.

If the family presents its problems transactionally, in terms of a relationship difficulty, it is still important to move very cautiously and not assume that each party will be prepared to agree that they are implicated in the marital, parenting or other relationship difficulties, other than as a victim. Pacing is all important. The family counsellor can only move at the family's own pace, however clearly he thinks he sees the way forward.

Stages of the First Interview

Beyond the overall aim of steering a middle course between collusion and confrontation such that the family agrees to come back, the family counsellor needs to attend to several other specific tasks during a first family meeting. One of the clearest accounts of the stages through which the first family interview should typically proceed is given by Haley.[5] He suggests that there are four: the social stage, the problem-eliciting stage, the interactional stage and the goal-setting stage. I will use this format for discussing the tasks that need to be accomplished during the first interview.

(1) The social stage. The family counsellor greets each member of the family and welcomes him or her to this first meeting. His initial role is to act as a good host, helping people to relax and feel at ease. It is a very good idea to let family members choose where they sit because, as has been

noted previously, the counsellor can pick up various clues as to the family's pattern of relationships, based on where and how the family members sit. It is usually best however if the counsellor keeps his observations to himself at this early point in his contact with the family. Premature or ill-thought-out comments or 'interpretations' are usually experienced as intrusive and hostile, however 'correct' they may be. The family counsellor needs to establish the ground rules of the family counselling process, all of which follow from his involvement with the family as a system rather than with a collection of individuals.

In his initial welcomes, the family counsellor tries to convey the message that each member is equally important and each has the right to be heard. No contributions from anyone will be discounted even if, as in the case of a young child or a mentally handicapped person, they can only be made non-verbally. Moreover, it is useful if the counsellor can show at an early stage that he will want to encourage family members to speak for themselves. It is often the case that mother and father instinctively speak on behalf of their children. It is useful if the counsellor addresses his questions or comments directly to even the youngest child and, if a parent replies, to suggest gently that it would be good if little Jane could say what she thinks for herself. After a while, family members will 'learn' this important ground rule and may even transfer it to their interactions outside the counselling sessions. Where family members lack differentiation and tend to fuse their ideas, beliefs and opinions one with another, this may be an important therapeutic step for them to take.

Another important rule to establish at an *early* stage is that private communications between one family member and the counsellor outside the sessions are unhelpful. Because the counselling task involves the whole family, it is inappropriate for 'secrets' to be communicated to the counsellor which he is then prevented from sharing in the counselling sessions with other family members. This does not mean that everything should be said in front of every member of the group, and it is important here for the counsellor to make a clear distinction between appropriate privacy and inappropriate secrecy. He may want to explain at this point that it is quite usual within a course of family counselling sessions, for some meetings to

be reserved for the married couple on their own without the
children, or for a session to be offered to each of the couple
alone with his or her parents.

Within this process of getting to know each other during
the social stage of the first interview, the family counsellor
needs to discover if every one knows why they have come.
Sometimes young children and even older ones have been
told that they are going on some outing and are quite confused
as to what is happening when they find themselves in the
minister's study. Helping parents clarify with their children
the general nature of the family meeting is important at this
preliminary stage.

(2) The second stage involves gaining some understanding of
what is troubling the family. The counsellor may already
have obtained one or more versions of this before the first
family meeting but it is important to throw it open to the
whole group so that everyone's different ideas are elicited.
Haley comments that,

> If therapy is to end properly, it must begin properly—by
> negotiating a solvable problem amd discovering the social
> situation that makes the problem necessary. The act of
> therapy begins with the way the problem is examined. The
> act of intervening brings out problems and the relationship
> patterns that are to be changed.[6]

Although this may at first appear a rather simplistic account
of the beginning of the counselling process, it nevertheless
succinctly states one of its early priorities. The problems as
the various family members see them have to be discovered
and the counsellor must help the family to feel that these
problems can be made somewhat more manageable than they
feel them to be at the moment. By the act of eliciting them
and engaging with them, the counsellor begins to make them
more manageable for the family and, by their joint efforts in
this first meeting, family and family counsellor begin to
discover the various possibilities that exist for change.

It is helpful if the counsellor first tells the family what he
already has learnt about them from the family member who
made the initial contact or from the third party who has
referred them. He can then move on to asking more about

their problems from the people who are present. He may throw this question open to everyone and see who responds or he may ask each member in turn. If he adopts the latter course it may be important to consider rather carefully how the family will interpret the order in which he asks family members' their opinion. For example, to begin by asking the youngest child may yield some interesting data and allow the child to offer his opinion 'uncontaminated' by the views of older family members. However, to do so may cut across the family's culture and sense of propriety. It may be important to challenge the family's rules for communicating but it is unwise to appear to insult some cultural norm if one can avoid doing so. Besides accepting at this early stage the family's own hierarchy of relationships, it is important to bear in mind at all times the fundamental aim of a first interview, which is to obtain a second one. One person in the group is often more influential in deciding whether or not the family will come back. The views of this person need to be accorded particular respect by the counsellor as he or she will be evaluating the counsellor's interventions in terms of whether they are likely to be helpful to the family in the future and whether it is both safe and worth while to return.

The counsellor should adopt an interested, open attitude and convey the message that all and every opinion about the family's problems is acceptable and of value. He should avoid offering his own opinions or answering questions about how the family's problems might be alleviated. He can simply say that he needs to hear a lot more from them before being able to suggest anything helpful. The counsellor needs to establish himself firmly in charge of the *process* of counselling whilst conveying to the family that they are in charge of its *content*. The 'what' belongs to the initiative of the family; the 'how' to the counsellor. This means that he must be prepared to ask a family member to stop telling their version of the story for a while so that others may also speak and in general he must act as a controller of communication. It is important that he asks family members what steps they have already taken to try and solve their problems, on the basis that it is pointless to try something again that has already proved unsuccessful. It is also useful, when faced with a statement such as, 'Our problem is Alison's refusal to go to school,' to ask which

other members of the family have had a similar problem with
going out or leaving home. This conveys the idea that
problems like this are seldom unique in a family and it has
the effect of reducing the scapegoating process and broadening
out the discussion beyond the identified patient. The nature
of the counsellor's questions can be instrumental in opening
out new considerations for the family, and some writers have
explored the way in which the counsellor's questions can in
themselves be made effective therapeutic agents because they
present the family with new hypotheses about its own
functioning.[7]

Handling the identified patient needs special care. The
counsellor should not focus his attention in any special way
on him or her, and it is best to avoid asking the identified
patient first about how he or she sees the problems in the
family. This person has already been elected by the family
group to be 'the problem' and the counsellor, while not
wanting to confront this view directly, should do nothing to
reinforce it. The counsellor may have to offer support to the
identified patient from time to time and diffuse the focus
from him or her if family members collude together in an
unremitting and destructive 'blame game'. It is, however,
often the case that during the second stage of the first
interview a variety of different views regarding the family's
problems will be offered and the family counsellor can then
move on to stage 3.

(3) At this point the counsellor shifts gear towards
encouraging family members to discuss the family's problems
among themselves. If he has successfully made contact with
each member of the group (Stage 1) and has managed to
encourage each person to voice his or her views of the problem
(Stage 2), this third stage should follow on quite naturally.
Family members will want to discuss and argue about the
differences that have been expressed and hopefully the
counsellor has been able to create a sufficiently safe and
accepting atmosphere for them to do so. As family members
begin to talk with each other, the counsellor can help by
suggesting that the two main protagonists in an argument
move so that they can sit next to each other. He may invite a
third family member to see if he can help the twosome

discuss their differences more productively. If mother and teenage daughter are arguing about whether the fact she stays out late is a problem or not, the counsellor can invite father to act as an objective mediator, helping mother and daughter to listen to each other and understand each other better. The counsellor can 'coach' father a little, if he hesitates to get involved or if he gets involved with one party against the other.

The more the family can re-enact its problems within the session, the better. Actions are more memorable than words alone and are the more natural means of communicating for children. For example, the family may be asked to role play the last row they had over the problem area. They should be helped to pinpoint the context precisely and re-create the situation in as much detail as possible: who said what to whom and when should be carefully portrayed. This enables family members to relive their feelings vividly and to give the counsellor an accurate picture of how each family member sees their problems. If the problem is such that it can be 'brought into the room' or registered symbolically in some way, this should be done at this stage. For example, while the family is discussing the inability of a child to go to school, the child may be clinging to his mother and acting as a barrier between his parents. The counsellor may ask the family to discuss how they are feeling about this clinging behaviour *right now* and in what way it is a problem and to whom. Asking the family to say who worries/gets angry most about the behaviour and so on down a worry 'hierarchy' provides important data and is more easily elicited when the problem behaviour is exhibited in the room in front of everyone.

(4) The final stage of the first interview is the goal-setting stage. What does the family want to change and how do they intend going about changing it? Hopefully, by this point, issues other than the specific behaviour of the identified patient have been opened up and again family members can all be encouraged to voice their views as to priorities. Family counselling needs to be a goal orientated, purposeful activity and it is at this stage that the counsellor needs to help the family to be as specific as possible as to the sort of changes they want to see happen. At this point and throughout the

counselling process it is important for the counsellor to affirm all the many efforts that the family has undoubtedly already made to solve their problems. People who present symptoms or problems do so because these are understood to be the best solution that can be found at that moment to some fundamental difficulty in their lives. The family needs to feel that the counsellor recognises the efforts it has already made to arrive at a workable solution. It will then be more prepared to consider trying something different. As Haley points out, 'problems . . . should be something one can count, observe, measure or in some way know one is influencing';[8] therefore the counsellor needs to help the family to say how much father drinks, how often, whom it affects most and why. He can then help them to decide what would have to change for everyone to feel that things were better.

Not every painful and problematic family situation is precisely amenable to this kind of analysis, and Haley writes from a structural/strategic approach to family counselling which will be discussed more fully in chapter 6. However, the more the counsellor can help the family to convert its vague aspirations 'to be a happy family' into the specific and the concrete, the more likely he is to be able to help them achieve meaningful changes in their relationship system. The task of family counselling is not to remove symptoms or solve individually presented problems, but to render them unnecessary to the way the family functions. The counsellor will always be searching for the connection between the symptom as presented and the more fundamental problems which undoubtedly exist within the relationship system as a whole. Nevertheless, the *route* to a happier and more productively functioning family system is always through the problem *as the family presents it.* Counselling goals must therefore also be framed within the terms of the problem as presented. If the counsellor adopts this strategy, the family will usually accept some widening of the focus of the counselling at a later stage.

Having established some initial aims for the counselling and enabled everyone to enter into a good enough agreement, the counsellor should end by deciding with the family the practical framework for further meetings. Should other family members be invited? How often should meetings take place? How long will they be? Where should they be held? Coming to some agreement about these practical issues gives both the family and the counsellor a secure framework within which to work. The details of this 'contract' for work may have to be altered or kept flexible, but unless there is some good reason for changing, the counselling sessions should normally take place at the agreed time, in the agreed place, with the agreed family members and finish on time. For most families (and counsellors!) about one and a quarter or one and a half hours is as long as everyone can be expected to work hard on tough, emotional problems, but it is long enough to enable each interview to pass through several important phases and come to some sense of closure. The counsellor should finish the first interview by checking whether everyone is clear about what has been agreed and making a date for the next meeting.

Notes

1. A. C. R. Skynner, 'The Minimum Sufficient Network', *Social Work Today*, vol. 2, no. 9, 1971.
2. G. Gorell Barnes, *Working With Families,* Macmillan 1984, p. 39.
3. W. Carr, *Brief Encounters*, SPCK 1985, p. 71.
4. C. Whitaker, 'The Growing Edge' in J. Haley and L. Hoffman (eds.), *Techniques of Family Therapy*, New York, Basic Books, 1967.
5. J. Haley, 'The First Interview' in *Problem-Solving Therapy*, San Francisco, Jossey-Bass, 1973.
6. ibid., p. 9.
7. M. S. Palazzoli et al., 'Hypothesising—Circularity—Neutrality; three guidelines for the conductor of the session', *Family Process*, vol. 19, 1980, pp. 3—12.
8. Haley, op. cit. p. 41.

FIVE

The Counselling Process

There are several different approaches commonly taken to counselling the family group and these will be examined in chapters 6 and 7. But first we need to look at some general issues that apply to the counselling process as a whole and to outline some of the typical 'events' which may occur along the way.

Having engaged the family's interest and motivation successfully, through an appropriate initial contact and an effective first interview, the counsellor should now have some reasonably clear idea as to the dimensions of the family's troubles and the way in which these might be approached. Sometimes of course it takes much more than one family meeting to get a clear picture of the family's difficulties or to arrive at a 'contract' of work with them. If we think of the counselling process as having three phases — the engagement phase, the middle phase and the termination phase — it is often the case that the engagement phase takes place over several interviews and merges into the middle phase of the process. Nevertheless, the counsellor should begin to feel quite early on that he has successfully joined with the family and that he and they are jointly undertaking a mutually defined task.

Throughout the course of the counselling, however short or long it may be, the counsellor will need to alternate between two overall strategies: on the one hand, maintaining the family's co-operation with the counselling process and, on the other, encouraging family members towards changing and restructuring the family's system of relationships. Restructuring techniques belong to a later discussion under the various approaches to family counselling. At this point we will confine our attention to techniques for maintaining the family's co-operation.

80

Efforts to 'join' the family are required most plentifully during the engagement phase, but go on being needed throughout the course of treatment. Individual family members and the family as a whole need continually to sense that, however tough the going gets, the counsellor is always on their side, always intent upon lessening the pain where and when he can, always struggling to be alongside the needs of each family member, understanding them and helping them as best he can. By a variety of delicate verbal and non-verbal actions, including humour, good eye-contact, touch and the offering of support and empathy to each individual, the family counsellor enables the family to keep coming to the sessions for sufficient time for change to occur. Whilst the counsellor's overall objective is to help the family to change its dysfunctional patterns of interaction, the change-producing strategies which he adopts must always be sensitively tempered with interventions designed to lower the stress and anxiety involved in change.

Whilst restructuring moves, by their nature, help to move the family on to something new, 'joining' strategies tend always to put the brakes on and maintain the status quo.

(1) The counsellor 'maintains' the family structure. For example, in a family where the structure is such that mother is the main communicator and c ominates the decision-making and rule-setting processes of the group, it may be that the counsellor is trying to help the family to restructure its relationships so that her husband is able to get his needs met in a more straightforward way and become able to take a more equal share in organising the family's life. But, while husband and wife are in the process of renegotiating their relationship, the wife in particular may need the counsellor's overt support while she struggles to relinquish her monopoly over this part of the family's life. The counsellor may seem to be colluding with the wife's resistance to change but in reality he will be helping the system to pause for a while and maintain the status quo while the wife's anxiety and distress subside. The alternative would probably mean that the wife would prevent further counselling sessions from taking place.

(2) A second important strategy for maintaining the family in

treatment and facilitating the counselling process is the way in which the counsellor 'tracks' the family's own material rather than introducing issues and concerns of his own. This is particularly important in the early stages but the counsellor is wise to continue to adopt this attitude of active passivity in terms of the actual *content* of the family sessions. The more the family is allowed to determine the agenda of the meetings and to decide upon the issues to be dealt with, the more they will feel that the counselling is attending to what is of primary importance to them. On the micro-level, the counsellor needs to find ways of encouraging and facilitating the expression of these issues by appropriate nods, smiles, and good eye-contact with whoever is speaking, without losing sight of what is happening within the group as a whole.

While the counsellor is allowing and actively encouraging the family to determine the *content* of what is being discussed, he must continually attend to the *process* that is occurring before him. While family members talk, he will be observing and noting the sequences of behaviour, the patterns of communication, the overt and covert leadership that is being displayed and the alliances and coalitions that exist between family members. The family counsellor needs to tune his ear and eye to the group processes of the family in the same way as the group counsellor does in his work with small groups. The family is a particular kind of small group, and throughout the course of counselling the family counsellor needs to attend to process as fully, and probably a lot more fully, than he attends to content.

(3) A third important means of maintaining the family in the counselling process is the counsellor's skill at adapting his style and whole bearing to the culture of each unique family group. The counsellor must find a way of overcoming his outsider status sufficient for the family to find him acceptable, trustworthy and 'homely' in a certain deeply personal kind of way. He must of course retain his all important objectivity and yet he must become an integral part of the system. This means that he must try to use language that is appropriate and congruent with that which is used by the family. He must match his mood to theirs, neither introducing an overbearing heartiness into a silent, depressed group, nor a

sombre, solemn tone where young children are lightening the family's mood by their humour and desire to play.

An experienced family counsellor will often quite unconsciously 'match' the way in which he sits with that of the family member with whom he is engaged. This matching of body posture is particularly useful when the counsellor is challenging or confronting a member of the family for he can then simultaneously convey, by non-verbal means, a sense of support and on-going alliance. An inexperienced family counsellor, still controlled by his own need to be helpful at any cost will often betray his own anxious efforts most obviously by the strident mismatch between the enthusiasm of his gestures and body posture and the laid back indifference of the teenage members of the family. Reflecting upon this sense of mismatch may help the family counsellor to regain his grip upon the humbling realities of family counselling— namely, that no matter how much he wants to help and rescue the family from its problems, he is ultimately merely the mid-wife to their own willingness and ability to make things different.

Whilst the family must always remain in charge of its goals, the counsellor is in charge of the framework of counselling. Moreover, whilst each family is unique, and this uniqueness must be addressed by the counsellor in the way he approaches them and their difficulties, there is also a sense in which the family counsellor will gain, through his experience, an understanding of the way families typically respond to certain kinds of stress. In particular, he will learn how families respond to the series of crises in their life cycle which were described in chapter 3.

This accumulated wisdom, together with a growing knowledge of how best to be effective, requires him to exercise his authority unequivocally in order to offer structure to the counselling and containment to the family. The family counsellor's role has been compared to that of the conductor of an orchestra or the producer of a play. The analogies are useful because they remind us that whilst conductor and producer alike must be in charge of the production, they are in no sense responsible for the content, purpose or aims of the play or symphony. Both writer/composer and conductor/

producer are essential parts of the whole but their roles and tasks are different. At different phases of the counselling, the counsellor's authority over the process will be more obvious than at others, but at all times the counsellor's task is to hold boundaries, set limits and keep the family group on course towards the aims and goals it has set for itself.

Various general factors will determine the way the counselling proceeds during the middle phase. Most of these concern the particular approach to family counselling that has been adopted and this will be discussed later. But other determining factors include the length of the counselling and the way the family manifests its resistance to change. Family counselling does not have to be a very lengthy affair and nothing that is said in this book should imply that, in undertaking some family counselling, the minister is automatically taking on a protracted and time consuming relationship with the family. A single family interview convened at a time of family crisis may be all that is required to unlock new resources and energy within the family. In fact, one meeting with the whole family may have far greater effect than a prolonged series of individual interviews with one or more family members. For example, two families reached crisis point when the father of a fifteen-year-old girl made pregnant by a seventeen-year-old boy threatened to kill the boy unless the police took him away and locked him up for his 'crime.' A single long interview, first with each family separately and then with the two families together, sufficiently resolved the immediate crisis to enable the two families to co-operate in helping this very young couple plan their new life together.

Some family counsellors choose to agree on a fixed number of sessions with the family during the initial contract, reviewing where things have got when the fixed number has been completed. A new contract may then be negotiated and another fixed number of sessions can be agreed. Others keep the contract open-ended and may build in a short review at the end of each meeting, checking whether the family wants a further meeting and emphasising the fact that counselling should only continue as long as the family is being helped. The intervals between sessions are usually longer than the weekly interval often chosen by individual counsellors. This is because family members need to have time to digest what has happened in the session and work on the material together. They are less reliant on input from the counsellor who is merely facilitating the operation of the system's own healing mechanisms. A two- or three-weekly interval is often favoured by family counsellors and, towards the end of the counselling contract, sessions may be spaced out further still so that the family and counsellor are gradually weaned away from one another.

Resistance to change will be a recurrent feature of counselling during the middle phase of the process. Primary resistance is manifested during the engagement phase, when, as we have seen, family and counsellor struggle towards achieving a common view of the family's difficulties, whereby the family, not the identified patient, is agreed to be the focus of concern. Having successfully negotiated this initial hurdle, both parties often enter a kind of honeymoon period during which the presenting problems get dealt with and the identified patient's symptoms improve. When greater efforts are made to bring about more fundamental changes within the family system, a variety of secondary resistances often arise. These include what has been called the 'absent member manoeuvre' when a key family member suddenly refuses to attend.[1] He often gives a series of apparently rational reasons why he cannot do so and the whole family colludes to defend his absence. Alternatively, the family becomes progressively more dependent upon the counsellor, who finds himself increasingly pushed to take the initiative and produce the motivation for continued work and change. Or again, the identified patient may become symptomatic once more and both family and counsellor feel depressed by the apparent return to square one. Or, another family member begins to exhibit a new set of problems or an unexpected threat is made by a marriage partner to begin divorce proceedings or by a young adult to give up work. Any of these events can be a normal part of the counselling process and the counsellor needs to interpret them in terms of the family's need to reduce the pace of change. The counsellor's task is to try to understand the meaning of the resistance and respond to it appropriately.

The third, or termination, phase of counselling may occur

as a planned part of the process or it may happen suddenly and without much warning. If counselling has gone on for quite a long time, the ending of the relationship between family and counsellor will hopefully be carefully planned, with each party preparing themselves for the separation. This may involve increasing the intervals between meetings. Sometimes it may be a good idea to offer a review meeting a year later to check up on how things are going. Sometimes however the counselling process is terminated abruptly by the family refusing to return. It may be possible for the counsellor to redress this situation by locating and acknowledging to the family some inappropriate intervention he has made which has made it difficult for the family to return. Often however, the family does not make further contact and the counsellor is left wondering what went wrong or whether the meetings up until that point had been of any help. Some studies have shown that many families who appear to drop out of counselling prematurely, have actually gained a good deal of help from the process but simply see no point in coming back.[2]

If a fixed number of sessions has been agreed, both parties will be clear when counselling is due to end. Even so, the counsellor should remind the family that sessions will shortly be coming to an end, so that everyone's feelings about termination can be expressed. If the counsellor has enjoyed working with a particular family he may be loath to part with them. If he has found the counselling painful and unrewarding he may be secretly glad that the work is coming to an end but guilty about his relief. In either case, the counsellor may need help from a colleague or consultant with whom he can discuss his feelings so that he can avoid letting them get in the family's way. This possibility will be discussed further in chapter 9.

Notes

1. J. Sonne et al., 'The Absent Member Manoeuvre as a Resistance in Family Therapy of Schizophrenia', *Family Process*, vol. 1, no. 1, 1962.
2. M. Soloman, 'Family Therapy Drop-outs: Resistance to Change', *Canadian Psychiatric Association Journal*, vol. 14, 1969.

SIX

The Structural Approach

We can now begin to consider the main approaches taken to helping restructure the family group. These cannot in reality be divided off from one another as neatly as the following discussion implies. Nevertheless it may be helpful to distinguish the main approaches to family counselling and reflect upon the types of family problem to which they are best suited. In the next two chapters we will examine the structural and strategic approaches to counselling the family, which are influenced by behavioural and communicational models of human interaction; in chapters 8 and 9 we will examine psychoanalytic and experiential approaches.

Structural family counselling emphasises the need to restructure the family group through the minute particulars of its 'here and now' interactions. It is a present-and-future-orientated approach to counselling and does not place much emphasis on the family's past history. Structural family counselling is influenced by behavioural and not psychoanalytic models, and its focus is directed to the observable, behavioural patterns and sequences between family members as they occur within the counselling sessions. The term 'structural' also indicates the way that practitioners who use this approach advocate the need to structure the process of counselling quite carefully. Counselling is time-limited—often in terms of an agreed six or ten sessions—and a contract is drawn up, outlining the main goals of the counselling.[1]

Structural family counsellors have introduced a range of specific techniques to aid in restructuring the family system. A useful technique advocated for early on in the counselling process is the re-enactment of the problem situation. The structural family counsellor tries to exploit the dramatic potential of the session and the family is asked to re-enact a specific occasion when they were encountering difficulties.

The counsellor asks the family to 'show' as well as to 'tell' what usually happens when problems arise in the family. The family may be further prompted by asking, 'When did this last happen? Will you show me what happened? Who was involved and who said what to whom?'

For example, the wife and children in a family are complaining that Dad seems to be getting more and more withdrawn from family life and his main involvement seems to be when he enters into verbal and physical fights with his teenage son. The counsellor asks the family to re-enact a typical sequence of behaviour that occurs around this stated behaviour. The family chooses the moment when Mum returns from her work as a community doctor and the children, Tracey aged nine and Dominic aged fifteen, return from school. Dad is a painter and works from his studio at home. The family re-enact the home-coming period yesterday afternoon:

TRACEY: Daddy, look at my nature exercise—I came top! Gosh what's for tea, I'm starving.

DAD: (*Walks out of the room but returns a minute later when he hears his wife come in.*)

MUM: Terrible day. Terrible man. I don't think I can go on if I've got to work with him another minute. Just steamrollers over everyone. (*Flops into a chair and lights a cigarette.*)

DAD: I was wondering if we could . . . (*breaks off as Dominic enters in a whirlwind*).

DOMINIC: Hi Ma! Got a super new tape. It's that group I told you about—They're going to make it—They've *got* to make it. You know, the one that Oliver is part of—he plays the lead guitar. Just fancy actually *knowing* the lead guitar in a group that's going to be really famous, Mum.

MUM: Darling, that's wonderful, come over here and show me. Did you have a good day? What's on this evening—I'll come and hear that tape if you're going to play it, after I finish my cigarette.

DAD: (*Slams out of the room.*)

The family was complaining that Dad had withdrawn from family life and was becoming increasingly bad-tempered, especially with Dominic. But the re-enactment of the behavioural sequence around the family's complaint, gives a much fuller picture of the meaning of Dad's withdrawal and bad temper. The structure of a healthy well functioning family system is described by Minuchin as one in which the boundaries between sub-systems are flexible but firm and the tasks and roles of individual family members are well differentiated.[2] He suggests that the executive sub-system of the family (normally the parents or some other adult pairing) needs to be firmly in charge and yet able to move flexibly from the sort of behaviour required where there are young children in the family to the different behaviour required when the children are becoming teenagers. In this family, we see no evidence of a clear boundary around the parental sub-system or any indication that it can take executive control of the family. Parents do not address each other at all, except one halting attempt on the part of father and each parent communicates (or fails to communicate) only with the children. Dominic is showing signs of being cast in the role of 'parental child,' a term Minuchin uses to describe a child who displaces a parent and fills his or her role in the executive sub-system. When, as in this case, the particular circumstance of gender and age are added to this alliance between mother and teenage boy, the situation is obviously ripe for conflict.

The counsellor's task is to help the family achieve its developmental needs by successfully negotiating the stage of the life cycle at which it finds itself. In general terms, Dominic must be relieved of his position of 'parental child' whereby he is acting as a substitute for his father in what should be the parental executive sub-system. The relationship between husband and wife needs to be strengthened in terms of their marital roles, and they need help in adopting parental roles that are appropriate to a teenage boy. The alliance between the children could be usefully strengthened and steps taken to prevent Tracey from filling the position of parental child which will hopefully be vacated by Dominic. The aim is to strengthen the boundaries between the two sub-systems in the family, so that the differing developmental needs of each can be more adequately met.

The structural approach to achieving these therapeutic aims will normally be undertaken through a series of carefully constructed tasks which the family is asked to undertake between family meetings. These tasks are given as a kind of homework assignment. A therapeutic task must have a clearly defined *purpose* in terms of the counselling goals. It is best if it can be *practised* in some slight way within the session and, if not practised, it should be fully discussed; and it must be capable of being *performed* within the family's on-going life outside the session. Often the task that is initially set may not at first be accomplished by the family—but in discussing what got in the way of achieving the task, counsellor and family will learn important new facts about the way the family is functioning and the obstacles standing in the way of progress.

For the family just described, the counsellor suggested that the husband and wife went out together once a week—either for a meal or to some other relaxing activity which they would both enjoy. The counsellor suggested this task as a way of addressing, head on, the inability of the couple to function as a marital pair. As a way of practising the task symbolically, the counsellor asked the family to change their customary seating, whereby the children sat between the parents, and instead, he asked the couple to sit together on the settee. They looked uncomfortable. Not surprisingly, when the family returned two weeks later, the task had not been accomplished. In the careful discussion which then took place, it became clear that the whole family had colluded in preventing the parents from going out. Tracey announced for the first time that she was afraid to go to bed on her own and that only her mother could make her feel secure. The parents revealed that they were afraid that Dominic would not look after Tracey properly and Dominic failed to reassure them that he would not get into a fight with her or make her cry. The counsellor spent some time during the session discussing with Tracey how she might help her do some more grown-up things and, in particular, what would help her overcome her fears. She said she wanted to feel secure that there were no burglars in the garden, so her father agreed to walk round with his torch each night to make sure. As a way towards strengthening the relationship between the father and Tracey, they were asked to sit together in the session and the father was asked to help Tracey talk about her fears. Tracey agreed to be put to bed by her father once a week, as a stepping stone to becoming a bit less dependent upon her parents. Dominic, who was saving up for a new bike, agreed to try to stop teasing Tracey in exchange for a small financial reward from his parents, each day he had not made Tracey cry. Mother, who was now sitting next to Dominic, was asked to be responsible for the financial transaction as a way of reducing the fights between Dominic and his father.

When, over the next few weeks, these tasks had been successfully accomplished, the counsellor reintroduced the idea of a weekly outing for the couple without the children. They remained reluctant but agreed to try. Despite a recurrence of the children's difficulties, the couple succeeded in having an evening out. When they came to the next session a new atmosphere in the family was evident. The couple were clearly surprised at how pleasant the evening had been, and although they remained cautious about the future of their relationship, they were eager to try another outing soon. Tracey came to the session with her hair done up in a bun, and by her more grown-up appearance and her pleasure at having succeeded in putting herself to bed several times, she gave several indications of her new willingness to become more independent. Dominic had begun to sense that his loss of a special relationship with his mother might be replaced by something better—a new independence from both parents and a growing ability to engage in progressively more adult relations with his peers.

This series of tasks was in fact the crucial therapeutic ingredient in helping a family who came with considerable, though concealed marital problems and where the children were unable to develop emotionally. After several more meetings, counsellor and family agreed to terminate the counselling process and the family seemed on course for continuing to work out some of its difficulties in a productive and useful way.

Notes

1. The main theoretician, practitioner and writer about this approach is Salvador Minuchin. The interested reader should consult his *Families*

and Family Therapy, Tavistock 1974, and *Family Therapy Techniques* (with H. C. Fishman), Harvard University Press 1981. G. Gorell Barnes writes as a British practitioner: 'Family Bits and Pieces: Creating a Workable Reality' in S. Walrond-Skinner, *Family and Marital Psychotherapy*, Routledge & Kegan Paul 1979.
2. Minuchin, *Families and Family Therapy*.

SEVEN

The Strategic Approach

The second approach to family counselling is the strategic approach.[1] Like structural family counselling, the strategic approach is behavioural and focused on the 'here and now' events that are occurring between family members. Counselling is usually quite short term and may be reduced to as little as one or two sessions. Unlike approaches designed to help the family *learn* new patterns of interaction (structural), gain *insight* into its past or present behaviour (psychoanalytic) or *experience* new ways of relating within the counselling session (experiential), the strategic approach is orientated towards *symptom removal* and rapid *behaviour change*. Whether the family learns, gains insight or has a new experience, would not be seen as relevant, although each and any of these might be deemed to be desirable spin-offs from the main focus of the counselling.

A most effective and frequently used technique, employed early on in contact with the family, is to suggest to family members that *all should try to remain as they are* and avoid changing their behaviour. The reason given to the family for this instruction is that this will enable the counsellor to understand the family's problems better and thus help him make more appropriate suggestions to them. In particular, the identified patient is asked on no account to change his behaviour or abandon his symptoms. A longish interval is usually set before the next session—perhaps three or four weeks or more. The effect of these instructions is often quite remarkable and the family will often return to the counsellor quite transformed—the identified patient's symptoms abated and the behaviour patterns which surrounded the identified patient radically changed.

Here we can immediately discern two of the theoretical constructs which underlie this approach. First, the counsellor is unashamedly *directive*. He or she takes charge of the counselling process, making suggestions and instructing the family as to what they should do and when. In this respect, the strategic approach is similar to the structural approach but is unlike both the psychoanalytic and experiential approaches. But second, the instructions given to the family in the above example were *paradoxical* in intent and in this respect the strategic approach uses techniques that are dissimilar to all the other approaches. Although the counsellor instructs the family not to change, his expectation is that they will change and that they will do so because the counsellor has asked them not to. Strategic counselling thus uses defiance-based techniques which are predicated upon the belief that all families are highly resistant to change and that only by utilising the family's resistance in a constructive way, will the counsellor have any hope of enabling their situation to change.

This is a challenging and a really rather remarkable set of ideas and runs counter to the main thrust of the counselling movement. Yet defiance-based change interventions are frequently to be found in ordinary life whereby the resistance of an individual or group is circumvented by the tact or skill of another. Mothers instinctively do this with young children; husbands with wives and vice versa. In fact, one of the reasons that these techniques are so effective in family counselling is that family members routinely employ them, often quite unconsciously, in their dealings with each other. *Prescribing the symptom* therefore often enables the family member to abandon it because he or she is asked to continue doing consciously what before he or she claimed was beyond control. The counsellor gives permision for the symptomatic behaviour to be exhibited—often with an encouragement to continue it for as long and as thoroughly as the individual would like. If one or more family members can successfully produce their symptoms 'to order' they can, by the same token, cease to be bound by them. The implication of this is that family members have more control over their situation than they have hitherto admitted and the counsellor may well underline this fact by using phrases such as 'when you decide to change your behaviour permanently . . .' or 'when you choose to discontinue having your symptoms . . .'.

It is often useful to add a slightly different ingredient into the situation by *putting new boundaries around the problem.* For example, a family comes for help with a five-year-old child who has frequent, prolonged and disruptive temper tantrums. The parents and the child are told that they should cease trying to overcome this problem and, for the time being, David should continue having his tantrum so as to help the counsellor get a realistic idea of the extent of the problem. However, so as to make life easier over the next few months, the parents should designate one room as 'the temper tantrum room' and whenever David begins to have a tantrum, he should be asked to go to the temper tantrum room and then encouraged to continue for as long as he wishes. When he has finished, he can come out and continue as normal with his parents.

Several aspects of the family's life together are addressed by this simple intervention. The parents are relieved of the fruitless battle to prevent the tantrums; David's behaviour is normalised and thus made a much less powerful weapon for him to use against his parents; on the other hand he is allowed, and indeed encouraged, to continue using it as an appropriate outlet when his wishes are frustrated; the parents are given a manageable task to execute — i.e. taking David to the tantrum room and their confidence as parents is increased. The essential characteristic of a symptom prescription is that the family is changed if they *do* what they are asked to do and changed if they *do not.* For if this family returns next session reporting that (as is likely) the tantrums have greatly decreased or ceased altogether, then clearly a major change has occurred. If, on the other hand, the temper tantrums continue as before, they are continuing at the behest of the counsellor and his 'pleasure' and 'warm congratulations' which would be expressed at the following session would underline the fact that the tantrums were now being exhibited, not as a weapon against the parents but as a means of pleasing the counsellor. Such a change of context radically changes both their meaning and their effect.

A paradoxical prescription can often be set in the context of a *ritual*, which may be quite long and complex and put a lot of demands upon the participants. Or it may be framed in such a way that it is simply long, repetitive and boring. For example, a family came for help because the wife was obsessed with fears of dying. She had undergone extensive physical investigations over the last few years and the GP was adamant that there was nothing physically wrong with her. He had referred her to the family counsellor, who invited her, her husband and two young children to come to the first session. It soon became clear that, because of his own experiences in his family of origin, being the eldest child with a much younger sister, the husband experienced his much younger wife as a child. On the other hand, he outwardly showed much distress at her inability to mother their two young children properly. An enormous amount of her time was spent either at the doctor's surgery, or in bed nursing minor ailments or round at a friend's house swopping medical worries or at home reading popular first aid and medical books to check what illnesses she really had. She believed that the doctors were hiding the truth from her and, even though she had had extensive tests in hospital, she believed she was suffering from one or several fatal illnesses.

The counsellor spent several sessions with the couple but directed most of her attention to the wife. She adopted a 'medical' approach, referring to the husband as the patient's relative. She did nothing to challenge the heavy investment in symptomatology on the part of the wife but simply agreed with them both how incapacitating the whole problem was for everyone. She then asked if the wife would be prepared to try something a bit different, even though it would probably sound a little odd at first—and whether the husband would help her. Without explaining what this might be, the counsellor sent the couple away to think about whether they would agree to undertake it and to come back next time and let the counsellor know.

When the couple returned they both agreed they would try. The counsellor then commented that, far from wanting to persuade the wife that there was nothing the matter with her, the problem, as the counsellor saw it, was that no one was taking her worries sufficiently seriously. If she was going to die, it was important that she prepared for this properly and because she was a wife and mother it was very important that she set aside time to make proper plans for her family. It would obviously help her make these plans if she knew more clearly the kind of illness she had and the amount of time left to her before she died. The counsellor therefore wanted her to spend several hours each day studying the medical books, talking to her well informed neighbour and then drawing up detailed plans for the way in which her husband and children were going to be properly cared for after her death. Because these tasks were so important, they must be done in a systematic way—not haphazardly as she had been approaching things up to now. Above all she *must work much harder at these tasks*. Far from worrying too much about her impending death, she was not taking the situation half seriously enough and this is what the counsellor was going to help her to do.

The couple were somewhat aghast at hearing these words and predictably were taken by surprise at not hearing the familiar efforts of doctors and social workers to soothe her fears and allay her anxiety. They carefully wrote down what amounted to an exact prescription of the wife's current behaviour, but hedged about by rules and rituals as to the times and places she should engage in her reading, worrying and planning work—all of which was to take up most of her day. As she would 'obviously have no time to cook or do any housework' the husband would have to take over most of these duties (all of which he was doing anyway). The couple were told that, so as not to interrupt this important work, and since there was nothing that she or anyone else could do for them anyway, the counsellor would not see them again for another six weeks.

Six weeks later, the couple returned for their next session. The following is an excerpt from a transcription of the video-taped session.

THERAPIST: O.K. I gave you two tasks to do since the last time we met, which was quite a long time ago— about six weeks, wasn't it?

WIFE: Yes.

THERAPIST: There were two tasks for you to do.

WIFE: Yes, well, the first task, of thinking solely of myself for an hour . . .

THERAPIST: Yes.

WIFE: That was very very *boring* . . . and I used to fall asleep.

HUSBAND & WIFE: Laugh.

THERAPIST: (*evincing surprise*) Oh. Um.

WIFE: But it seems to have *done the trick*! I'm not . . .

HUSBAND: You got fed up with worrying, didn't you.

WIFE: I did. I got to the stage where I just felt . . . oh, so *what*! I can't control what's going to happen any more — well, I can't control it, anyway.

THERAPIST: Um.

WIFE: And I've started thinking rationally now, you know, when I've got something wrong, like if I've got a cold. Now going back a couple of months I'd have thought, 'Oh, I've got a cold — it must be something far worse' — but I just laugh at myself now and think, 'How stupid. I've got a cold — just like everybody else gets a cold.'

HUSBAND: And the fact that she hasn't even had a cold for six years is beside the point!

WIFE: A year — a year last February it was.

THERAPIST: Um. So am I hearing that right that you . . . er . . . as you know, the two bits of the task were for you to spend one hour each day on your own worrying about all the things that might happen to you and the illnesses that you might have and to concentrate your mind on that; and the second task was to spend several hours checking out how many things that you thought you'd *got* in the way of illnesses and to keep a record of these. Now, am I hearing that right — you say that you don't seem to have had any feelings that you've got things wrong with you?

WIFE: I haven't had any . . . well, when I *read*, I have thought 'Oh, I wonder if I've got that,' but now I think to myself, 'Don't be stupid.'

HUSBAND: You seem to have been more relaxed recently.

WIFE: Yes, a lot more relaxed.

HUSBAND: For the last two or three weeks, actually.

WIFE: Yes, much better. The worrying has been reduced by at least 80 per cent. I just don't think about it any more—*occasionally*—but then I think most people do.

THERAPIST: Yes—I mean, I'd feel a bit anxious really if things had got better that quickly, so I'm rather glad that occasionally you still do.

WIFE: Oh, yes.

THERAPIST: So it's now 80—20; 80 per cent—20 per cent?

WIFE: Yes—but before it was *all the time*—even when I was doing my work, I'd be worrying.

THERAPIST: Yes, that was our base line, wasn't it.

WIFE: But I don't get the *panic* now as much as I used to. I still get some—it's true I do—but um, it's not the overwhelming *panic* that I used to get.

HUSBAND: After doing the task for about ten days, you got completely fed up of worrying, didn't you, and you wondered if it was worth the bother, didn't you. You said, 'I'm not going to *worry* any more—I simply can't stand going on worrying like this'. But you sort of carried on doing it—not *every* day.

WIFE: Um. Some of the time I did worry—but what I was doing with the set time for worrying—well it seemed to sort of flush it out.

THERAPIST: Yes. Mm.

WIFE: It's still *there*—but not *overwhelmingly*.

THERAPIST: Yes. Did you notice any difference? Er, some days I expect you worked harder at the task than others, probably. Was there any difference in the effect that that had?

WIFE: No. But if I don't think about it—if I didn't spend the hour on my own—well, I never did make it last an hour—I just ran out of illnesses after about half an hour.

THERAPIST: Um—the first half an hour. You managed to find enough illnesses to fill about half an hour.

WIFE: But after a while I kept thinking, 'I've been through that one and . . . it was *boring!*' (*Laughter.*)

THERAPIST: Yes. Yes. (*To husband*) Did she work hard at it, Denys? Did she attack the task with vigour?

HUSBAND: Yeah—I mean—er—the first couple of weeks she
            certainly did it and worked hard at it. She
            probably didn't work so hard at it after that
            because she reached the stage where she thought
            this is absolutely silly to think like this.
WIFE: No one can have that much wrong with them!
HUSBAND: Yes, she said to me, 'This is getting silly—I don't
            need to worry about these things any more.' There
            certainly seems to have been some sort of impact
            made on her—quite soon—after only a couple of
            days—but certainly after a week—she got com-
            pletely fed up with worrying. She's now going to
            worry that she's got nothing to worry about!
THERAPIST: Well, I'm sure you're right to be worried about
            that because, well things are often a flash in the
            pan—there are no magic cures to things but the
            thing is, as I said right at the beginning, to take
            things a step at a time, to take things slowly.
WIFE: Mm. But there's no guarantee that it's *not* going
            to come back—after perhaps a little while.
THERAPIST: Mm. No. No. Indeed it certainly isn't possible to
            have any copper-bottomed guarantees. All we
            can do is just try some different things out. But,
            er—you were both pleased at the difference, am I
            getting that right?
WIFE: Yes.
HUSBAND: Yes. Oh, yes, yes.

It is clear that the wife made quite a dramatic move away
from the fears that were obsessing her and the change is clear
to both husband, wife and counsellor. It is of course of
enormous importance that the counsellor does not show any
amusement or indeed pleasure, but merely a continuing
concern and puzzlement that things have changed. (Since
paradox is indeed puzzling this need by no means be a
feigned attitude.) In this excerpt, the counsellor carefully
examines all aspects of the task and the way it has not been
executed. She then makes an important intervention by
cautioning against any great optimism and she *'prescribes a
relapse'* by suggesting that, in her experience, such rapid and
dramatic changes do not normally last and they must both be

prepared to return to square one. However if they were feeling satisfied with things as they were, she could only wish them well and hope for the best, though there was indeed probably little that could be hoped for.

At this point, the couple became quite upset with the counsellor and said that they had begun to realise quite a lot of new things about their relationship over the past few weeks and could they not continue having counselling sessions to talk about these. Hesitantly the counsellor said she supposed that they could. From this moment on there was no recurrence whatever of the wife's obsessions and the GP confirmed that she never now came to the surgery except for an occasional visit for a real ailment in one of the children. The couple worked hard on their marital relationship for several more sessions, during which time it became considerably more adult and with a lot more equality and sharing between them. At follow-up, a year later, they were continuing happily unintruded upon by the wife's fears of death and effectively tackling the many emotional and practical tasks of bringing up their young family.

Several aspects of strategic work are illustrated by this case:

(1) The symptom is prescribed—in other words the wife is instructed to continue doing exactly what she is doing anyway.

(2) It is hedged about within a ritual—she is to retire to a special room at a special time to undertake an hour's concentrated worrying each day as well as engaging in all the other activities which surrounded her symptoms.

(3) The counsellor introduced the symptom prescription within a frame of reference that was acceptable to the couple—she adopted a 'medical' approach and used the resistance of the identified patient position as a manoeuvre to redirect the couple's emotional energy towards their relationship.

(4) She built up towards an acceptance of the prescription by engaging their compliance with the task first, before they knew what it was, so that some of their resistance to her interventions would be overcome in advance of receiving the prescription.

(5) The counsellor took the view that it was good that things

were changing slowly, and that even if the couple were
reporting that things were 80 per cent better, it was good that
they were not 100 per cent better. This again helps to
overcome the couple's resistance to change by pitting the
therapeutic effort paradoxically against change instead of for
it.

(6) In a similar way, the counsellor agreed that there were no
copper-bottomed guarantees that the problems were *not* going
to return, implying that they may *well return* — an intervention
which is both realistic and paradoxical simultaneously.

Several techniques routinely used in the strategic approach
to counselling families are more mildly paradoxical, but are
strategic in the sense that they are carefully planned and
targeted to gain a particular result. The placing of a *positive
connotation* on what would normally be considered to be
undesirable or unacceptable behaviour is an effective means
of reducing the family's sense of threat and rendering the
scapegoating of one or more family members less powerful.
The object of a positive connotation is to make explicit, in a
benign way, the relationship between the identified patient's
symptoms and the family's pattern of relationships. An
important point about placing a positive connotation on
apparently unacceptable behaviour is that it registers an
important truth about such behaviour which always underlies
its more obvious negative characteristics.

For example, in a family where a teenage girl is staying out
late and driving her parents to distraction, the counsellor
might point out how thoughtful the girl was to ensure that
her parents stayed cemented together by their concern over
her. If they were not so worried and preoccupied with this
concern, they might be drifting apart now that the children
were leaving home. Such a statement would in all likelihood
have a great deal of truth in it because, by the very nature of
the life cycle changes occurring in a family moving into Stage
5, the 'empty nest' position, there are often particular stresses
on the marital relationship. The positive connoting of the
daughter's delinquent behaviour will come as a shock to
everyone and this usually enables the family to see and hear
the connection between the identified patient's problems and
the family's relationship needs in a new way. Moreover, the
fact that the counsellor is viewing the girl's behaviour in a

positive light and encouraging her parents to do so too, reduces the power of its intended negative effect and therefore makes it less attractive. The girl's conscious *intention* is probably not to be helpful to her parents, even though this may be the *effect*. She is therefore likely to reconsider whether she should continue with it. If she ceases, the question arises as to whether the effect on the parents' marriage will then become negative in the way that the counsellor has predicted. The answer to this is that it probably will not—for the counsellor will have been careful to positively connote the parents' response as well as the girl's behaviour, and because once the circular, interconnecting pattern within the family relationship system has been *named*, the power of each part of the pattern ceases.

Placing a positive connotation upon everyone's behaviour in the family system is a special case of *reframing*, a technique frequently used in the strategic approach to family counselling. 'There is nothing good nor bad but thinking makes it so.' This line from Hamlet indicates the idea underlying this technique, i.e. that it is often possible and therapeutically productive to separate out the *concrete facts* from family members' *perception* of those facts. Whilst it is often not possible to change the facts, it may be possible to change family members' perception of the facts. As Watzlawick *et al.* point out, 'successful reframing must lift the problem out of the "symptom" frame into another frame that does not carry the implication of unchangeability'.[2]

For example, in chapter 3 I referred to a couple who were struggling with stage 4 of the family life cycle. This couple, who had been married for over twenty years, came for help because the husband had started an affair with a twenty-six-year-old girl. The wife had a close relationship with their two late-teenage children, whilst quarrels between them and their father were frequent. As the father's genogram was explored, it became clear that he had had repeated experiences of death and illness in his family. His father, mother and grandfather had all died when they were in their late fifties of heart attacks and the husband had a forboding that he, now in his mid-fifties, had only a very few years left. The wife had undergone a series of abortions before the couple married and soon after the two children were born, she had been bereaved of her mother, whom she described as her 'best friend'. Her mother was only sixty-five. The couple seemed burdened by guilt, regrets and a variety of ghosts from the past and fears for the future. One of these 'ghosts' was the husband's daughter by his first marriage, whom he had not seen since she was a baby. The previous year he had made a long journey abroad to try to find her, but with no success. It seemed that he had somehow 'lost' all three of his young adult children and was doomed to die without connecting with the next generation.

At this point, he started the affair. The girl was exactly the same age as his daughter from his first marriage. His wife was deeply distressed since she could not see how their long-standing relationship was so seriously flawed as to warrant the intrusion of this new relationship. For her it was a disastrous and inexplicable event, irrevocably threatening to their relationship and her own sense of wellbeing. She had however kept her feelings to herself for the past year — unable to express her shock, rage or distress about the affair.

Gradually, the counsellors developed a series of hypotheses which might allow the couple to view the affair in a different light and to reframe its meaning. They suggested that both the husband and wife had experienced serious bereavements at critical stages of their life cycle which had been left unresolved. These cast a doom-laden shadow over their future which, although they found it hard to put into words, both recognised and expressed at a deep level. The counsellors suggested that both husband and wife had unconsciously taken constructive steps to combat this shadow and thus to save their relationship. The wife had formed a close friendship with their grown-up children, while the husband had started a new relationship with a young girl. Both had found a way of connecting up with the life and vitality of the next generation, thus warding off the threat of destruction and death. But the problem, as the counsellors saw it, was that the solution that each had chosen was excluding and painful to the other. Whilst the husband's affair excluded his wife, the wife's closeness with the children excluded him from being a father. (A characteristic reframe which counsellors, using a strategic approach often use in their own analysis of the family's situation, is to wonder how far the family's solution to the problem is now the problem and conversely, how far the problem can be regarded as the solution to the problem!)

These hypotheses created a new, benign frame which the counsellors used to describe the behaviour of both Jack and Jane and which constructively reframed in a positive light the behaviour of each partner in relation to the marriage. Each began to view the behaviour of the other as having some meaning and purpose in terms of the family relationships instead of being experienced as a calculated attack on the other person. Each could then begin to learn from and listen to the other instead of expending all their energies on defending their own position.[3]

Notes

1. Important books describing this approach: J. Haley, *Strategies of Psychotherapy*, New York, Grune & Stratton, 1967; C. Madanes, *Strategic Family Therapy*, San Francisco, Jossey-Bass, 1981; M. S. Palazzoli et al., *Paradox and Counterparadox*, New York, Jason Aronson, 1978; P. Watzlawick et al., *Pragmatics of Human Communication*, New York, W. W. Norton, 1968.
2. P. Watzlawick et al., *Change*, New York, W. W. Norton 1974.
3. R. Bandler and J. Grinder, *Reframing*, Real People Press 1982.

EIGHT

The Psychoanalytic Approach

Whilst the structural and strategic approaches emphasise the need to alter behavioural sequences and effect rapid behavioural change, the psychoanalytic approach is concerned to help family members gain insight into their dysfunctional patterns of behaviour and into the kind of relationship patterns they have inherited from the past.[1] Like other forms of counselling which are derived from a psychoanalytic base, the psychoanalytic approach to family counselling investigates the connection between past and present patterns of behaviour and subscribes to Freud's maxim that those who do not understand the past are doomed to repeat it. Again, like other forms of psychoanalytically-based counselling, this approach to helping families recognises the part played by unconscious factors in determining behaviour. Instead of focusing only on conscious patterns of behaviour in the here and now, it seeks to understand the interlocking and systemic nature of the unconscious processes occurring between members of the family group. Shared dreams, phantasies, symptoms, defence mechanisms and family members' interlocking pathology are all of interest to the psychoanalytically-oriented family counsellor.

Family Myths

A family comes for help because of the refusal of the eight-year-old boy to go to school. It soon transpires that the mother has suffered from agoraphobia since the death of her sixteen-year-old daughter in a motorbike accident. She is unable to leave the house unless she is with her mother who lives nearby or with her little boy. After several family sessions it becomes clear that a number of tragic accidents occurred in the previous generation around the time when the mother was born and that her mother had suffered from agoraphobia when she herself was only a small child. The family myth seems to be that the family will survive if it huddles together and has as little as possible to do with the outside world. The myth is passed down through the female side of the family and the countervailing pull of the two psychologically strong husbands in each generation is not powerful enough to overcome this dominating family myth.[2]

Family myths are powerful determinants of family inter-action, and yet they remain largely unconscious within the shared inner life of the family group. The family myth usually enables the family to avoid having to face up to some frightening theme which is unconsciously perceived to be an overwhelming force threatening the existence or continuity of the family. The counsellor's task is to enable the family to gain insight into the meaning of the myth and thus to gain freedom from its constraints. When the family becomes aware of the family myth and the avoided theme which the myth conceals, much previously inexplicable behaviour on the part of family members becomes suddenly understandable and logical.

For example, the little eight-year-old boy who was refusing to go to school was doing so in order to protect his mother from her fears. Equally, his mother's agoraphobia enabled her to stay at home and protect her youngest child in a way she had 'failed' to do for her sixteen-year-old. Father could leave home to work and socialise because he was secure in the knowledge that his loved ones were safe. Maternal grandmother could experience, in her daughter's family, a satisfying antidote to the life-threatening events that had occurred in her own family of origin. In other words, all received secondary gains from the demands made upon them by the family system's emotional needs. Yet everyone was held in a rigid homeostasis and none of the family members could develop, either in terms of their own inner needs or their intra-familial relationships.

The Genogram

An extremely useful tool for helping the family to understand the way in which the past affects the present is the family tree or genogram.³ It not only reveals the transmission of family myths, but also the behaviour patterns, family rules and roles that are passed on from one generation to the next. Many family counsellors will routinely construct a genogram with the family early on in the counselling process as a way of gathering and recording the relevant family history. Often there is so much material generated during discussion with the family that it is wise to reserve two separate sessions, to construct the genograms of each parent's family of origin. Ideally, the genogram is drawn up on a blackboard or flip chart so that every member of the family can see how it is developing and join in with comments or questions.

Figures 3 and 4 illustrate the symbols that can be used in constructing the genograms of the parents of two young women, Sally and Clare. The counsellor draws the family tree up on the board, asking for names, ages, relationships, deaths, occupations and any information that appears to be important and interesting. Family members contribute information from their knowledge or imagination, and misperceptions can be clarified and new information given as different family members discuss and argue about their different ideas of the family. The counsellor needs to look at several particular aspects of the family's growth and development, since they usually yield important insights. First, dates. How do important dates in the family connect with one another, especially the dates of entries and exits from the family system? In this family we can see how individuals become ill when illness is needed to absorb the family's attention and how marriages and pregnancies take place after the deaths of older relatives. Second, the counsellor should help the family examine what Toman calls the 'family constellation' and the kind of 'fit' that operates between the marital pair in this and other respects. The place that each member occupies in the birth order provides a markedly different experience of family for each person. The experiences of eldests and youngests, for example, differ markedly, as does the family experience of someone who is an only child compared with someone who has several siblings. In the family illustrated in Figures 3 and 4 we see how extra-ordinarily consistent is the experience of being either an eldest or a youngest sibling.

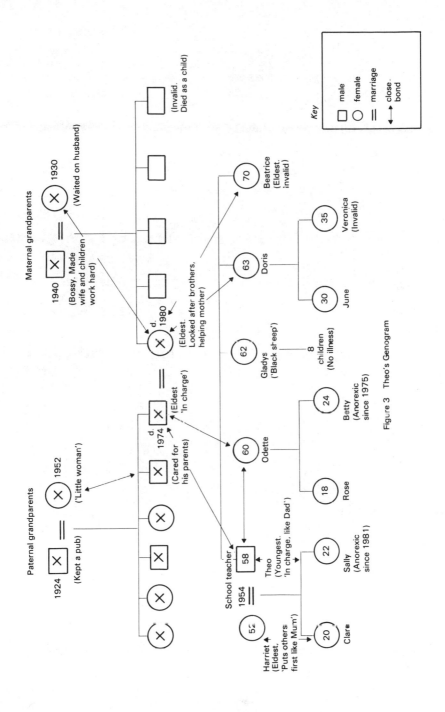

Figure 3 Theo's Genogram

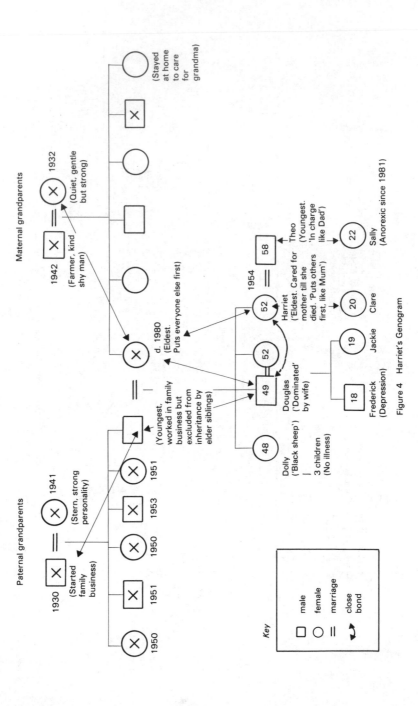

Paternal grandparents

Maternal grandparents

1930 ☒ = ◯ 1941
(Started
family
business)

(Stern, strong
personality)

1950 ◯
1951 ☒
1950 ◯
1953 ☒
1951 ◯

(Youngest,
worked in family
business but
excluded from
inheritance by
elder siblings)

1942 ☒ = ◯ 1932
(Farmer, kind
shy man)

(Quiet, gentle
but strong)

◯ □ ◯ ☒ ◯
(Stayed
at home
to care
for
grandma)

◯ d. 1980
(Eldest.
Puts everyone else first)

Harriet ('Eldest. Cared for
mother till she
died. 'Puts others
first, like Mum')

1954
◯ 52 = □ 58

☐ 49   ◯ 52
Douglas
('Dominated'
by wife)

◯ 48
Dolly
('Black sheep')
│
3 children
(No illness)

☐ 18   ◯ 19   ◯ 20   ◯ 22
Frederick Jackie Clare Sally
(Depression)   (Anorexic since 1981)

Theo
(Youngest.
'In charge
like Dad')

Figure 4 Harriet's Genogram

Key

□ male
◯ female
= marriage
↩ close
    bond

Marital Choice

The psychoanalytically-oriented family counsellor will also be concerned to help the family examine the gaps between phantasy and reality in the way that the couple come together and the expectations each has of the other and of other family relationships. In this family Theo married Harriet for the specific purpose of having children and in order to continue to receive the care from a woman he had received from his mother and sisters. Harriet married Theo in order to be able to continue to care for a husband and children in the way she had cared for her younger siblings, and to re-enact the life of her saintly and martyred mother, whom she idealised and after whom she longed to pattern her own life. An obviously complementary fit existed between Theo's and Harriet's needs until new and frightening ingredients such as Sally's life-threatening illness compelled the couple to reassess their priorities.

It is interesting to discover whether each person's choice of a mate is based upon a symmetrical or complementary 'fit' between their respective positions in their families of origin and to what extent the 'fit' reinforces functional or dys-functional patterns laid down in the family of origin. Toman suggests that couples who have had complementary experiences in their families of origin are more likely to find that the marital relationship evokes familiar patterns of response.[4] These may be used helpfully as a launch-pad for developing the new marital relationship or they may introduce into the new relationship, dysfunctional patterns from the past. For example, if, as is the case with Theo and Harriet, one member of the couple has had experience of being amongst the younger sibling group and the other amongst the elder ones in their original families, they will be more inclined to transfer to their family of procreation the familiar patterns, roles and rules that they learned in their original families. In Figures 3 and 4 we see a strong pattern of eldests and youngests marrying one another with a strong encouragement therefore for both Theo and Harriet to bring to their marriage other familiar patterns from the past.

The work of Dicks and others at the Institute of Marital

Studies, London[5] has also helped us understand some of the unconscious determinants of marital choice. The instant 'chemistry' that appears to operate between individuals may also be linked to the unconscious need to find someone who is either *like* the self, but in an idealised form, or *unlike* the self and thus supply a deficiency that is dimly perceived to exist in the self. If exercised too strongly, problems can arise from both kinds of unconscious determinant. Couples who are attracted on the basis of an idealised part of the self may continually be disappointed that their partner does not live up to their expectations. On the other hand, couples who are attracted on the basis of dissimilarity, may be threatened by the difference and unable to cope with it at close quarters. For example, women like Harriet who choose husbands who are self-assertive and aggressive may perceive their need to become more assertive themselves and hope that they may 'acquire' some of this from their mate. But the actual experience of living in close proximity to so different a personality structure may create a high level of anxiety in both partners. Couples who come for help where the relationship is predicated upon dissimilarity, often need help in arresting a retreat into 'more of the same' behaviour on the part of each which will progressively widen the gap between them. Ultimately, the kind of marital 'fit' experienced by the passive, martyred Harriet and the domineering, masterful Theo will lead to the sado-masochistic relationship of increasing violence and passivity only too familiar to clergy, social workers and other helping agencies.

Themes from the Past

Some of the themes and patterns from the past that are revealed in Theo and Harriet's genogram are:

1. Parent-child bonds are stronger than marital bonds.
2. Women care for the needs of men in their roles as daughters, wives and mothers.
3. Women should be strong and intellectually bright but 'know their place'.
4. Children care for elderly relatives.

5. An invalid child focuses the love, concern and attention of everyone and fills a vacuum left when other emotional needs have been taken care of.
6. Conflict is too dangerous and destructive to be expressed overtly.

These themes are to be found in both Theo and Harriet's families to a greater or lesser extent, and it is not difficult to see why a young woman like Sally is put into a classic double-bind. On the one hand she is the 'apple of her Father's eye' because she is the firstborn, a much wanted child after seven years marriage, in a family where children are idealised. She is intellectually very bright and her natural impetus is to get on and get out of her family into adult life. On the other hand, the family rule is such that children (and female children in particular) must stay at home to look after parents and women must 'know their place' and always allow men to be in charge. She resents her mother for allowing herself to be trampled upon both by her father and by herself and her sister — for her mother is thus providing a role model for Sally which she wants to reject. She enjoys her father's constant attention yet resents his interference in her affairs which holds her back from becoming a woman. She senses that it is children who are important and that she must therefore remain a child (by not eating and by staving off the normal changes of puberty). Yet she picks up the contrary message that she must grow up and do well so that her father can be proud of her intellectual abilities, like his father was of him. The genogram can be used to indicate the alliances and conflicts between family members and to bring to light the avoided themes such as the part played by psychiatric or physical illness, delinquency or violent death. In this family, illness is used as a defence against having to face up to the more ambiguous demands of loving a healthy, strong and assertive child or marital partner. The less challenging demands of a sick and helpless individual enables everyone to avoid the conflict and ambivalence inherent within mature, loving relationships. Thus the challenge for the family counsellor is how to enable the family to allow the anorexic symptom to be abandoned and how to enable family members to relate to each other as mature, autonomous adults.

Family Transference

The psychoanalytically-oriented family counsellor will want to help the family examine the way in which individual family members project on to each other feelings that belong to the self and also transfer on to one or more family members images from the past.

For example, a family came for help because the young teenage boy was fire-raising. The older siblings were now grown up and had successfully left home to get married and find work. Adrian had been born after a ten-year gap and long after his parents had given up the thought of further children. Soon after he was born, his mother began to say how like Adrian was to her Uncle Ronnie, her mother's much younger brother who was now dead. Ronnie had been partly rejected by *his* mother and had run away from home when he was fifteen. He had joined the army when he was old enough and had retained a reputation in the family for being a wild and unpredictable 'black sheep'. Father, mother and Adrian were locked into a transference of roles from the past generation to the present. Some headway was made by using a genogram to discuss the relationships that existed in the different generations in order to help the family to distinguish the past from the present. However, it was not until the two older siblings joined the sessions, each of whom had a positive memory of Uncle Ronnie, that the family began to make progress.

The family counsellor identified the task as: (1) distinguishing Adrian from Ronnie in the minds of the parents and relieving him of the projections of feeling and the transference of role with which he was burdened; (2) identifying positive features in Uncle Ronnie's personality and helping the family to assimilate a more realistic picture of his behaviour. The older siblings were able to supply some very positive memories of how their uncle had appeared to them to be, and his 'irresponsibility' became redefined as a 'sense of fun' and his 'escapades' as bravery and adventurousness. More important, the parents began to realise that they had unwittingly groomed Adrian to play a similar role for which, like Ronnie, he was now scapegoated. These new insights enabled the parents to view and therefore relate to Adrian differently. Gradually, as he experienced a fuller acceptance from them, his delinquent behaviour subsided and he was able to become his own person instead of living out the role and personality of another.

The influence of 'ghosts from the past' or the 'shadow of the ancestor', as some family therapists have suggested, is more powerful if the individuals concerned are literally dead.[6] It makes it more difficult to check phantasy against reality, since they cannot literally be invited to the sessions. As in the case of Adrian, however, it is important to locate resources within the wider family network which can puncture the one-sided picture that is being transmitted. It may also be important to make the dead person's presence as real as possible within the sessions, by leaving a spare chair for him or her and asking, at different junctures of the interview, what he or she would have said or felt. Whatever the situation which the family is presenting for help, the family counsellor needs to remember that each family member brings to his relationships with the others a series of internalised images from other relationships which are then transferred on to their current experience of the family. The task of the counsellor is to point them out as he or she becomes aware of them and help family members to examine them, clarify them and work them through so that they can be sufficiently unburdened from the past to relate more productively to each other in the present.

Notes

1. Important books describing this approach: N. W. Ackerman, *Treating the Troubled Family*, New York, Basic Books, 1968; S. Box *et al*, *Psychotherapy with Families*, Routledge & Kegan Paul 1982; A. C. R. Skynner, *One Flesh—Separate Persons*, Constable 1976.
2. J. Byng-Hall, 'Family Myths Used as Defence in Conjoint Family Therapy', *British Journal of Medical Psychology*, vol. 46, 1973.
3. The construction and use of a genogram is well described by S. Lieberman in *Transgenerational Family Therapy*, Croom Helm 1979.
4. W. Toman, *Family Constellation*, New York, Springer, 1961.
5. H. V. Dicks, *Marital Tensions*, Routledge & Kegan Paul 1967.

6. N. L. Paul and G. H. Grosser, 'Operational Mourning and its Role in Conjoint Family Therapy', *Community Mental Health*, vol. 1, 1965, and R. D. Scott and P. L. Ashworth, 'The Shadow of the Ancestor', *British Journal of Medical Psychology*, vol. 42, 1969.

NINE

The Experiential Approach

The fourth major approach to family counselling is what has loosely been called the 'experiential' approach.[1] It is characterised by the use of a variety of action techniques and it often involves the counsellor using his own personality freely and flexibly in his relation with family members. The aim is to *make the session itself* a therapeutic experience that touches the emotions and feelings as well as the family's cognitive set.

There are obviously things in common between this approach and both the structural and the psychoanalytic approaches, since the structural approach conceives of the family therapy session as a sort of *laboratory for experimenting* with change and the psychoanalytic approach aims to help family members *re-experience their past* so as to be less burdened by it. However, although the family counsellor who adopts an experiential approach will draw on both the other approaches, his primary aim is to provide a new experience for the family. He or she will place considerable importance upon his or her own personal counselling because only a continuous attention to the self will enable his or her own personality to be free enough to attend appropriately to the emotional needs of family members and engage in a therapeutic relationship with them.

In this approach, the counselling proceeds through the mutual and less structured participation between counsellor and family. Learning and insight are always less important than actual experiencing. The counsellor will use the whole range of his personality make-up to achieve shifts and realignments in the family's network of relationships. He or she will be fatherly/motherly in relation to the 'child' selves of family members and will use his or her sexuality to engage the sexually dormant or repressed aspects of family members' 'adult' selves. For example, a male counsellor might flirt a

Family Matters

118

little with the wife in order both to encourage a disinterested
husband to 'compete,' as well as to demonstrate to the
husband that he, the counsellor, finds her attractive. The
message to the husband is 'Why don't you?'—but it is the
experience of seeing another man engage in a flirtatious
relationship with his wife that may help him rediscover what
has got lost. Similarly, the counsellor may respond maternally
to a frightened insecure self that is hidden inside an
apparently strident and dominating parent. In so doing, the
counsellor may be able to demonstrate to a hostile adolescent
that his parent is vulnerable and in need of care at times.

There are obvious traps in this kind of approach. For
example, if the counsellor is seen as a more attractive, potent
male by a husband who feels inferior and insecure, he may be
made to feel even more inadequate. Great sensitivity and self
awareness are clearly required. Again, the counsellor may
want to model more appropriate and productive behaviour to
various members of a family, but he must make sure that he
does not demonstrate behaviour that is out of reach for family
members, so making them feel more helpless and hopeless
than before. But, given care and sensitivity, the counsellor's
use of him or herself in this way is a powerful therapeutic
tool. For example, a family was referred to a child guidance
clinic because the little four-year-old girl Louise was failing to
thrive and one or both parents were suspected of physical
abuse. Both parents found physical touch very difficult. They
were in their mid-twenties and both came from emotionally
and materially poor families. The mother was unable to hold
or cuddle her little daughter or even have her on her lap.
Neither parent touched each other, although they did not
argue or have any particularly negative feelings towards each
other. They seemed to lack models of intimacy or ways of
expressing affection or care.

After one or two sessions the counsellor began to pick up
Louise and hold her on her lap. She praised her for her little
drawings and scribbles she began to make as she gradually
felt more at home in the sessions and she pointed out to the
parents how positively Louise responded to this praise.
Gradually the counsellor suggested that they all four could
play with the toys together on the floor and that she and the
parents could let Louise show them what fun it was to play

again with sand and water. The fact that the counsellor, a high-status person in the eyes of this young couple, did not find this kind of behaviour silly or undignified, gave them 'permission' to try it themselves and to begin to engage with the child parts of themselves which had been abused and disconfirmed when they were children.

Gradually the counsellor suggested she might help the mother to have Louise on her lap for a few moments and that between them they might brush her hair and tie her ribbons. Falteringly, the mother copied whatever the counsellor did and gradually the fear of touching Louise began to melt away. The mother suffered from quite a lot of stiffness and pain in her neck brought on by the tension of struggling to make ends meet, ward off social workers inspecting her handling of Louise and being an acceptable wife to her husband. The counsellor asked if her husband ever massaged her neck. When she said no, the counsellor offered to show him how. The wife found the massage a wonderfully relaxing and enjoyable experience and, after some hesitation, the husband agreed to continue it. The session ended with the wife doing the same for her husband and the husband then massaging the counsellor's neck as a way of demonstrating his newly acquired skill—in which he felt immediate pride and a great sense of elation. After only three or four sessions, this little family was transformed, not only by their newly experienced abilities to express the love and care they had felt but could not show, but also by the whole experience of being loved, respected and enjoyed by the counsellor in a mutually satisfying therapeutic relationship.

Family Sculpting

A technique that is often employed in this approach is that of family sculpting.[2] It enables family members to express emotions and feelings that are deeply experienced, yet cannot be expressed. Each family member is asked to place the others in a 'tableau' which represents his or her view of how the family is. The 'sculptor' is encouraged by the counsellor to place each person in relation to the others so as to portray as many of the complexities of the relationship as possible, through the physical posture and the facial expressions which the sculptor asks each family member to adopt. The counsellor explains to the other family members that they should allow themselves to simply become 'clay' in the hands of the sculptor and, even if their view of the network of family relationships is very different, they should, for now, simply help the person who is doing the sculpting to express his or her particular view as accurately as possible. By using their bodies to create a three-dimensional representation of their relationships, family members use the physical space within the session to recreate symbolically the emotional space between them. A great many hidden feelings can be expressed in a short time and yet, because the technique does not rely upon being able to express complex and subtle thoughts in words, it enables children and other less verbal members of the family to take a full share in describing and helping to change the family.

Family sculpting is a useful way of enabling the family to describe its problems. It can also be used to help each person to show very graphically what *changes* they would like to see happen and the ways in which the family could be altered to make it feel happier and more productive. It can sometimes be useful to take photos of the different family members' sculptures, to compare them with each other at a future session or to help review the progress of counselling by looking back to how the problems showed themselves in the sculpture when the family first came for help.

The following case may help to illustrate the ways in which family sculpting can be used. John, Marion, Collette and David came for help. It was John's second marriage, and Collette (aged fifteen) was the daughter of his first wife Jodie who had now remarried and had returned to live in America. Sometime after Jodie had left, John had had an intense affair with Megan lasting about a year until Megan had a breakdown, was admitted to a psychiatric hospital and a few days later committed suicide. John's grief at losing Jodie had been compounded by the guilt of having and then losing Megan. A year later he met Marion and they began living together.

Their relationship was exciting and fulfilling. Marion was an artist and taught art at a college where she had met John. Whilst being 'different' and rather 'wild', Marion also harboured strong needs for security. Her father had walked out of the family when she was four and she had been brought up by her mother and maternal grandmother. Life had felt uncertain and it seemed that love had to be earned. She developed a strong dependent Christian faith, though she had ceased to practise her Roman Catholicism when she met John. From childhood she had longed to marry and create the secure and happy family life she had lacked as a child.

From the start therefore she had wanted to marry John and to begin a family—but he was reluctant to enter again the full commitment of marriage. He felt fated in some strange way and felt that the death of Megan had put him under a curse. However, after two years they had in fact married and soon afterwards their first child David was born. Their relationship began to get into difficulties almost as soon as they married and became more acutely stressed by the seemingly never-ending demands of the baby. Marion devoted herself to her new role of mother unstintingly, whilst John felt progressively distanced from both his wife and his son. During the first family session John, who seemed most obviously in pain, was asked to sculpt the family. He put Marion and David holding each other tightly in one corner of the room and himself as far as possible away. When asked how this made him feel, he said 'bereft and abandoned'. When asked what he could do about these feelings he felt that, although he could reach out with one arm to try to stretch over towards Marion and David, his feet were glued to the floor and he could not actually move. Marion was then asked to sculpt her picture. It was now that an entirely new factor was introduced. She placed herself and David close together but 'matched' this pairing by placing John at a distance but paired with his teenage daughter Collette. (In creating the tableau one of the two family counsellors substituted for Collette.)

It transpired that a few months earlier Collette, who had been living with her mother in America, had suddenly returned to Britain saying she wanted to live with her father. Collette's arrival had produced an entirely new situation which both relieved and exacerbated the problems. Whilst Marion's close alliance with David, now four, all but excluded John, he now had a ready made ally in the teenage daughter from his first marriage. Each parent therefore had formed a symmetrical relationship with one of the children, which gave each a sort of uneasy comfort but which made the task of healing the marital relationship more complex.

Marion saw the relationship between John and Collette as intense and excluding of her in the same way that John felt Marion and David's relationship to be. Asked what she would like to do in the sculpture to change the situation, Marion placed John behind Collette with his hand on her arm, guiding it towards making a finger-tip touch with Marion who had stretched out her arm to Collette. Marion felt that John was getting in the way of Collette and Marion making any positive relationship and, although she would have preferred Collette not to have returned, she saw realistically that the best hope for them all was for Collette and she to be able to get on.

Now that the counsellors were aware of Collette's presence they invited her to the next session. The family were again asked to do some sculpting. This time Collette sculpted her picture of the family. She put her father in the middle of the room with one arm stretched out to her mother and his other stretched out to his second wife, Marion, and their child David. The counsellors pointed out that John looked very uncomfortable and they encouraged Collette to get her father to 'solve' his problem. The result was that he stretched harder in both directions, but with no hope of getting into touch with either Marion or Jodie. The counsellors asked Collette to place herself in the sculpture and she put herself in a sort of mobile whirl—trying to support her mother in America, her father in his pain and her step-mother who seemed to her both to want a relationship with her *and* to be rejecting her. It transpired at this point too that Collette would have loved a closer relationship with David and had often offered to babysit or put him to bed but Marion would never allow this.

Participating in Collette's sculpture moved John deeply. He asked to try again and this time he sculpted a picture which showed himself in the middle of the room stretching out with one hand to Marion and David and with the other to Collette who he placed not very far away from Marion and David. Behind him he put one of the counsellors to represent Jodie, stretching out and holding on to one shoulder, and the other counsellor to represent the dead Megan, holding on to the other. After further thought, he put both Jodie and Megan standing on chairs behind him and pulling him down and back with all their power. Here for the first time, John was able to express the strength of his feelings of guilt and sadness at the rupture of these two previous relationships and the way that these feelings were holding him back from entering fully into his second marriage.

These sculptures provided the family and the counsellors with material on which to work for several sessions. The whole family had been deeply moved by watching and experiencing each other's viewpoint and the particular pain that flowed from the different experiences of each person. Over the next few months John spoke at length of his pain and guilt, Marion talked of her early feelings of deprivation and each began to understand the way in which the past affected their ability to relate to each other in the present. As they watched each other struggle they drew closer together, and this was helped forward by Marion gradually allowing Collette to take a share in caring for David. David, who had been extremely demanding in the sessions of Marion's attention, gradually began to remain at home in Collette's care, and the sessions appropriately moved into marital sessions for Marion and John on their own.

It is often possible to introduce ideas from other kinds of counselling for short periods of a family session. For example, the technique of helping a family member to speak to another who is dead or otherwise unavailable, using an empty chair to represent that person, can usefully be adapted from Gestalt therapy. The purpose is to help the family member to re-experience the feelings and pain and, with the help of the family group, to work the feelings through to a resolution. Even when these feelings relate to the past and pre-date the individual's life in the current family group, their effects are always interactional. More importantly, current family members can, when they become aware of the individual's difficulties stemming from the past, help in the process of resolution. The family group is potentially a force for healing and therapeutic change, and one of the tasks of the family counsellor is to help it fulfil this role. Unlike many other approaches to counselling, whether with individuals or with families, counsellors using the experiential approach would normally end the work with the family by checking out with them what had been helpful or unhelpful to the family; they would talk over mistakes and misunderstandings between them and the family which may have arisen and share with the family their own learning and growth that had occurred as a result of the work. This more equal, participatory relationship between family and counsellors is characteristic of the experiential approach and is well described by Whitaker and by McCluskey.[3]

Notes

1. Useful works of reference relating to this approach are: C. A. Whitaker and D. V. Keith, 'Symbolic-experiential Family Therapy' in A. S. Gurman and D. P. Kniskern, *Handbook of Family Therapy*, Brunner/Mazel 1981; E. De'Ath, 'Experiential Family Therapy' in S. Walrond-Skinner, *Developments in Family Therapy*, Routledge & Kegan Paul 1981.
2. P. Papp, 'Family Sculpting in Preventative work with "Well" Families', *Family Process*, vol. 12, 1973; J. Hearn and M. Lawrence, 'Family Sculpting', parts 1 and 2, in *Journal of Family Therapy*, vol. 3, 1981 and vol. 7, 1985.
3. U. McCluskey, 'Theme-focussed Family Therapy', in S. Walrond-Skinner and D. Watson, *Ethical Issues in Family Therapy*, Routledge & Kegan Paul 1987.

TEN

Therapists or Pastors?

In the Introduction I tried to clarify the different ways in which an understanding of family therapy may help the pastor in other areas of his or her ministry. Yet much of what has been written in this book so far might suggest that every parish priest, minister and pastorally involved lay-person should equip themselves to become family therapists. As well as being quite impractical, given the wide-ranging tasks and roles that the full-time minister must carry, such an idea would be quite inappropriate. There is overlap between the working areas of the professional psychotherapist or counsellor and those of the pastor, but the areas of concern which belong to each need to be kept distinct. While the full-time professional family therapist is a method-oriented specialist, providing an expert service in family therapy for the families who are referred to her, the pastor, by contrast, has a multiplicity of contacts with families who present a huge variety of needs and for whom a family therapy approach would often neither be possible nor appropriate.

The Church is intensely interested and concerned about the family, yet she remains highly ambivalent. On the one hand she idealises the notion of family, using family imagery to describe both the Church as a whole and the local congregation. On the other hand she separates family groups up according to gender and age. Both responses to the family prevent the minister from exercising his or her pastoral ministry in the fullest way. 'Try for one moment to empathise with a widower or a single person, a single parent or a gay person and to imagine what this obsession with the family means for them,' remarks Green sharply.[1] Idealising the family also has the effect of down-grading other kinds of intimate relationships, putting them either 'beyond the pale' (homosexual relationships) or allowing their importance to remain insufficiently noticed (friendship). In neither case is the minister or the congregation able to provide these relationships with adequate support. On the other hand, much of the potential inherent in the family's mixture of gender, age, skills and interests gets lost because of the Church's propensity to divide and segregate the sexes and age-groupings for worship, social events and learning.[2]

It is true that the minister may find that his natural point of contact with his parishioners is in terms of family sub-systems or individuals—with mothers and toddlers at the pram service; with men at the monthly men's supper; with young people at the youth club or women at the Mother's Union. Routine pastoral visiting too may have to take place at a time when only part of the household is at home. Family members do need opportunities to group with others of the same age, sex and particular interests as themselves. But networks of intimate relationships—whether they are conventional families or other intimate groupings—generate life and energy beyond the sum of their parts if encouraged to meet together with others for study, worship and social life. A church social club, for example, is greatly enriched when young and old share activities together, and less reinforcement of sexual stereotyping occurs when couples in the church meet together rather than in the traditional male and female groupings.

Even more important is the minister's ability to retain an internal image of the natural system in his mind in his dealings with individuals. Some members of the minister's congregation and people in the wider community will be quite isolated. They may need help through a one-to-one relationship or through contact with their peers though, especially when elderly, they may also gain enormous help from a minister who is able to 'see' them as still part of a family network, now dead or dispersed and who can help them to talk about regrets and joys, lost opportunities and longings for reconciliation. However, few members of the congregation will have absolutely no family network to which they belong, and most of the minister's contacts will be with visible individuals who are nevertheless inseparably embedded within an invisible social system. For example, it is still the case that the majority of the members of most congregations are women. Their menfolk, where they exist, remain at home. Yet the impact and interventions of the minister, through his preaching, through the liturgy and through his pastoral care will be mediated to them through the individual who is designated by the family to be their 'contact with the Church'. As in individual counselling or psychotherapy, the counsellor has an effect upon the individual's family system but he cannot be sure of *what* that effect might be.

An awareness of these systemic effects is important because, as in any other form of individual contact, he or she may unwittingly contribute to the deterioration of the relationship system in which the individual family member is embedded. For example, two young women who are friends start coming to church. The minister is naturally delighted. He makes sure that they are introduced to other young adults and that they are inducted into the church's network of groups for newcomers. They make friends quickly, obviously enjoy coming to church and ask to be confirmed. The minister has visited them in their homes and on one occasion has met each of their husbands who show no interest in church but are happy for their wives to attend. But over the following months the church draws their wives' attention further and further away from them and, more fundamentally, begins to have subtle effects upon the wives' values and priorities . . . Some greater understanding of the way in which families operate as systems might have reduced the minister's initial enthusiasm and altered his approach.

The minister, trained in family dynamics, will be made more aware of the dangers inherent in the above situation. He will also be able to recognise more easily a disguised cry for help by the family. In some situations, a family's cry for help may seem far removed from the problem as it is presented. For example, a middle-aged woman telephoned to say that a strange tapping noise was to be heard at her windows. This had started a few months before. She wanted to know if the Vicar would come and bless the house. He agreed to visit. In the conversation which ensued, the woman explained that her husband had left home to live with another woman and that around this time the window tapping had begun. She felt bereft of her husband and exploited by her teenage children who refused to pay any rent even though they were both in work. The Vicar did indeed bless the woman's house as an initial acceptance of her 'presented problem'—but he continued to meet with her to talk about the family and began to explore ways in which she and they might be helped.

Sometimes the withdrawal of a request may indicate that there are difficulties in family relationships. For example, a couple who had asked to have their baby baptised phoned up before the priest's visit to say that they no longer wanted to proceed. The priest visited anyway and discovered that the couple were having a lot of problems and were on the verge of splitting up. They had thought that 'it wouldn't be right to have the baby christened while we are like we are'. The priest suggested that they went ahead with the baptism because God's love and acceptance extended to them all especially during their times of difficulty. He also suggested that they might begin to talk about their marriage and how some of their problems might be helped.

Perhaps the most natural way in which the minister has contact with families is through the liturgical acts of the Church and the Church's ministry surrounding the occasional offices of baptism, marriage and funeral rites. In one of the few books which endeavours to explore in detail the connection between worship and pastoral care, Green points out the many opportunities which are afforded by liturgical acts to enable people to understand and manage the significance of crucial life experiences. He discusses the power of the Church's liturgical rites and symbols both to reveal and to conceal meaning and in helping to handle the ambiguities of human experience. Everyone has to confront at some point, and on some level of intensity, the paradoxical experiences of sexuality, birth, separation, defeat, death and the question mark over life after death. Yet, as Green points out, the Church does not always help people integrate their life experiences with their experience of God—however tenuous that experience might be. As a result, the liturgy's potential as a vehicle for coping with fear, isolation and meaninglessness is often unfulfilled. He suggests that this is partly because of the Church's fear of fully accepting the dark, shadow side of human nature.

The same retreat from violence, sexuality and fear may empty the potentially rich symbolic acts of baptism, marriage and the funeral rite of much of their power for healing and growth for the family. And yet if these shadowy levels of human experience can be addressed, through an understanding of the systemic relationship of conscious and unconscious and of the different parts played by family members, the minister has rich opportunities for using a family approach productively in his response to requests for marriage, baptism and the funeral rites. It is this ministry which we will now briefly examine.

Marriage

If one considers the amount of time which most parish clergy spend in connection with weddings, baptisms and funerals, it is at once obvious that, whether or not he plans to be, the average priest or minister spends a considerable amount of his time involved with families. Preparing couples for marriage provides the most obvious example.[3] The distinction is often made between marriage preparation and pre-marital counselling, but in practice it is hard to know in advance of beginning work with a couple whether the nature of the work will be chiefly educative, preventative or therapeutic. So far as one can make this distinction at all, it might reasonably be said that the emphasis in preparing a couple for a first marriage is chiefly educative and preventative, whilst in helping a couple to embark on what is a second marriage for one or both of them, more therapeutic work will be involved.

However, it is important not to equate marriage preparation with marital therapy even though the two may share some common techniques and approaches. Even when preparing couples for a first marriage, however, the boundary between these three different emphases is not always clear. Various studies have suggested that there does not seem to be any correlation between undertaking marriage preparation with couples and preventing divorce or marital break-up. But, as Friedman suggests, 'failure of pre-marital counselling to affect the divorce rate today may be due primarily to the fact that the approach is often directed toward the *couple's relationship'*.[4] For it is not the couple in isolation, but the whole family system of each of the prospective partners that offers the potential for effective pre-marital work. The Church often seems extraordinarily myopic in its separation of the marital sub-system from the family. Nowhere is it more important to redress this misdirected emphasis than in pre-marital work.

In coming for marriage preparation, the couple are entering upon a new phase in their lives, and the minister is offering to help them negotiate an important new stage in their life cycle. Many couples are probably expecting little more from the minister than *wedding* preparation, but if they are expecting something more, then it certainly is not therapy. They have come to him or her with their joys not their problems, and if they expect anything it is a few signposts which may help them make the transition to the married state. For the minister however it is a precious opportunity to help the couple face marriage with more realism and more awareness of its opportunities and challenges.

If he or she has begun to adopt a systems approach to the marital and family situations which need help at a later stage, he will naturally and properly want to transfer these insights to the different task of marriage preparation. Whether he normally prepares couples together in a group or in individual meetings, he will want to see how far the theoretical models and methods of family counselling can help him prepare couples for marriage more effectively. His knowledge of systems theory will suggest to him that the couple will be helped if they gain more understanding of the circular, interdependent nature of experience in a relationship and that, when things go wrong, the 'blame game' method of trying to solve the problem is always counter-productive. Helping the couple to learn something about the way family systems work, helping them to discuss how to handle conflict, argue productively and 'fight fair' will be of enormous help in laying a good foundation for their relationship—even if such matters can only be touched upon in marriage preparation. (Such work is of infinitely more value than talks by 'experts' on mortgages, health and sex because it connects with far deeper emotional realities and engages with them in the 'conception' stage of their relationship.) The minister will want to build into his meetings with the couple some questions to them which deepen their awareness of the difficulties they may encounter and the resources they can call upon to help them.

The reason why the family approach is of crucial relevance to helping couples before marriage is that, as Friedman points out, 'the emotional phenomena of engagement and disengagement (from previous relationships) are the opposite sides of the same coin.'[5] Each of the pair has to separate sufficiently from their families of origin to enable them to engage in their new relationship. The heart of marriage preparation therefore needs to be directed towards the interface of past and present and be set within the context of the family system as a whole.

Resources for the future are built upon the past, so it is helpful to get the couple to identify the patterns they have learned about marriage and parenting from their two families of origin. To help them do this it may be useful to construct a genogram of each partner's family of origin and to talk about the rules and roles and patterns which seemed to work for their parents and grandparents and those which did not. Doing this work has several purposes.

(1) It raises to conscious awareness some of the dysfunctional rules and patterns which get unconsciously transmitted from one generation to the next.

(2) It introduces the idea that these patterns do not *have* to be replicated — the couple can increase their area of choice as to how they want to develop their own unique relationship.

(3) In talking about each other's families of origin in front of the other person, each can learn more about their partner and the social and emotional context from which he or she comes Each partner can be helped to understand more fully the reasons why they have become the sort of people they are and why they need the sort of partner they have chosen.

(4) The minister will have the opportunity to convey the idea that marriage is a bonding between two *families* and not just between two *individuals*. If there are negative feelings about this marriage amongst one or other of the couple's families these need discussing openly, if possible in a face-to-face meeting. The couple need to work out how they will approach such negative feelings in others and to discover resources of mutual support and loyalty both within their relationship and amongst their relatives and friends.

(5) Most important of all, the minister can help each partner identify the ties and pulls within the families of origin which may get in the way of a thorough bonding in their new

relationship. Young couples usually have particular difficulty in separating sufficiently from their parents, and many a young wife or husband finds that he or she has needed to run home after the first row or has been abandoned by their partner for this reason. Some cultural contexts provide a more sympathetic ambience than others. Families who still live close together on large housing estate areas may find nothing odd about a young wife spending her day time round at her mother's while her husband is at work or, if unemployed, with his mates. Each partner needs however to be encouraged to share their feelings about their own needs and to set out to provide, *within* the relationship, security and containment for their partner's emotional needs.

The minister will make use not only of his understanding of systems theory and of psychodynamic ideas as to how the past affects the present, he will also be able to help the couple to anticipate some of the ways their movement through the life cycle will affect their relationship. For example, he may ask them to think about what each may feel like when the first baby arrives. It is usually a new idea to realise that threesomes are quite different from twosomes. Helping them to talk about 'what happened' when the woman's sister had her first baby or the man's best friend had his, we raise to their awareness how each may feel. Reflecting upon their own potential feelings and the feelings of the other will help them prepare for this new situation. For example, it is often very difficult for either to realise how closely bonded the woman will feel to her newborn baby and how difficult this experience may be for the husband. It is also important for him to know that his feelings of being temporarily displaced are normal and natural and that they can be put to good effect, enabling mother and child to become more separate when this becomes part of the developmental needs of both the child and the couple. It is he who must then 'displace' the child and reclaim the central place in his wife's sphere of attention if all three members of the family are to be able to develop appropriately towards the next stages in the life cycle. Sculpting can be used as a tool to illustrate graphically and rapidly how such changes in a triangular relationship may be brought about. It is useful to give the couples one or more check-lists to fill in separately about how well they think they know each other; about their sexual needs and about the sort of problems they might anticipate experiencing. These can be given to the couple after each session and the material generated by them used in the following discussion sessions with the minister.[6]

New Marriage after Divorce

Changes in the Anglican Church's marriage discipline have meant that many more priests and ministers are contacted by couples wanting to marry in church, while one or both parties have a marriage partner still living. Here the boundary between the educative and therapeutic functions of marriage preparation all but dissolves, and it is helpful to consider this work as a form of brief therapeutic involvement undertaken at a time of crisis in the couple's life cycle. This allows the minister to draw fully upon the theoretical models of family counselling as well as on those of crisis theory. The salient characteristics of this work are that (1) it is short-term, (2) it is goal-orientated and highly structured, and (3) its therapeutic thrust will normally be directed towards one or two focal issues which emerge quite quickly and clearly as the meetings get under way.[7] Enabling a couple to embark successfully on a new marriage after one or both have been divorced will mean that in every case a lot of attention must be directed towards resolving past hurts and healing what remains unhealed. It may be important to make use of the Church's sacrament of reconciliation or to offer the couple a ritual for dissolving previously made vows.

An average of five sessions will normally allow some significant work to get done. A typical plan for the sessions goes as follows:

1. Discussion about why they want to marry in church; their beliefs; how they met and what draws them and attracts them to one another—all designed to focus on the positive and optimistic hope for their new marriage.
2. Genogram of one partner. It is often a good plan (if only one partner has been married before) to draw the genogram first of the partner who *has not* been previously married, as it gives the couple more time to settle into a

relationship with the minister before having to deal with the potentially highly charged material of the first marriage.

3.   Genogram of second partner.

4.   Discussion of potential strengths and weaknesses of this relationship—what is going to be the central issue they will need help with handling?

5.   What resources do they have in themselves and what resources can they call upon in others to help them handle their potential difficulties?

The following case illustrates the use of a family counselling approach with a couple preparing for a new marriage. In the first session, the ministers discovered that Alan, aged twenty-eight, and Rachel, aged twenty-three, had met eighteen months earlier at a Christmas party. Alan was the son of regular and extremely committed church-goers and came from a large and mutually supportive family network. His mother showed her feelings easily and was warm and outgoing; his father, whom he said he took after, was a quiet man who kept his feelings to himself. Six years earlier Alan had fallen in love with his first cousin Kate, some one whom he had known since childhood and whom he met regularly at the many family get-togethers. Alan's parents and siblings had been strongly opposed to the marriage, feeling that the blood tie between them was too close to make marriage a proper relationship for them. On the whole they were glad when this marriage broke down and delighted when Alan met Rachel and they decided to marry. In the second session the minister constructed Rachel's genogram. It materialised that she came from a violent, aggressive family where there had been lots of rows. Until her parents divorced when she was seven, she had frequently been hit about by both parents. After the divorce she became very close to her father, only to 'lose' him to his new wife when she was eleven years old. At the same time, her mother remarried and she described how she felt that both parents had chosen others to live with rather than live with her. At nineteen, she met Ken and they decided to marry. One month before the marriage she discovered she was pregnant and Ken, without any discussion of his feelings about this new situation, promptly deserted her and found another girlfriend. Obvious themes from Rachel's genogram were that:

(1) People one loves will choose to be with others, creating in Rachel a sense of grief and jealousy.

(2) Men are unreliable, inscrutable and desert her.

(3) Marriage is violent and upsetting and is somehow 'fated'.

In the third session the ministers constructed Alan's genogram. He had come from a warm and stable home and had close relationships with his older sister Jackie and younger brother Daniel. When he was fifteen the first of two major tragedies struck the family—Jackie had a severe road accident and was physically and mentally damaged for life. During the five months she was in a coma, Alan found it hard to visit her and yet felt guilty about his inability as well as criticised by his parents. Gradually Jackie recovered to the point when she returned home as a semi-invalid and the family reorganised itself around this new situation. Despite the disapproval of his parents, Alan left home to marry his cousin. But two weeks before the wedding, tragedy struck the family again. Daniel was killed in a motorbike accident. Alan and Kate decided to go through with the wedding, but for Alan the experience was obliterated by his grief and guilt at Daniel's death. His grief could not be properly expressed both because of his parents' need to claim a priority for theirs and because of Kate's need for love and attention. He not unnaturally proved unequal to the emotional burdens laid upon him and Kate deserted him for another man two years later. Alan returned home to his parents and some of the rift between them began to heal. Obvious themes from Alan's genogram were that:

(1) People one loves leave or are taken from one, leaving a sense of unfocused guilt and unresolved grief.

(2) Feelings are too complicated to show or to share and are best kept inside.

(3) Marriage is an uncertain haven from the problems presented by other relationships and is somehow 'fated'.

In sessions 4 and 5 the minister and the couple looked at the two genograms, comparing them and the themes which seemed to arise out of them. Both Rachel's and Alan's first wedding plans had been severely disrupted, and both had been deserted by their former partners. Both came to this

marriage with more anxiety and dread than they had realised—
but, as they talked and shared their previous experiences
with the minister, their half acknowledged fears that this
wedding too would be 'fated' became much easier to express.
Rachel expressed her anxiety that Alan would not talk about
his feelings (a fact that had proved disastrous in her first
relationship) and Alan began to see how he had been well
taught (by his father's example and by his parents' overwhelming needs around the two family tragedies) to keep his
feelings to himself and to barely let himself know what they
were. Rachel could see how it was going to be difficult for her
fully to trust a man after being deserted by both her father
and her fiancé. Both began to see how they could help the
other to tackle some of these important emotional tasks.

In the fifth session, the minister helped the couple to look
at the resources they had to offer each other. Alan might be
able to 'teach' Rachel that men could be reliable, faithful and
caring, while she might be able to 'teach' Alan that she would
be a safe receptacle for his feelings and would handle them
with sensitivity and care. Each might be able to help the
other to work on unresolved relationships in their families of
origin. Rachel might be helped to reconnect with her two
'lost' parents which she grieved for so much, and Alan needed
help in finding appropriate ways of relating to his ex-wife
who was still his first cousin and who, in this close-knit
family, it would be necessary for him to meet up with quite
frequently. In the process of helping Alan work this out,
Rachel would be helped to come to terms with her feelings of
jealousy about Kate, which in turn would help her resolve her
feelings about her father's second wife and Ken's girlfriend,
both of whom had displaced her. There was much emotional
work to be done if this couple were to be able to build their
marriage on a realistic and solid base. At the end of the
session, the minister set the couple two specific tasks. Alan
was to write a letter to his brother Daniel and go and read it
out to him at the graveside—expressing all the grief and
regrets he had been unable to express so far. Rachel was to
make contact with both her parents and ask her father if he
would give her away at the wedding. In a review session, held
about four weeks before the wedding, the couple looked
relaxed and unburdened. Both tasks had been accomplished

with great success—Alan had begun his grief work with the help of a good deal of support from Rachel and she had had a moving and very constructive meeting with each of her parents, introducing them to Alan. On the great day itself, both families united to support and launch this couple into their new life together.

Baptism

Birth and death represent major crises of accession and dismemberment in the life cycle of the family and, instinctively, people reach out to ask for help in interpreting their significance and meaning. As Carr has pointed out, 'the range of possible reasons for coming to the Church seeking baptism for a child is as great as the style with which the approach may be made.'[8] In every case however, as Carr goes on to comment, the request for baptism is one that is concerned with a significant event that has occurred in the parents' lives and in the lives of the wider grouping of relatives and friends in which their immediate family is embedded. The birth of a child may or may not be a cause for celebration, but its arrival and entry into the family system significantly affects every other member of the system and every relationship which has already been formed. Nothing will ever be the same again. If, for all the excellent reasons suggested by Carr, the minister takes as his starting point the *fact* of the parents' parenthood and the significance of the child's new life in terms of its joy and its cost, then he or she will at once be led into helping family members begin to explore the meaning and significance of their new roles, relationships and responsibilities. Here it should be noted that the task is not to make use of the baptismal request as an entry point into potentially dysfunctional processes in the system. The baptismal request is not *ipso facto* a cry for help, although it *can* be in some situations. The minister's approach must obviously be oriented in the first instance towards responding to the request for *baptism itself* in the way which will most appropriately assist the family in meeting its needs at this point in their lives.

Depending upon the way in which the minister structures his baptism preparation, he may be able to increase the opportunities for contact with the family's social grouping in a very natural way. Parents will usually choose godparents from members of their extended family or significant psycho-social network. These people are 'identified' by the parents as being a necessary way of fulfilling the demands of the baptism ritual. Some times they are powerful authority figures in the family whose 'blessing' is required at each important juncture of the family's life. Their choice represents the parents' obedience to a well established, if implicit, family rule. Sometimes the invitation to be a godparent is given in an effort to reconcile some long-standing quarrel that has occurred between friends or between two branches of a family. In the case of a single parent — usually the mother — the choice of godparents may represent her desire to surround her child with the security and acceptance that she may feel is lacking because of her unmarried status. In these situations, the request is often made for very large numbers of godparents. The task of the minister is to help the family, through the liturgical and theological tools at his disposal, to explore the meaning and significance of the choices, decisions and half-formed ideas which they are moving towards.

In some cultures, all decisions regarding the children are the province of the mother. Whilst accepting the family's manner of presentation, the minister may be able to 'give permission' for more peripheral family members, including father, to talk about his feelings, hopes and fears for the child and show how these might be expressed liturgically and ritually during the baptism. Where several requests for baptism are received each month, most ministers are able to offer at least one meeting for a group of parents and godparents together at the vicarage or church hall. This meeting may focus upon some instructional film or other material which gives information about the meaning of baptism, church membership, etc. If the minister is aware of the significance and wider implications of the birth for the whole family system, he will be able to introduce ideas which speak to family members' covert or unconscious needs. During the discussion time and when he speaks formally he can, for example, address issues of change in family members' roles and relationships, the acceptance of new intimacies and new separations, the naturalness of anger and guilt when faced with these changes, the possibility for new beginnings in old relationships and the hope for healing and new life. A home visit made after the general meeting will give him the opportunity to follow up these themes in terms of the way they apply specifically to each particular family.

Bereavement and Death

If the minister is helped by an understanding of the dynamics of family systems in his work with parents who request baptism for their children, he will be helped even more profoundly in his normal ministry to the bereaved. The death of an individual is always a crisis of dismemberment for the family system to which he or she has belonged. Nor does death end his or her membership of the family in an emotional sense for, as we have noted in earlier chapters, deceased family members can exert an even more crucial influence over the living than when they were themselves alive. Helping the family to take the first steps along the road to resolving their relationship with the deceased is therefore an important piece of prophylactic work. The loss of a family member will often bring into consciousness the family group's sense of identity *as a family* and as an entity over and above the sum of its parts. A family interviewed on a television series on bereavement brought this point home vividly. The little eight-year-old daughter had been killed in a road accident. Mother described how, shortly afterwards, the family had sat down together and decided that as they were 'no longer a family' it would be best if they all committed suicide. It seemed to them at that point in their experience to be the only reasonable thing to do.

It is sometimes easier to see how and why the crisis of death and bereavement can be approached most productively in terms of the whole family system, by noting the appalling consequences for the family's ongoing life when things go wrong. A family asked for help two years after the death of their five-year-old daughter. Father had been the chief caretaker for the three children while mother went out to work. He therefore felt acute guilt at the death of Jenny. In the first family meeting he alternately held his head in his hands or stared into space. He was angry and mute, while mother and Frances (aged 9) and William (aged 14) were barely more able to tell the family's story of emotional arrest during the past two years. It seemed that, since Jenny's death, Father spent most of his time in his study, working for an Open University degree. William also shut himself away for long hours and had no friends, whilst mother spent most of her time at work. Frances had regressed to a state of dependency upon her mother and needed her to put her to bed each night. However, Frances seemed also to represent the family's desire to continue living. She acted as a sort of gentle go-between within the family—spending time with each of the others and also providing a link with normal outside contacts by visiting her friends in neighbouring homes. Apart from this, the only family 'outing' was a weekly visit to Jenny's grave. Frances and William had begun to protest against these visits, though the parents usually insisted. It seemed to the family counsellors that each family member was endeavouring to bear the responsibility and consequences of Jenny's death by themselves in a position of emotional isolation from the rest of the family.

The emotional separation was maintained by a series of mutual projections, each family member holding another responsible for Jenny's death and for the consequent dislocation of their lives. It appeared that the family had had no help or support at the time of Jenny's death. The husband's family, from whom he was partly estranged, lived abroad. The wife's parents were dead and she was an only child. She was a doctor and her colleagues appeared to expect her to be strong enough to cope without outside help. The family were committed atheists and chose to handle the funeral service by themselves, without involving a priest or minister. The only contact they had had with an outsider was with an undertaker. He was apparently embarrassed and unable to cope effectively with the death of this young child, and so their contact with him left the family angry, hurt and depleted. These experiences had become frozen over the past two years, and the family came for help in a state of mutual resistance and silent pain. The counsellors concentrated upon enabling family members to own their projections of guilt and responsibility and then to test the reality of these feelings against objective fact. Through talking and sharing their feelings, and through various exercises and tasks suggested by the counsellors, family members were able to provide each other with the possibility for healing and new growth. After six months counselling help they were now having regular family outings, time together as a couple and a first family holiday. Frances had developed more age-appropriate behaviour. Her night fears had abated and she now felt comfortable about putting herself to bed on her own. All four family members had 'unfrozen.' They were able to talk about Jenny in a natural and loving way as a continuing member of the family, and their obsessive weekly visits to the grave had ceased.

The amount of time which a minister can spend upon the sort of prophylactic work which would have greatly relieved this family's later problems is of course very minimal. Nevertheless, because bereavement—especially the tragic, untimely bereavement of a child—represents a major acute crisis, only a small amount of help offered appropriately at the *right time* is required to prevent the effects of long-term stress.

Even if the minister's contact is limited to one visit before the funeral and one visit afterwards he nevertheless can offer a great deal of help to the family as it begins to negotiate the process of bereavement and to move from separation, through transition to reintegration. In his pre-funeral visit he may need to support some family members in voicing their needs and gently challenge the family rules which appear to be preventing them from getting those needs met. For example, a family member may wish to visit the dead person and view the body even though other members of the family do not approve. Conversely, a family member may want to absent himself from the family's visit to the Chapel of Rest. The minister can helpfully suggest that different family members may need to choose to do different things at this point and that these differences do not reflect criticism of the choices made by others or disrespect for the deceased.

Because people's defences are impaired at a time of acute crisis and they are often emotionally labile, family members may wish to talk about past family problems, old quarrels and misunderstandings both between themselves and the deceased and between other groupings in the family. Family members may express terrible regrets for the past and may seek the assurance of forgiveness. They may also indicate ways in which healing of past broken relationships might be begun. For example, a minister visited the family of an elderly man, Freddie, who had died of multiple sclerosis. He had lived with his daughter and son-in-law for the last four years and they had nursed him devotedly until his death. It transpired that Freddie's wife had deserted him after discovering the diagnosis and, after thirty years of a marriage which had appeared to work well, she had moved in to live with a young man of twenty-three. The daughter, son-in-law and her two younger sisters were outraged by their mother's behaviour and yet grieved for the disrupted relationship with her. They were angry with their mother but, more importantly, they longed for a means of restoring contact with her. The minister offered to visit her—an offer which everyone was eager to accept. She found the mother paralysed by her conflicting feelings of guilt, grief and anger. She talked with the minister about the shock of discovering that Freddie had an incurable illness and the inner knowledge that she could not face nursing him. She had realised for the first time her own increasing age but longed for a last chance of irresponsible and care-free happiness. The minister told her of her daughters' sadness and desire to restore contact and that, if she wanted to, they would welcome her to Freddie's funeral and to a family gathering at the house afterwards. After the minister's visit, the mother went to visit her elder daughter and son-in-law. They talked for some time and it seemed to have been a profoundly important experience for all of them. The mother did not attend the funeral but said she would sit in a nearby church while the funeral was taking place. In her sermon at the funeral, the minister was able to touch upon themes of reconciliation and forgiveness and the new opportunities that can emerge, even out of the grief of bereavement.

Notes

1. R. Green, *Only Connect,* Darton, Longman and Todd 1987, p. 100.
2. The Church of England's General Synod Report, *Children in the Way*

(1988) is a recent attempt to encourage all-age learning in the Church and so counteract this tendency.

3. See P. Chambers, *Made in Heaven?*, SPCK 1988, for a full discussion of the various approaches to marriage preparation.
4. E. H. Friedman, *Generation to Generation*, Guilford Press 1985, p. 92.
5. ibid., p. 91.
6. Various packs which include audio-visual material have been produced for use in marriage preparation. One of the most comprehensive of these is the one produced by the Church Pastoral Aid Society, 'Side by Side'.
7. W. Kinston and A. Bentovim, 'Creating a Focus for Brief Marital or Family Therapy' in S. Budman, ed., *Forms of Brief Therapy*, New York, Guilford Press, 1981.
8. W. Carr, *Brief Encounters*, SPCK 1985, p. 68.

ELEVEN

Supporting
the Counselling Process

Working with families is a reflexive task — for almost every one of us is, or has been, a member of a family ourselves. In chapter 1 we looked at the ways in which the counsellor's own experiences of family provide an important reservoir of knowledge about the ways in which family groups function. When we come to consider how the process of family counselling may best be supported, we need first to note the resources and needs of the counsellor's own family. In theory, the counsellor's own intimate network is his chief support. His family or other intimate network should provide the place where he can unwind, receive love, care and attention and be renewed for his ministry of counselling families.

In practice however the juxtaposition of demands made by his role as a minister and his tasks of family counselling may create in him more needs than this family network can reasonably handle. As a minister, he lacks many of the boundaries around his time and presence which are available to his secular counterparts. Appointment systems and waiting lists are inappropriate means of protecting himself, and the fact that much of his work is reactive rather than proactive limits the degree to which he can structure his working day as tightly as the full-time family counsellor. As a minister engaged in counselling families he becomes the recipient and container of family members' projected feelings. As part of the counselling process, family members will test out his authenticity, his empathy and his emotional stamina by using him as a container for their negative feelings, their fears and their hates and, as the process continues, he will be caught into a transference relationship which will often be made up of the transferences of several family members simultaneously.

Although transference does not develop to the same extent as in individual counselling, the family counsellor may nevertheless experience that temporary sense of personal disorientation brought about by being viewed by one or more members of the family as a punitive parent, an irresponsible adolescent or a rebellious child. The counsellor's management and use of these transferences will be part of the process whereby he helps family members to own their own feelings, distinguish their past experiences from present and take back into the family group the interpersonal relationship experiences which belong within rather than without. Box, in discussing the way in which the family counsellor must necessarily act as a container for these processes, describes the demands upon the counsellor as follows:

> The therapist in the transference has to be able to tolerate the family's frustrations as well as his own and to help the family 'modify' rather than 'evade'. In order for containment to occur, the therapist needs to retain his own sense of 'goodness' or effectiveness, despite the family's projection of the opposite into him; he needs to tolerate the doubt that is being created and, like the mother with her baby, to hold the unwanted feelings until they can be relayed back to the family in a form which may be assimilable.[1]

Clearly, this is no mean task and it deeply affects the inner life of the family counsellor. He or she therefore emerges from a day's work, when perhaps two or three family groups have been seen, with a multiplicity of conflicting feelings which have been stirred up inside by the projections of family members. In addition, the counsellor's own countertransference of feeling responses to family members may further complicate the feelings he is left with at the end of the day.

To all this we need to add a further aspect of life which forms part of the complex whole of the counsellor's emotional experience—that is, his day-to-day *real life* experiences in his own family. In an odd and extraordinary way, it often seems to be the case that the material with which the family counsellor is dealing with in the families he is trying to help, may reflect or mirror rather closely the personal issues he is struggling with in his own interpersonal relationships. This stems from the fact that there are a limited number of general

themes which underpin the detailed working out of family life
and the counsellor is almost certain to encounter one or other
that resonates only too closely with his own current
experience.

This fact contains both a threat and a hope. The counsellor
may feel threatened about the closeness of the two worlds in
which he moves but he may also realise the hope and
opportunity which this juxtaposition affords. If, for example,
the counsellor is struggling with the destructiveness of her
own covert, castrating power which acts as a substitute for
appropriate assertiveness in her marital relationship, she
may be able to learn, alongside the wife in the family she is
trying to help, ways in which this can be expressed and
integrated into her own marital relationship in a more
constructive way. This will only be possible if she is not
overwhelmed by the potential *threat* of the wife's similar
difficulties. If she is able to recognise the similarity for what
it is, she may be able to turn it into *hope* and a tool for growth
for both the wife and for herself.

Supposing however she is unable to see the parallel between
her own situation and that of the wife? She may find it very
difficult to cope with the husband's inevitable projections
onto her of his own feelings regarding his wife's behaviour.
These feelings will replicate those which are expressed by her
own husband and she may find herself caught into the same
circular process whereby she acts in a controlling way towards
the husband and he becomes passively angry and
progressively unable to assert his point of view. The
dysfunctional processes of the couple she is trying to help
will then compound her own marital problems.

To reduce the possibility of such an undesirable situation
occurring, it is important that the minister is able to talk over
his family counselling with an experienced consultant or
supervisor. The role of the consultant is to listen, to interpret
and to help the minister work through the emotional meaning
of the counselling experience with each particular family. In
the above example, the consultant would help the minister to
become aware of the similarity between her own and her
clients' situations and to reflect upon how this similarity
could be used positively both in the counselling itself and in
her own personal life. The consultant will help the minister to

become aware of the family's transference and the minister's countertransference experiences and to look for the ways in which the family's own shared defences, group myths and avoided themes may resonate with the minister's own experiences in his family of origin and current family. The act of seeking out a consultant with whom to talk over one's family work is an act of professional responsibility because, for the reasons already enumerated, it is often very difficult to separate out the experiences of the family one is trying to help from one's own past or current familial experience.

The consultant will help the minister examine his own prejudices, biases and stereotypes which arise from his earlier relationship experiences and which can seriously interfere with his ability to help couples and families. An important example of such a bias is the bias towards patriarchy. Sexual stereotyping is something with which we are all deeply imbued. Feminist writers have drawn attention to the ways in which women have been elected to present emotional and psychological problems on behalf of others and have then been punished for doing so. Counsellors are no more immune than others from sexual stereotyping and, because of their influence over the family's handling of sex roles, they may need special help in dealing with these problems in themselves.[2] Racial biases, too, may also need help.

The consultant should also be able to assist the minister review his goals for each family, select appropriate methods for moving towards those goals and determining the point at which the counselling process has made reasonable progress towards achieving the goals set by himself and the family. As I mentioned in chapter 5, the minister may need particular help from the consultant when he arrives at the termination phases of the counselling process. The consultant can help him separate out his own needs to continue with or to abandon a family from *their* needs to continue or terminate the counselling process. Such decisions are often hard to make and difficulties may stem from the fact that it is unclear as to whose needs are being met and how.

The minister may prefer to discuss his work with families in a group of his own peers. The group needs to be small enough to enable each person to have sufficient time to devote to each family situation. Provided that this can be achieved, group supervision has much to recommend it as a way of supporting family counselling. First, the model of the group is a more congruent one than the individual model of one-to-one consultancy. Second, the group's behaviour may reflect the behaviour of the family being discussed and the minister may be able to learn more about the way his family is functioning by observing and questioning the supervision group. Third, the supervision group can be used for the minister to 'try out' his ideas with the family. The group can role-play the members of the family and give the minister feed back as to whether or not his interventions are being experienced by them as helpful and effective. He can use group members to sculpt the family, so that he can show them more clearly the way the family group interacts. They in turn can then be more accurate and realistic about their suggestions to the minister. He can also use a group sculpture to experiment with different ways of helping the family to change and to increase his understanding as to the effect of his potential interventions upon the different sub-systems in the family.

The consultant and group will need to attend not only to the case material which the minister is presenting but also to the three interlocking triangles of family group, minister's own family and the congregational system. The focus of interest and concern will often need to be on the *relationship* between two or more of these three triangles. For example, when the minister begins to undertake some family counselling, he will obviously need to spend a considerable amount of time with just two or three family groups. If his pattern of work prior to that was to visit his church members regularly, this pattern may have to be altered and his routine visits reduced. Members of a congregation will normally accept the need for intensive involvement with the sick or bereaved but they may feel angry and envious of the attention devoted to couples and families with marital and child-focused problems. These arouse less sympathy than the sick or bereaved and they may invoke criticism and attack. Because there may be relatives or friends of the couple in the congregation, the minister may feel constrained by their influence and anxious lest they become alienated or hostile as a result of his interventions with the couple. Obviously his aim should be to act systemically and to include these relatives within the ambit of the sessions. If hitherto the congregation has been used to a minister who has allowed relationship difficulties to be denied and hidden from view, his concern for these aspects of his church members' lives may be seen as intrusive, however sensitively he approaches them.

Likewise the changes that occur in the minister's own family will have an effect upon the interrelated system of his church congregation. For example, a bachelor priest suddenly announced his intentions of getting married. The parish had had a succession of bachelors and therefore few parishioners had had any experience of a married priest. During the three years he had been the parish priest, he had become the object of a variety of romantic phantasies belonging to both male and female parishioners. In particular, a middle-aged woman who was diagnosed as manic-depressive and whose mental health was always in a state of precarious balance, had entertained the phantasy that she might one day become his wife. Similarly, a male member whose own marriage revolved around a triangle between himself, his wife and his mother, had coped with his own repressed homosexual needs by building up a close, supportive and confiding relationship with the priest. The priest's announcement of his engagement shattered the hopes and dreams of both these members as well as others in the congregation. The woman was hospitalised for some weeks and the man became withdrawn and hostile. He became instrumental in provoking and leading a variety of criticisms of the priest's ministry and, unused as they were to having to share their parish priest with a wife or children, the parishioners voiced their resentment of his wife by criticising the priest's absence from a range of community functions.

Friedman discusses the way in which the minister, faced with these kinds of pressures, may often need to enlist help if he is to be able to manage the dynamics of these interlocking triangles productively. He suggests that there must be an effort to become less reactive to and anxious about the content of specific charges levelled against him and to concentrate instead on the *underlying processes* by doing some of the following:

To get some emotional distance from the two major interlocking emotional systems, his family and his congregation; to try to maintain a non-anxious presence with both by reducing his own anxiety about being the one who must satisfy both groups; to shift responsibility for the 'problem' to other members of the congregational family in a way that would not polarize; to keep up his own personal level of functioning by shifting his energy to doing what he enjoys and is good at; and to seek an opportunity in the future to focus those members who are most 'hostile' (i.e. intense towards him) onto unresolved issues in their own families, perhaps during some celebration of a rite of passage.[3]

As well as receiving proper supervision or consultation, the minister may also need to engage in the counselling process for himself. Receiving help himself and becoming the recipient of the counselling process is not indicative of failure; it is an indispensable tool. Just as the individual counsellor receives counselling himself as part of the ongoing development and support of his work, so should the family and marital counsellor regard the need for appropriate personal help as being integral to his work. The most appropriate kind of therapeutic help is to receive family or marital counselling himself. This enables his family group to develop their own resources and strengths for dealing with the pressures and challenges described earlier. Unfortunately, there is insufficient acceptance on the part of the Church of the *minister's* need to receive therapeutic help himself — especially when he is taking on the counselling of individuals, couples or families. Such resistance by the institution springs from guilt and fear, yet it must at all costs be overcome if ministers who have gifts and a desire to work with couples and families are to receive proper support.

A most important means of getting ongoing support for one's marital and family counselling is to work with another counsellor. Almost every case that has been described in this book describes work conducted by the author, working as part of a co-therapy team.[4] For purposes of clarity in describing the actual techniques of treatment, the co-therapeutic aspect of the work has not been highlighted.

Nevertheless, it remains a highly significant ingredient of my own practice and that of many other family and marital counsellors. It is probably true to say that co-therapy, defined as two counsellors working together simultaneously with a family, is practised more frequently by those who work from a psychoanalytic, existential or theme-focused approach than those who work from within a strategic framework. The latter tend to work alone or with the help of a consulting team.

The advantages of working as a co-therapy pair relate both to the needs of the counsellors themselves and to the needs of the therapeutic process. Working as part of a co-therapy pair means that each counsellor has an inbuilt means of gaining ongoing support and oversight, and a co-therapy relationship allows an integral system of checks and balances on the work of each counsellor to operate. Each enables the other to receive support and affirmation for his interventions with the family, and each offers to the other a means of testing out his or her perceptions and hypotheses concerning the family's functioning and treatment goals. Co-therapy makes the therapeutic task significantly less isolating, more productive and more enjoyable for the counsellors, all of which can only enhance the quality of their work with the family. Moreover, a co-therapeutic approach to family counselling, enables the counsellors to help each other prepare *before* the session and debrief *afterwards* much more fully and accurately than simply giving an account of the work with the family to a consultant at a later date, important though that is.

A co-therapy relationship takes time to develop and it will be some while before each person feels able to be entirely open in his or her thinking with the other and to be able to give and receive criticisms as well as appreciation of each other's work. Like a marital relationship, which it closely resembles, trust and commitment grow imperceptibly, as much through the gaps between words as through the words that are actually exchanged.

The right choice of a working partner is important. There is some evidence to show, for example, that the family is best served if the two counsellors are roughly equal in their counselling experience.[5] Many family counsellors favour a male/female partnering as this offers obvious advantages in terms of understanding the male and female members of the marriage or family group. It also allows the counsellors to role-model appropriate and functional interaction for the family, based upon a marital and/or parental role model with which the couple or family can begin to identify. Some family counsellors have experimented with working with their own marriage partner and this model is frequently adopted in marriage preparation work. Married co-therapists undoubtedly have some unique advantages but they also face particular hazards, and it should not be assumed that the minister's husband or wife will automatically make an ideal counselling partner. The partner should certainly have the same degree of training or preparation for counselling, and serious consideration needs to be given to the potential effects on the couple's own relationship. The couple should certainly be prepared to discuss their work and its effect upon their relationship regularly with a consultant.

The two main advantages of working with another counsellor when counselling the family may be summarised as follows:

First, it aids in the practical task of 'managing' what may be quite a large group of people, often made up of a wide mixture of ages, interests and motivation. Two counsellors working together makes it possible for one to get involved with the young children for example, sitting on the floor with them and helping them to communicate their feelings to the adults, perhaps through interpreting the meaning of their play or drawings. If sculpting is being used as a treatment or diagnostic technique, one of the counsellors can get involved in the sculpt, taking the place of the family member whose sculpture it is, while the other helps the family member to express his feelings, pain and hopes for the future through developing the family tableau. Two counsellors working in partnership means that there are two pairs of ears and eyes available and neither has to feel responsible for absorbing and making sense of the whole mass of complex data which the family group will offer. Moreover, the two counsellors will often perceive and understand the meaning of the family's interactions differently, because of differences in their own life experiences, gender and beliefs. For the relationship to work, there needs to be a reasonable measure of congruity

between the counsellors in terms of their values, beliefs and
what the purpose of the therapeutic endeavour is perceived to
be. Beyond that, however, their *differences* in perception will
help them to arrive at a more accurate and comprehensive
understanding of the family's difficulties and of their goals.

Second, the co-therapy model is more appropriate to family
counselling than working alone as a single therapist. It injects
into the counselling situation a *relationship* and this
immediately focuses the concerns of the group on to the
interactions *between* people rather than the individual
experiences of family members. The co-therapists, whether
they are male/female or a same-sex pair, can use their
relationship to role-model for the family functional communication, cooperation and different ways of handling disagreement and conflict constructively. They can demonstrate
ways of admitting ignorance and owning responsibility for
mistakes by doing so in front of the family and, by the same
token, they can demonstrate ways of forgiving the other and
accepting vulnerability or weakness. One counsellor can build
upon an intervention made by the other, increasing its
perceived validity or power. Similarly, one counsellor may be
able to clarify an intervention made by his or her colleague,
rewording it if he senses that the family has not understood
or saying that he himself does not understand and asking his
colleague for clarification. If the co-therapists are male and
female they will have particular advantages when working
with conflicts over gender role or with sexual problems. The
female counsellor will be able to understand something of the
inbuilt tendencies in society and in marriage to stereotype
women in ways which reduce their freedom and creativity.
Likewise the male counsellor will be able to identify with the
negative consequences of these tendencies on himself. The
female counsellor will be able to help the wife discuss the
physical aspects of her sexual experiences more easily just as
the male counsellor will be able to help the husband to talk
about his. More importantly, the male/female co-therapy pair,
by their own relaxed discussion, will be able to model for the
couple how sexual matters can be approached without
embarrassment and with humour and ease.

Despite its many advantages, the development of a
satisfactory co-therapy relationship capable of performing

some or all of these functions does not occur without some effort. If co-therapy is to act as a support to the counselling process and to each of the counsellors, the counsellors must be prepared to take time to work at their relationship and to discuss its ongoing development. Several difficulties may arise:

(1) Probably one of the most formidable difficulties which a pair of counsellors must confront is when a family attempts to split the co-therapy team. Often the scapegoating process, being acted out within the family, will be transferred to the co-therapy team. One of the counsellors will become the recipient of the family's negative feelings and will be either humoured, attacked or covertly disqualified. The other counsellor may begin to collude with the family in scapegoating his colleague. The counsellors will need first to become aware of what is happening and then try to work out how far the family's need to split them into good and bad objects relates to the reality of their interventions or to an irrational activity concerning unconscious processes operating within the family system. It may be the case that one of the counsellors experiences strong negative feelings towards one or more of the family members and acts these out through critical or non-empathic interventions. Clearly this problem belongs to the counsellor and not to the family and needs to be worked with in terms of gaining more awareness of his or her own countertransference experiences. On the other hand, where the negative experience of one of the therapists appears to derive from the family's projections, these need to be understood and worked on with the family so that they may be helped to relate this understanding to their own family dynamics. Such a task presupposes that the two counsellors have become sufficiently free of the need to compete with one another either for the good will of the family or for the position of being 'the more effective counsellor'. Competition and rivalrous feelings are common experiences in co-therapy teams, especially when the team is newly formed. They are disastrous only if they are not faced, understood and worked through.

(2) The second difficulty, related to the first, is the way in which a co-therapy team may begin unconsciously to mirror the dysfunctional patterns of the family group. For example,

when working with a couple where the husband was unable to accept that his wife had a reasonable complaint against his dismissive and chauvinistic attitudes towards her, my colleague and I found that he was becoming a more dominant influence in the sessions whilst I was becoming progressively more silent. When I did speak, the husband turned away and then undermined my comments with word or look. His wife, on the other hand, sat forward eagerly and hopefully on the few occasions I ventured a comment. It was not until we sat down and examined the conflicting feelings stirred up in us by the jarring and atypical flow of our own interaction that my colleague and I became more fully aware of the wife's predicament and the way in which we had been induced to mirror the interaction between the couple.

(3) The co-therapy team—especially when it is made up of two fairly inexperienced family counsellors—may try to use the team as a protective device. To an outsider the two counsellors appear to be huddling together against the strength and perceived hostility of the family group. The counsellors may develop a kind of symbiotic tie, where differences between them are experienced as fearful and attempts at differentiation by either counsellor are frowned on by the other. One of the difficulties for the family in this kind of over-close, mutually protective co-therapy relationship is that, as in a fused marital relationship, where the children feel rejected and excluded, the family group can begin to feel painfully outside the closeness and harmony of the co-therapists' relationship. Faced with this kind of relationship between the counsellors, the propensity of family members to retreat into dysfunctional and exclusive pairings will increase and the capacity for growth for all members of the treatment group will be reduced.

People sometimes ask whether a co-therapy team should structure its relationship in any formal way. Normally, the answer is no. Much of the value of using two counsellors to work with a family simultaneously is derived from the manner in which their relationship develops responsively to the needs and the difficulties expressed by the family, in ways in which we have already noted. If for example the two counsellors plan that one should take the lead and the other play a more observational role, much of their spontaneity will be reduced.

Obviously it is important that the counsellors spend a little time before each session discussing the most effective way of moving the family towards the treatment goals at each particular stage of the process. But each should then feel free to intervene and respond to the material offered by the family in his or her own way. A debriefing time after each session, during which some notes are written up about what has happened and what needs to be worked on next time, is absolutely essential. It will be during the debriefing session that the counsellors can raise matters that feel problematic in their relationship as well as in terms of how the counselling is progressing.

As is the case with other kinds of counselling, the family counsellor must learn to disengage from the family at the end of each session. He needs to clear his mind and his heart of the burden that they have placed upon him, so that he can move on to the next claim upon his time and attention. For the minister, responsible for a wide-ranging number of tasks in the parish and in the congregation, this may mean that his next duty is quite unrelated to family counselling. Since family counselling is likely to occupy a very small percentage of his weekly ministry, it is all the more important that he or she develops techniques for taking leave of this emotionally draining work and becoming free to engage fully and effectively in whatever duty presents itself next. He will be helped in doing this if he schedules his family counselling sessions at the time of day at which he works best and if he leaves sufficient space beforehand to prepare for the session and sufficient time afterwards to disengage from it.

He needs to be able to forget about the session, in the confidence that he will have the material available for recall before he meets the family again. This means that he must develop a quick and easy method of record-keeping. My own preference is for a card index system combined with some diagrams. Small cards limit the amount of notes one can make to the bare essentials—a brief note on the process of the session; any startling new data that the family has shared and any tasks that were set and which must be inquired about in the next meeting. I also note down themes or issues which, given a suitable opportunity, need to be attended to during a future meeting. I fold the family's genogram up with the card and, if new material relating to the past has been revealed, I include it on the genogram, expanding and developing it as necessary. I do not believe it is possible to work effectively with families without keeping a record of each session; on the other hand, the average time I spend on writing up the record is five minutes — occasionally as much as ten minutes if the material is particularly complex. The record needs to be written up *immediately* after the session. Good record-keeping is one of the most reliable tools that a family counsellor can enlist in support of the counselling process. Combined with a congenial co-therapist and an effective consultant, family counselling can be one of the most stimulating and rewarding aspects of the minister's work.

Notes

1. S. Box et al., *Psychotherapy with Families.* Routledge & Kegan Paul 1981, pp. 160—1.
2. P. Chesler, *Women and Madness,* New York, Doubleday, 1972; I. K. Broverman, 'Sex-role Stereotypes and Clinical Judgements of Mental Health', *Journal of Consulting and Clinical Psychology,* vol. 34, 1970; W. R. Gore, 'A Relationship Between Sex Roles, Marital Status, and Mental Illness', *Social Forces,* vol. 51, 1972.
3. E. H. Friedman, *Generation to Generation,* New York, Guilford Press, 1985, p. 195.
4. It is important to use the term 'co-therapy' not 'co-counselling', as the latter has a specific usage which is quite different from what is being described here. Techniques of co-therapy are described well by M. Holt and D. Greiner, 'Co-therapy in the Treatment of Families' in P. Guerin, *Family Therapy,* New York, Guilford Press, 1976, and E. Dowling, 'Co-therapy: a Clinical Researcher's View' in S. Walrond-Skinner, *Family and Marital Psychotherapy,* Routledge & Kegan Paul 1979.
5. D. G. Rice et al., 'Therapist Experience and "Style" as Factors in Co-therapy', *Family Process,* vol. 11, 1972.

TWELVE

Towards a Theology
of the Family

This book is based on the presupposition that the family in some form or other is an essential human institution and that it can only be fully understood and assisted by engaging with it as a natural social system of interdependent relationships. But the Christian minister has to take a further step and examine the kind of role the family might play in God's purposes for human beings. We must therefore now review the nature of this role and the extent to which the concept and reality of the family can be derived from biblical and theological sources.

Families have existed in some form or other within all cultures and in all periods of history, from the earliest societies known to human beings. Because no human group has been discovered which does not practise some form of family life, we must begin our construction of a theology of the family from the premise that the notion of family lies at the heart of the creative purposes of God. It appears to have been in the very nature of the created order that God's loving care of his creatures is first expressed through the gift to them of an intimate group, whose members are tied to one another by blood or emotion or both. Anderson comments: 'The family is a necessary component of creation. Despite wide diversity of form and function throughout human history, the family has fulfilled God's intent to provide a context for creation and care in order to insure the continuity of the human species.'[1]

In the second chapter of Genesis we find that the family stands at the climax of the created order. The human being is created male and female and each is put into relationship with the other. As a consequence of their relationship, they are given the gift of fertility and the ability to procreate other members of their species to which they will also become intimately related as parents. 'God blessed them and said to them, "Be fruitful and increase, fill the earth and subdue it" ' (Gen. 1.28 NEB). Far from being predicated upon the separate, autonomous individual, the creation stories of Genesis make it clear that the original form of humanity is not even simply individuals-in-relationship, living together in some kind of family structure. The original form of the human species is *co-humanity*. Human beings are created to become one flesh, separate persons — both their unity and their individuality being equally necessary and receiving equal emphasis. Loneliness and lovelessness are viewed as intrinsically incompatible with being human. 'It is not good that man should be alone'; for a human being who is not rooted in intimate, interdependent *relationship* is not fully human. But more crucial still, a human being alone is not a reflection of the image of God. ' "Let us make man in our image and likeness" . . . So God created man [Adam] in his own image; in the image of God he created him; male and female he created them' (Gen. 1.26 – 7 NEB). The plural noun 'Adam' is used to describe human beings, and it is as a male — female representation of co-humanity that God's image is to be reflected.

It appears to be the case that God envisages the family as a vehicle for transmitting both his care and his sovereignty. The command to be fruitful and increase is in order to fill the earth with human beings and subdue it to the will and purposes of God. The family is to convey God's will and his Presence to the world through the image that he has imprinted upon it and its members. It is clear too from the Old Testament that the family continues to be seen as the basic building block of social life in ancient Israel. The family was a religious as well as a social unit, and its membership included not only husband and wife and unmarried children but also the married sons, their wives and children, the family's slaves and their families. Polygamous arrangements were quite common. With the formation of Israel as a nation and the innovation of monarchy, the great tribal units broke up, but the smaller immediate family group remained of central importance within Hebrew society. The purpose of marriage was the continuation of the family, and various devices were adopted to ensure that this primary function was maintained. Barrenness was a disastrous affliction, and an individual's inability to procreate constituted a major crisis for the family and an implicit threat to the community as a whole. God's saving acts to Sara and Hannah are mediated through his gift to them of children, and their failure to conceive, which was experienced as a curse and disruption in their relationship with God, was thus expiated. The family was the unit through which the cultic acts of the community were most clearly and regularly expressed — the covenanting of God's relationship with Israel through circumcision and later through the memorial of the Passover. The task of the family was to hand on the law and traditions of the community from one generation to the next and, as such, it was the primary vehicle by which God's will was made known to his people.

The family's internal relationships are seen as a parallel and mirror of the overriding relationship between God and Israel itself which is that of a father to his child. 'Israel is my first-born son. I have told you to let my son go, so that he may worship me' (Exod. 4.22 NEB). Over and over again it is the image of God's fatherhood which overshadows the other images of God's relationship with his people, such as kingship. God's fatherhood is inherent in the act of creation itself, and in the passage from Exodus, as elsewhere, his fatherhood of Israel — his *first-born* — is further seen as prefiguring the fatherhood which will be reclaimed in relation to *all* peoples, when his Son — the Christ — reinstates the family relationship between God and humanity. Here we need to note that this image of fatherhood does not in any way exclude or deny the complementary feminine image of motherhood. Various contemporary theologians (Maitland, Ruether, Fiorenza)[2] have drawn attention to the fact that although the image of God's fatherhood is a crucial one, indicating the familiar and personal relationship in which we stand with him, it should not be used (*pace* Oddie)[3] to indicate maleness in terms of human gender.

The Old Testament enables us to see the family earthed in the original creative purposes of God and as a primary vehicle for transmitting his will and his law to his people. The New Testament and the later doctrinal developments of Christianity provide us with rich avenues for expanding our theology of family and our understanding of its purpose and role in God's plan. Three important Christian images relate helpfully to our understanding of the nature, function and purposes of the family—these are the Trinity, the Holy Spirit, and the Kingdom. The Trinity provides a model of *relationship,* the Holy Spirit a model of dynamic *process,* and the Kingdom enables us to understand the family's *ecology* by revealing the limitations of the family and its necessary location within the context of God's wider demands and purposes.

The Trinity

By far the most important of these three images is that of the Trinity. The nature of trinitarian relationships is most fully expressed in the farewell discourses of St John's Gospel (chapters 16 and 17). Here we are given a model of relationships which postulates *intimacy without fusion* and *differentiation without separation.* The relationship between the three Persons is one of equality and mutual love. The functions of the Persons are clear and boundaries are firm but permeable. The intimate union between the Persons is given as a model for the unity and oneness of Christ's followers with God and with each other: 'May they all be one: as thou, Father, art in me, and I in thee, so also may they be in us, . . . I in them and Thou in me, may they be perfectly one' (John 17.21, 23). Yet the Father, the Son and the Spirit are each differentiated from the others by their role and function. The Holy Spirit 'will confute the world, and show where wrong and right and judgement lie' (John 16.8). Yet he will not operate as an autonomous, separate Being but as One who is in intimate relationship with the Father and the Son. 'He will not speak on his own authority, but will tell only what he hears' (John 16.13). The Son holds a specific role and executes particular functions. He holds sovereignty 'over all mankind, to give eternal life to all whom thou hast given him' (John 17.2). 'I have glorified thee on earth by completing the work which thou gavest me to do' (John 17.4). Yet the Son's role and function is always framed within the relationships between the Three Persons as a whole. 'I came from the Father and have come into the world. Now I am leaving the world again and going to the Father' (John 16.28).

Some interventions by one of the Persons require clearly differentiated functioning on the part of each. The Son must 'leave' his Father in order to 'come' into the world, and the Father, by implication, must let him go. The Son must leave the human brothers and sisters he loves because 'If I do not go, your Advocate will not come, whereas if I go, I will send him to you' (John 16.7—8). The pain of separation is sometimes required if maturity and growth are to be achieved. 'It is for your good that I am leaving you' (John 16.7).

An important thrust of contemporary theology is this emphasis on the social nature of the Trinity, which provides us with an important model of God *as relationship.* One might say that the most crucially distinctive feature of Christianity, as compared with Judaism or Islam, is that God is conceived of not as a unitary being but as a relationship. Various contemporary theologians (Moltmann, Jenkins)[4] have examined the implications of the notion of God as Trinity and have perceived the extraordinary richness and power of the Trinitarian model, symbolising as it does both the vertical, transcendent and the lateral, immanent dimensions of the Godhead. But particularly in its ability to keep these two contrary dynamics in relation to each other, Moltmann and other major theologians have drawn attention to the power of this image of God for our own times. Thus, for Jenkins, the Trinity stands 'not for a doctrine but for a way of life'. It is not hard to understand how this should be, because beyond all the subtleties of debate and the heat and noise of doctrinal controversy, the doctrine of the Trinity yields two magnificently simple and luminous truths.

The first is that the Christian God is a social God and, as Kenneth Leech puts it, 'the doctrine of the Trinity is essentially the assertion of the social nature of God'.[5] Although both the economic and subordinationist notions of the Trinity yielded crude models of monarchianism based on the supposed hierarchical order of the three Persons, the Trinity that 'emerged' from the early Councils and which is captured for us in 'Quicunque vult' is that of a God who is not a remote, autocratic monarch but a God who is a community of equal interacting Persons. In Leech's words: 'The doctrine of the Trinity is an assertion that within the Godhead itself, there is society and equality of relationships and that humanity is called to share in that divine life.'

Second, the unity of the Trinity is a *differentiated* unity, where the distinctions between Persons are clearly retained despite the unity of substance which all three equally share. This differentiation was strongly asserted when it seemed that the contrary concept of modalism might hold the day. Thus the Trinity portrays for us the paradoxical nature of all intimate relationships—the need for differentiation within unity; for autonomy within interdependence; for individuality within community. The Trinity holds in tension these contrary, necessary forces, and is in some vital sense an expression of the essential characteristics of Godhead in terms of loving interdependence, equality and reciprocal relationship.

Thus, Leech and others argue from the doctrine of the Trinity the fact that *relationship* not *individualism* is at the core of Christianity because it lies at the core of the Godhead himself. Just as the Genesis image of the human being is that of co-humanity, so the Trinitarian imagery of God indicates that the pattern for our continuing mode of being human is to live and grow in *relationship*. Intimate relationship is the only means by which God can live out his Divine Life, and it is therefore the only means by which human beings can live out their humanity. This is because God is himself love, and love presupposes the need for relationship. Since love cannot be experienced or expressed in the absence of another, love requires the continuous existence of relationship.

The Holy Spirit

Our second image for constructing a theology of the family is derived from the nature and operation of the Holy Spirit. The Holy Spirit's mission and ministry involve three spheres of activity: (1) in the work of creation itself, where the Spirit is seen as 'brooding over the face of the deep' (Gen. 1.2), helping, alongside the Word of God, to bring the created order into being; (2) in initiating, sustaining and continuing the incarnated life of Christ in and through the Church and her Sacraments and (3) in being the continuous 'giver of life' to the world, whereby the whole of the cosmic order is sustained and brought painfully to ultimate perfection (Rom. 8). It is the third activity to which we will pay particular attention, for it is here that the Spirit's work continues to act upon the whole created order and the whole of human kind. Modern theologians (Pannenberg, Teilhard de Chardin)[7] emphasise the Spirit's cosmic mission. Teilhard de Chardin describes the immanence of the Holy Spirit in the geosphere, the biosphere and noosphere, and others have underlined the way the effects of the Spirit's work can be witnessed in the struggles and triumphs of the secular world, which bring about new institutional forms and structures (including new forms and structures of family life); new areas of consciousness; new refinements of conscience and new energy for tackling the particular problems of contemporary society, those of peace and justice and the continuous search for truth.

J. V. Taylor, in his study of the Holy Spirit's function and role, suggests that in understanding better the role of the Spirit we are helped to understand the meaning and organisation of systems.[8] Since the family counsellor's understanding of the family group is, as we saw in chapter 2, centrally predicated upon a theory of systems, Taylor's work is of particular interest and relevance. Beginning from the Spirit's creative function, both in the original formation of the world and continuing into the present, Taylor describes the Holy Spirit as the great Go-Between, *connecting* one element with another, *communicating* between particles, *creating* the dynamic processes of relationships and systems. 'The Holy Spirit is the invisible third party who stands between me and the other, making us mutually aware.'[9] The Holy Spirit acts throughout the created order as the principle which enables systems to operate as 'more than the sum of their parts'. Thus, in understanding how the universe operates systemically we are better able to understand the particular function of the Holy Spirit, and vice versa.

'As a believer in the creator Spirit,' comments Taylor,

I would say that deep within the fabric of the universe therefore, the Spirit is present as the Go-Between who confronts each isolated spontaneous particle with the beckoning reality of the larger whole and so compels it to relate to others in a particular way; and that it is he who at every stage lures the inert organisms forward by giving an inner awareness and recognition of the unattained.[10]

And in turn, the Holy Spirit's particular role in the Divine purposes is better able to help us conceive of the systemic relatedness of things and persons. If the Spirit is the connecting principle, the Go-Between which lies on the *inside* of things and in the dynamic *processes* of life, then we can convincingly connect our family therapy theory with our theology. For the operation of the Spirit points us unequivocally towards a systemic understanding of relationships and suggests that our model of family is authentic, not only in its mirroring of the Trinity but in its respect for the special role of the Spirit.

The Kingdom

Our third image is that of the Kingdom, and here we need to examine the meaning of the Kingdom and the relationship between this concept and the purpose and function of the family. Important as family imagery is in the Old and New Testaments and in Christian doctrine, the importance of Kingdom imagery must be brought to bear upon it. Moreover the claims of the Kingdom must be used as a measure for understanding the degree to which the family can truly be seen to be central to Christian belief and practice. Part of the construction of our theology of the family must therefore entail an effort to discern the role and limitations of the family in the Divine task of redemption and salvation.

The Christian understanding of the redeemed community brings with it a set of imperatives which, if engaged with seriously, open out whole new possibilities for individuals living in intimate relationship. They offer a purpose, goal and the means for achieving that goal. Through consciously setting out to live for the other, rather than pursuing the apparently direct route to self-fulfilment the paradox central to all relationships is laid bare; self-fulfilment is only achieved through bringing to fruition the fulfilment of the other. The *purpose* of the human family is to enable that paradox to be struggled with and lived. More specifically, it is to mirror the Trinitarian family in the intimacy and yet differentiation of its Persons; in the mutual self-giving of its love and in its focus of loving care for those who lie beyond its boundaries. The *task* of the human family is to nurture its members so well that they are able to leave their Father's house and engage in the struggles of the Kingdom—bringing about God's radical peace and justice in the world. The *goal* of the human family is to bring its members to fulfilment in body, mind and spirit, understanding that the consummation of this task will nevertheless only take place in the context of eternity.

The time dimension is crucial in understanding the potential conflict between the demands of the family and the demands of the Kingdom. This is a struggle to which Jesus alludes repeatedly and which may confront the individual with sharp and unavoidable conflict. Many times in the Gospels we find that the claims of the Kingdom are set over and above the claims or obligations of family life. St Luke tells us that Jesus, as a boy of twelve, clearly believed that his obligation to be 'in his Father's house' overrode his obligation to be with his natural parents. In chapter 4 of St Luke, Jesus is described as experiencing the difficulty of following his own particular mission within the inhospitable bounds of his own home territory—a familiar problem of young adulthood. In chapter 8 we listen to him diluting the special claims that his own family are wanting to make on him and generalising the natural claims of blood and kinship to embrace all who 'hear the word of God and obey it'. He sees his own earthly life as one which is cut loose from both the security and the ties of the home (Luke 9.58) and specifically rebukes those individuals who respond to his call, by asking leave to attend first to their legitimate family obligations (Luke 9.59—62). More specifically, he directly attests to the fact that he has come not to bring peace but division, and he illustrates these divisions in terms of the natural family (Luke 12.51—4). In Matthew 10.37—8 and Luke 14.26 Jesus conceives of the Kingdom of Heaven as making claims on his followers which demand that they love him more than parents or spouse, brothers or sisters, and these demands are reinforced in Matthew 19.12 when he asserts that some individuals will be called to forgo marriage and family completely for the sake of the Kingdom.

The family does indeed play a vital role in enabling the individual to move beyond the self, by learning to relate to others and by struggling with the paradox of autonomy/inter-dependence. But the demands of the Kingdom will always call the individual to move on and out of his or her family of origin and to engage with the varied tasks of adulthood in creating and recreating the surrounding social order. One of these tasks *may* include the formation of a new tier in the family life cycle and creating a new link in the family's ongoing chain. But it may also include eschewing the more obvious forms of family life and joining instead a monastic order or a commune or breaking new ground in new and unfamiliar situations with a few companions or alone. The early Church clearly believed that the newly inaugurated Christian order dictated that some individuals should live beyond and outside family life. This otherwise unnatural sacrifice seemed logical and necessary, both because of the supposed imminence of the *parousia* and because of the need for total commitment if the embryonic Church was to survive. The continuing history of the Christian Church bears ample testimony to the fact that the family can claim to exercise only a modest role in the outworking of our salvation and sanctification and that after the eschaton it will apparently have no role at all (Mark 12.25).

We are now in a position to summarise the ingredients of a theology of the family and to examine how its main constructs relate to the theory of family systems.

(1) *Ubiquity.* The family prevails over all others as the pre-eminent social structure into which most human beings are born and live out most of their lives. It must therefore be taken with the utmost seriousness by the pastoral counsellor. The *fact* of family is supported both by the theory of systems and by the theology of creation. The theory of systems suggest that both organic and inorganic matter is organised systemically— therefore we should expect human beings to be organised systemically in a series of inter-related

systems. The theology of creation demonstrates the way in which individual human beings were originally conceived of by God as being *in relationship* with each other. The essential and fundamental 'isness' of relationships and of the family system must therefore attract primary interest from the pastoral counsellor and demand his attention over and above his concern for individuals.

(2) *Non-Summativity*. The basic construct of systems theory is that the whole is more than the sum of its parts, and in chapter 2 we tried to demonstrate the way in which individuals can only be properly conceived of as being parts of a dynamic relationship. Systems theory, psychodynamic theory and communication theory can all be invoked to support this premise. Non-summativity, or wholeness, involves achieving a balance between intimacy (without fusion) and differentiation (without separation) and it requires the establishment of clear roles and boundaries between individual sub-systems. We have drawn upon the model of the Trinity to support these constructs theologically and to provide a theological understanding of the family counsellor's pastoral task.

(3) *Process*. In chapters 2 and 3 we noted how a system is composed of both its lateral and vertical networks and that its identity is established by its structure, its content and the processes that occur within it. The process of change is best helped forward by attending to the processes that occur *between* sub-systems rather than to the system's content or structure. Process can be conceived of in microcosm ('what is happening between these individual family members now') or in macrocosm ('what is happening to this family as it proceeds over time from one stage in the life cycle to the next'). To support this argument theologically we have drawn upon the special role and function of the Holy Spirit as Giver of Life, acting as the continuous 'Go-Between' within the myriad organic and inorganic systems which make up the cosmos. We saw how the Spirit exists and operates at the core of process and how this fact highlights the centrality of process as a factor in our understanding of and intervention in systems.

(4) *Variety.* Throughout the book we have referred to the family's variety both in terms of its membership and its forms. The family is composed of an intensely varied group of individuals in terms of gender, age, resources, roles, talents and purposes. It is the family's internal variety which provides it with energy for growth and change, but its variety also serves to bring stress and conflict.

We noted in chapter 2 how the family needs to arrive at a continuous balance between stability, or homeostasis, on the one hand and growth, or morphogenesis, on the other. This requires the fluid, flexible yet secure handling of differential roles and tasks between family members. If roles and tasks are allocated and held on the basis of stereotyped views of what is appropriate for women or men, children or parents, old or young, homeostatic mechanisms will prevent change and growth. If, on the other hand, there are no patterns and rules by which family members relate to each other, no one can experience the stability and security which are equally necessary for growth to occur, and variety to be maintained. Likewise, the *fact* of family continues over time and between cultures but the *form* of the family must be infinitely various if it is to adapt to changes and pressures from its supra-system.

To understand the concept of the variety in family membership and form, we have drawn upon the variety of God's creation itself and on the particular variety in sexuality which was part of the original creation of humanity and which is expressed as well as transcended within the Godhead himself. In chapter 1 and at other points in the book, we have also noted the essential variety in family forms and have stressed the need to avoid holding up one particular form as being the one which God intends. Jesus in fact sat very lightly to the family (defined in any narrow sense). His few comments about it are mainly disparaging and he showed no inclination to found one himself.

In their construction of a social theology of the family, Anderson and Guernsey draw attention to the fact that 'one never grants to order as a social structure of reality the perfection and absolute quality that is reserved for God alone', and, 'The authority of the creative Word of God never passes on to the form of its embodiment.'[11] In other words,

although the family can rightly be seen to be part of the
original creative purpose of God for human beings, the family
as an institution must not be sacralised, nor must any
particular form of it. On the contrary, the variety in family
forms should be accepted and delighted in, as Anderson
suggests, because it is a sign of God's extravagance. It is
indeed the quality and depth of loving human relationships,
not their form, which reveal something of the perfection of
God's own love.

(5) *Ecology*. In chapter 2 we noted how the family system is
made up of a variety of sub-systems and is in turn embedded
in a supra-system, its environment. The family's ecological
environment has been likened to a set of nested structures
(Bronfenbrenner) or to a series of Chinese boxes (Skynner),[12]
each one residing inside the next and circumscribed by its
boundary. Through the operation of positive and negative
feedback, the family system must remain in dynamic
relationship with its environment and thus be capable of
adaptation to it. There must be a continuous flow of
communication over the boundary between the family system
and its environment. This is achieved by interaction between
one family system and another, between family systems and
other human organisations and between the changes of family
membership brought about by crises of accession and
dismemberment whereby family members join and leave.

In terms of a theology of the family, the family's environment also includes the demands of the Kingdom and of life
after death, and both the demands of the Kingdom and the
context of eternity provide an essential framework for the
family's ultimate purposes and goals. We are repeatedly posed
with a contradictory challenge: the family's own relative and
more limited goals must be confronted by that which lies
beyond and which is offered as a further and fuller goal to
which human beings are beckoned. And it is this further and
fuller challenge which the family counsellor must hold in
mind when helping couples and families move towards
maturity and growth. God calls individuals out of relationships as well as into them, and one of the tasks of the family
counsellor may be to undermine the idolatrous worship of
family life that can so easily become a substitute for

responding to the claims of the Kingdom. The family is the usual means of providing the individual with the environment he or she needs to grow in wholeness and holiness. It is an enabling mercy whereby human beings are nurtured and loved, challenged and stimulated by visions of hope and of glory — yet it is only the means and never the end. It is part of the now but not yet of living the Kingdom, and it will only perform its true function if it enables its members to transform the world into Christ's Kingdom of love and justice and peace for all.

Notes

1. H. Anderson, *The Family and Pastoral Care*, Philadelphia, PA, Fortress Press 1984, p. 15.
2. S. Maitland, *A Map of the New Country*, Routledge & Kegan Paul 1983; R. R. Ruether, *Sexism and God-Talk*, SCM Press 1983; E. S. Fiorenza, *In Memory of Her*, SCM Press 1983.
3. The contrary view is stated by W. Oddie in *What will Happen to God?*, SPCK 1984.
4. J. Moltmann, *The Trinity and the Kingdom of God*, SCM Press 1981, and D. Jenkins, *The Contradiction of Christianity*, SCM Press 1976.
5. K. Leech, *The Social God*, Sheldon Press 1981, p. 6.
6. ibid., p. 7.
7. W. Pannenberg, *Jesus, God and Man*, SCM Press 1968; P. Teilhard de Chardin, *The Phenomenon of Man*, Fontana 1959.
8. J. V. Taylor, *The Go-Between God*, SCM Press 1972.
9. ibid., p. 19.
10. ibid., p. 31.
11. R. S. Anderson and D. B. Guernsey, *On Being Family — a Social Theology of the Family*, Grand Rapids, MI, Eerdmans, 1985, p. 21, 22.
12. U. Bronfenbrenner, *The Ecology of Human Development*, Harvard University Press 1979; A. C. R. Skynner, 'Boundaries', *Social Work Today*, vol. 5, 1974.

Bibliography

Ackerman, N., *Treating the Troubled Family.* New York, Basic Books, 1968.

Bateson, G., *Steps to an Ecology of Mind.* Granada 1972.

Bateson, G., *Mind and Nature: a necessary unity.* Dutton 1979.

Bentovim, A., Gorell Barnes, G. and Cooklin, A., *Family Therapy: Complementary Frameworks of Theory and Practice.* Abridged edn, Academic Press, 1987.

Berger, P. L. and Berger, B., *The War over the Family.* Penguin 1984.

Boszormenyi-Nagy, I., *Invisible Loyalties.* New York, Brunner/Mazel, 1973.

Boszormenyi-Nagy, I., *Between Give and Take.* New York, Brunner/Mazel, 1986.

Bowen, M., *Family Therapy in Clinical Practice.* New York, Jason Aronson, 1978.

Box, S., Copley, B., Magagna, J. and Moustaki, E., *Psychotherapy with Families: an analytic approach.* Routledge & Kegan Paul 1982.

Capra, F., *The Turning Point.* Wildwood House 1982.

Carter, E. and McGoldrick, M., *The Family Life Cycle.* New York, Gardner Press, 1980.

Dicks, H. V., *Marital Tensions.* Routledge & Kegan Paul 1967.

Dominian, J., *Make or Break: an introduction to marriage counselling.* SPCK 1984.

Fisch, R. et al., *The Tactics of Change.* San Francisco, Jossey-Bass, 1982.

Gittins, D., *The Family in Question.* Macmillan 1985.

Gorell Barnes, G., *Working with Families.* Macmillan 1984.

Gurman, A. S. and Price, D. G., *Couples in Conflict.* New York, Jason Aronson, 1975.

174   *Bibliography*

Haley, J., *Problem-Solving Therapy*. San Francisco, Jossey-Bass, 1973.

Haley, J., *Leaving Home*. New York, McGraw-Hill, 1980.

Hoffman, L., *Foundations of Family Therapy*. New York, Basic Books, 1981.

Lewis, J., Beaver, R., Gossett, J. and Phillips, V., *No Single Thread: psychological health in family systems*. New York, Brunner/Mazel, 1976.

Laszlo, E., *Introduction to System Philosophy*. New York, Gordon & Breach, 1972.

Lieberman, S., *Transgenerational Family Therapy*. Croom Helm 1979.

Minuchin, S., *Families and Family Therapy*. Tavistock 1974.

Minuchin, S. and Fishman, H. C., *Family Therapy Techniques*. Harvard University Press 1981.

Morgan, D. H. J., *Family, Politics and Social Theory*. Routledge & Kegan Paul 1985.

Neil, J. R. and Kniskern, D. P., *From Psyche to System*. New York, Guilford Press, 1982.

Palazzoli, M., Boscolo, L., Cecchin, G. and Prata, G., *Paradox and Counterparadox*. New York, Jason Aronson, 1978.

Paolino, T. and McGrady, B., *Marriage and Marital Therapy*. New York, Brunner/Mazel, 1978.

Pincus, L. and Dare, C., *Secrets in the Family*. Faber 1978.

Poster, M., *Critical Theory of the Family*. Pluto Press 1978.

Rapaport, R., Fogarty, M. and Rapaport, R., *Families in Britain*. Routledge & Kegan Paul 1982.

Satir, V., *Conjoint Family Therapy*. Palo Alto, CA, Science and Behavior Books, 1964.

Satir, V., *Peoplemaking*. Palo Alto, CA, Science and Behavior Books, 1972.

Segal, L., *What is to be done about the family?* Penguin 1983.

Shorter, E., *The Making of the Modern Family*. Fontana 1977.

Skynner, A. C. R., *One Flesh, Separate Persons*. Constable 1976.

Skynner, A. C. R., *Explorations with Families*. Methuen 1987.

Treacher, A. and Carpenter, J., *Using Family Therapy*. Blackwell 1984.

Wallerstein, J. S. and Kelly, J. B., *Surviving the Break-up.* Grant McIntyre 1980.

Walrond-Skinner, S., *Family Therapy—The Treatment of Natural Systems.* Routledge & Kegan Paul 1976.

Walrond-Skinner, S., ed., *Family and Marital Psychotherapy: a critical approach.* Routledge & Kegan Paul 1979.

Walrond-Skinner, S., ed., *Developments in Family Therapy.* Routledge and Kegan Paul 1981.

Walrond-Skinner, S. and Watson, D., eds., *Ethical Issues in Family Therapy.* Routledge & Kegan Paul 1987.

Watzlawick, P., Beavin, J. and Jackson, D., *The Pragmatics of Human Communication.* New York, W. W. Norton, 1967.

Watzlawick, P., Weakland, J. and Fisch, R., *Change: Principles of Problem Formation and Problem Resolution.* New York, W. W. Norton, 1980.

Index